THE FANTASY SPORTS BOSS 2016 FANTASY BASEBALL DRAFT GUIDE: EARLY OFFSEAS0N EDITION

By The Fantasy Sports Boss Staff

TABLE OF CONTENTS

1. Editor's Note..Page 3
2. 2016 Draft Sleepers...Page 5
3. 2016 Draft Busts..Page 9
4. Top Rookies..Page 13
5. Ten Burning Questions..Page 17
6. Tommy John Risky Pitchers For 2016............................Page 21
7. Position Rankings and Analysis....................................Page 24
    - Catchers..Page 24
    - First Baseman..Page 39
    - Second Baseman...Page 66
    - Shortstops...Page 83
    - Third Baseman..Page 98
    - Outfielders..Page 115
    - Starting Pitchers...Page 168
    - Relief Pitchers...Page 254
8. The Final Word...Page 266

EDITOR'S NOTE

To Our Readers:

It is that time once again. A time where another fantasy baseball season approaches with a blend of excitement, anxiety, and all-around optimism. Undoubtedly the highlight of the grueling six-month season comes even before the first game becomes official. I am talking of course about the annual extravaganza known as the fantasy baseball draft. Whether you are getting together with your buddies among drinks and wings at your favorite establishment or you're simply sitting in front of the computer making your selections in solitude, the draft is without a doubt the most exciting and at the same time, crucial part of the season. Nail the draft and you set yourself up nicely right out of the gates. Fumble away the draft and you potentially place yourself behind the eight ball before the first pitch. It is with that backdrop that we once again bring you our annual draft guide which is jam-packed with everything you need to take home your league's trophy. The usual features are back once again such as our annual draft busts, sleepers, top rookies, ten burning questions, and of course our award-winning rankings and analysis. In addition, we have used a more advanced analytics approach to our player profiles this season, which is especially helpful for those in daily leagues. Also you talk about big. Our draft guide comes in at a whopping 3 pages this season which is unmatched anywhere else in the industry. Finally, you won't find another draft guide out there with a full paragraph devoted to all the fantasy baseball-worthy hitters and pitchers. While most guides have a few sentences on each player, we delve in fully with up to a full page dedicated to certain guys.

Of course the draft is just the first step in the long process of finishing on top of your league and that is where part 2 of our analysis comes in. Our draft guide is just a supplement to our daily fantasy baseball coverage through our website at www.thefantasysportsboss.com. Be sure to bookmark our site so that you can follow along all season as we stay on top of all the latest happenings and share with you our online features.

Once again let me take the opportunity to thank all of you for your support and dedication which has surely helped us reach the heights we have today and we wish you nothing but the best of luck this season.

Sincerely,

Michael E. Keneski

The Fantasy Sports Boss

www.thefantasysportsboss.com

P.S. Be sure to keep an eye out for our "Post-Free Agency Draft Guide" edition due out sometime in January.

2016 FANTASY BASEBALL DRAFT SLEEPERS

By Michael E. Keneski

If you were to poll those who are habitual participants in fantasy baseball (or fantasy sports as a whole for that matter) what they think is the most exciting part of the game beyond the draft, invariably the answers most given would be the annual sleepers that we all simply must have. Each and every season a crop of hitters and pitchers become the object of serious affection for those who enlist in fantasy baseball leagues and the competition is often very fierce for these still-unproven commodities. In fact the battle to get your hands on these players often results in their draft prices skyrocketing, thus lessening the potential "sleeper" impact. Be that as it may, we still can't help ourselves from paying for potential. It is a mistake that even seasoned players make but the allure to pick up the next instant star like Mike Trout, Ryan Braun, or Jose Abreu is just too much to resist. So with that said, here is our 2016 Fantasy Sports Boss All-Sleeper Team. Of course we are doing nothing but adding to the hype when it comes to these names but we feel strongly in the potential for a good number of them to exceed their draft positions this season. Once again we exclude players who have yet to make their first appearance in the major leagues as those individuals belong in the Rookie Report.

Michael Conforto: There is big power potential here as Conforto has been universally acclaimed as one of the very best young sluggers in the game. In the heat of a pennant race, Conforto did just fine in his rapid promotion from Double-A to the Mets in 2015 and seems poised for a long run of 25 home runs and a .290 average.

David Peralta: The Arizona Diamondbacks have an insane collection of power/speed outfielders, let by All-Star A.J. Pollock and supplemented by a young group that includes David Peralta. While Ender Inciarte has more speed than power, Peralta has the edge with the home runs. Combine burgeoning power in a great ballpark with a good batting average and Peralta looks ready to break through in 2016.

Rougned Odor: It was a tough start to the 2015 season for Rougned Odor, as an early pronounced slump necessitated him being sent back to the minor leagues for more seasoning. Odor made it back quickly enough however and immediately began hitting ropes all over the field. Turning just 22 in February, Odor has massive upside as a power/speed second baseman.

Jarrett Parker: The next Joc Pederson resides in the same NL West Division as Jarrett Parker is taking the same path to the majors as his counterpart with the Los Angeles Dodgers. While Parker strikes out at a ridiculously high rate that will make his average a liability, he has massive speed and developing power that can lead to a 15/30 campaign as soon as this season.

[margin note: SF OF]

Greg Bird: The Yankees have done nothing but drool over the potential of power-hitting first baseman Greg Bird and we began to see what all the fuss was about when he replaced an injured Mark Teixeira during the second half of 2015. Bird would go on to hit 11 home runs in 178 at-bats and his future seems certain as a 25-30 long ball asset. Unfortunately Bird will begin the season in the minors if Teixeira is healthy since Alex Rodriguez mans the DH spot. Still that will help keep the draft price down to more affordable levels which makes Bird a tremendous buy since it is only a matter of time until Teixeira gets injured again.

[margin note: start in minors]

Steven Matz: Joining Matt Harvey, Noah Syndegaard, and Jacob DeGrom in the amazing collecting of hard-throwing young pitchers on the New York Mets is lefty Steven Matz. While Matz has fought through a bunch of early injuries in his career, his stuff is considered ace-level by anyone who has seen him throw. With Matz a part of the rotation to begin the 2016 season, the upside is significant.

[margin note: SP 5th starter]

Ender Inciarte: Joining David Peralta from the Arizona outfield on this list is the speedy Ender Inciarte who is a classic leadoff guy right on down to the .300 average and good stolen base ability. There is not a heck of a lot of pub associated with Inciarte yet due to inconsistent playing time but he could do a 2015 Gerard Parra breakout if the playing time works itself out.

[margin note: OF Traded to Atl]

Blake Swihart: Young catchers with upside are the rarest of commodities and that usually means an extreme draft price has to be paid in order to secure their services. This is not the case though with Boston Red Sox backstop Blake Swihart who has shown the ability to hit for average coming up the team's system, while also possessing developing power and good speed for a catcher.

[margin note: C]

Justin Bohr: In this era of pitching dominance, it is always a smart strategy to pick up power whenever and wherever it presents itself. Even the Miami Marlins had to be surprised when Justin Bohr proceeded to hit 23 home runs in just 446 at-bats last season. Bohr has the look of a slugger who is capable of maybe a bit more in the home run department in 2016 and his very cheap draft price makes him a tremendous late round buy.

Tyler Lyons: Any St. Louis Cardinals prospect is worth your attention no matter the position but Tyler Lyons looks like a solid sleeper candidate for 2016. Lyons did well during his first foray into the majors last season, registering a 3.75 ERA and 9.00 K/9 in 60 innings. While Lyons is no Carlos Martinez, he has enough potential to deserve our attention.

Joe Ross: Bad job by the Washington Nationals not making 2011 first round pick Joe Ross more a part of their 2015 rotation plans. Tyson's younger brother did a terrific job in his 76.2 innings last season in putting up a 3.64 ERA and 8.10 K/9. The pedigree is certainly there due to his draft slot and Ross is hinting that more numbers are on the way.

Randal Grichuk: The Cardinals also have a good power prospect on their hands in Randal Grichuk who smacked 17 home runs in just 350 at-bats as a rookie in 2015. While Grichuk is a hacker right on down to the high K rate, 20-plus home runs seems a lock in 2016.

Jimmy Nelson: The Milwaukee Brewers' Jimmy Nelson certainly took some lumps during his first full major league season in 2015 but the overall result was impressive. Nelson's 4.11 ERA was a bit high but he got better as the season went on and he was a big strikeout guy in the minors. We have not seen the best the kid has to offer just yet.

Raisel Iglesias: There is some big-time strikeout potential here as we saw in August when Iglesias thrust himself into the consciousness of the fantasy baseball community by registering three straight games of double-digit K's. Overall Iglesias struck out 104 batters in 95.1 innings which points to a future as a possible 180-plus K guy. Electric arms like this don't come around often and the miserable season in Cincinnati and lack of innings from Iglesias could still have his hype a bit dimmed.

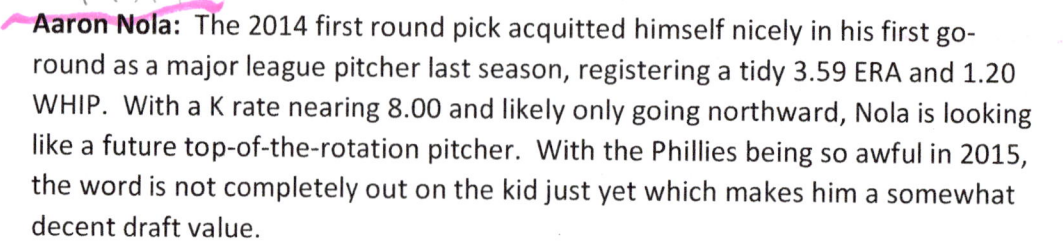

Aaron Nola: [Phil] [SP] The 2014 first round pick acquitted himself nicely in his first go-round as a major league pitcher last season, registering a tidy 3.59 ERA and 1.20 WHIP. With a K rate nearing 8.00 and likely only going northward, Nola is looking like a future top-of-the-rotation pitcher. With the Phillies being so awful in 2015, the word is not completely out on the kid just yet which makes him a somewhat decent draft value.

Each one of these players has a very bright future ahead of them and 2016 could very well be their coming out party. The draft price is not out of control for anyone on this list either which is why we put each of them here in the first place. As always don't reach for the moon for any one player but the upside is very promising among this group.

2016 FANTASY BASEBALL DRAFT BUSTS TO AVOID

By Michael Wong

No matter how hard you try, completely avoiding the dreaded fantasy baseball draft bust is almost impossible. Whether it is injuries, slumps, trades, or any other factor, investing in a player who fails to supply their anticipated numbers is more than a simple annoyance. Depending on how high in the draft you selected such a player, the results can be disastrous and set back your roster in a major way. We say every year in these pages that steering clear of draft busts is never an exact science. Sometimes simple bad luck is to blame. However there are certain players each and every season who carry more risk than others and thus making investments in those hitters and pitchers can be more than a bit dicey. It is with this thinking in mind that we put together our "2016 Busts to Avoid List" for you to study and store away in your brains so that you can avoid some of these potential land mines. A year ago in this space we included the following names on our bust list that ultimately went right along with our prediction:

Adam Wainwright: suffered torn Achilles which reinforced our spring belief Wainwright would have difficulty holding up physically off recent heavy usage seasons.

Matt Holliday: Offensive numbers continued to slide and second-half was completely injury-marred.

Steve Pearce: Nailed this one as we told you all that 2014 was a major outlier campaign for the journeyman Pearce that was not to be believed. Pearce went belly up right away in April to validate this one quickly.

Yadier Molina: While Molina still hit for average, his power vanished almost completely as we correctly said his name brand would outpace his actual production.

Jon Singleton: It didn't take long for Singleton to make us look smart on this bust pick, with his sky-high K rate sending him back to the minors for more development at the start of the season.

Victor Martinez: We screamed to the rafters that the 32 home runs Martinez hit in 2014 would go down as one of the all-time outlier campaigns and that is exactly what happened. Martinez' power plummeted back to his career norms and he dealt with ongoing knee issues.

Michael Cuddyer: This was an easy one as Cuddyer went from the offensive haven that was Coors Field to spacious Citi Field. By the middle of the season Cuddyer was hurt yet again which became another factor in us calling him a bust candidate, not to mention eventually turning into a platoon guy who played only against lefties due to horrific Jason Bay-like numbers.

Dustin Pedroia: Pedroia started off with a bang as he smacked two home runs in the opener but it was all downhill from there which was no surprise to us. Once again the slight Pedroia showed that all those years of manning second base with his smallish body took a major toll on his health as he spent a large chunk of the year on the disabled list with more injury woes. Now a complete shell of his former All-Star self.

Jimmy Rollins: Yes Rollins kept hitting home runs but his speed declined sharply and all season he could barely hit over .200 as his 2014 mini-comeback was nothing but a one-year mirage.

Mat Latos: Despite getting moved to spacious Miami, we didn't like Latos' ill health and declining stuff. After getting hit very hard to begin the season, Latos ended up on the DL with more injuries. A trade to the Dodgers when he returned did not do much to save his season either as they eventually DFA'd him.

That made it 10 names we correctly tabbed as 2015 draft busts and so we more than helped you steer clear of quite a few troubling players heading into the season. Of course we missed on a few such as Russell Martin, Joey Votto, and our biggest miss being Nelson Cruz but overall it was a very accurate analysis. So with that said, let's see who makes the list for 2016:

Jason Kipnis: Kipnis has now alternated good and bad seasons over the last three years but his 2015 "comeback" was not as impressive as it looks on paper. For one thing, Kipnis won't go near his .303 average as he got there last season through a very lucky .356 BABIP. In addition, Kipnis hit just 9 home runs and saw his stolen base rate plummet with only 12 in his 641 at-bats. When the average drops this season, the light power/speed numbers will stand out more as a negative. Throw in an increasing tendency to get hurt and Kipnis is sizable risk.

Hector Santiago: A tremendous first half run by Hector Santiago when he registered a 2.33 ERA soon turned into a very ugly 5.47 second half mark as fatigue became an issue. With career-long control problems and the feeling that opposing batters began figuring him out the second half of 2015, Santiago is very dicey even at the back of your rotation.

Matt Harvey: Already with a Tommy John elbow surgery in his past, Matt Harvey presents risk due to the fact he went well past the 180-inning recommendation he had coming into the 2015 season. With the Mets making it all the way to the World Series, Harvey sailed past 200 frames and now sets himself up for a "bounce" where the numbers slide a bit or injury takes hold in 2016. The K rate dipped slightly as well last season which adds to the red flags.

Daniel Murphy: It was no doubt an amazing power display put on by Daniel Murphy as he went yard in six-straight games during the first two rounds of the postseason as he helped the Mets advanced to the Fall Classic. However that run was incredibly fluky since Murphy's career-high in home runs is just a mediocre 14. Some will draft Murphy higher than they should this season due to his postseason run and that would be very foolish considering the career trends. Throw in the fact Murphy's brief time as a base stealer looks finished already and it becomes easy to understand avoiding the veteran unless he comes at his standard past draft price.

Brandon Phillips: After pretty much everyone wrote him off going into 2015, Brandon Phillips had a nice comeback season when he began running again and hit for average. It reeks of a "last hurrah" campaign though as Phillips is now in his mid-30's.

Matt Carpenter: One of the most surprising numbers coming out of 2015 was the 28 home runs and 101 RBI collected by St. Louis Cardinals third baseman Matt Carpenter. Clearly swinging for the fences now that he was manning third base full-time, Carpenter has a lot to prove in terms of showing the 28 bombs were no mirage. Always steer clear of classic outlier performances such as this.

Mike Moustakas: Another outlier number was seen in the .284 average from Kansas City's Mike Moustakas in 2015. A major average drain since coming into the majors, Moustakas' career trends scream out that he will be back to the .250-.260 range this season which changes the overall statistical outlook.

Carlos Gomez: Still young at the age of 30 in December, Carlos Gomez' body betrayed him completely in 2015 as he got into only 115 games and was hobbled throughout the year. Guys who are build on speed like Gomez are always threats to decline early which is something to keep in mind. When you also look at how Gomez' home run rate dropped last season, we are more leery than ever on the guy's outlook.

Carlos Gonzalez: Finally figuring out how to stay healthy, Carlos Gonzalez had a ridiculous 2015 by slamming a career-high 40 home runs. Counting on Gonzalez to stay healthy two years in a row is asking for the moon and the 40 home runs for now are in the outlier bin.

Hanley Ramirez: While we always have a soft spot for Hanley Ramirez throughout his stellar career, his body now is falling apart as evidenced by two straight injury-marred campaigns. The speed is almost vanished as well and the average is slipping sharply. With shortstop eligibility now out of the picture, Ramirez is losing a majority of his past appeal.

Jacoby Ellsbury: There may not be a more overpaid and injury-prone player than New York Yankees outfielder Jacoby Ellsbury. With his legs betraying him, Ellsbury pretty much is useless to you since steals and runs are his best asset.

Of course we are not saying to avoid every one of these names completely but instead just be cautious when weighing whether or to not to include them in your draft plans. The downside here can be very ugly given the issues we already identified and looking for more stable investments is the much better way to go. Some players are simply too risky to buy into and thus there is really no reason to give yourself more headaches in an already stressful season.

2015 FANTASY BASEBALL ROOKIE REPORT
By Michael E. Keneski

2015 proved to be a banner year in fantasy baseball when it came to rookies. Whether you were talking about pitchers or hitters, the 2015 rookie class did its part to impact the fantasy baseball season and supply some significant value to their owners. And it is the allure of the rookie hitter or pitcher that continually brings forth a massive amount of attention each season as we all try to zero in on the next Mike Trout or Matt Harvey. The top rookies almost always bring about intense competition at the draft, oftentimes inflating such a player's value above where it should be considering their untested status. However there also are a much bigger class of rookies who don't garner as much attention and that is where some massive payoffs can arrive. So with all that said, let's take a look at the top rookies for the 2016 fantasy baseball season as we examine their potential impact and forecast when they could arrive on the scene.

THE BIG TEN

1. Corey Seager: Having already had a cup of coffee debut with the Los Angeles Dodgers at the end of last season, the smooth-swinging shortstop is universally praised as a future star. With power that already is starting to bloom and with an advanced hitting approach that should net a string of .300 batting averages, Seager could have immense value this season at a shallow position.

ETA: April 2016

2. Lucas Giolito: While he has a Tommy John elbow surgery in his past, the package is all there for Giolito to be a front-end starter real soon. Blessed with immense size at 6-6 and 255 pounds, Giolito is a bulldog on the mound whose fastball touches 100. A knee-buckling curveball complements the heater and will make Giolito a future 200-K monster. All the kid needs is an opportunity and he will an impact player right out of the gate.

ETA: June 2016

3. Julio Urias: The best left-handed pitching prospect in the game hands down. Urias features a three-pitch repertoire that he repeats with ease, with a fastball that routinely sits in the 93-95 range. Lacking the pure heat of Lucas Giolito, Urias has a bit more movement on his offerings which generate plenty of strikeouts. Has to better develop his changeup to join the advanced fastball and curve. Control lacking at times, especially when Urias tries to dial it up. On the small side at 5-11 and 180 which could lead to some injuries.

ETA: September 2016

4. J.P. Crawford (SS-Phillies): Cousin of Los Angeles Dodgers outfielder Carl Crawford. Good contact skills but power still developing. Runs well but not great. Won't be an overly big stolen base guy. Could hit for a solid average right away but power/speed ability up for debate. Still a bit of a project but has nice ceiling at the shallow shortstop spot.

ETA: August 2016

5. Tyler Glasnow (SP-Pirates): Power pitcher all the way. Glasnow trying to replicate development of Gerrit Cole in terms of using high heat to generate a high level of strikeouts. Control is a big problem at times though and calls into question how high the ceiling can go. Also had has some injury concerns in the past, with some questioning his rough delivery.

ETA: July 2016

6. Trea Turner (SS-Nationals): The Washington Nationals have a potential shortstop gem on their hands with the two-way Trea Turner. Has the inside track to be the team's starting shortstop from Day 1 this season with the Nationals not interested in bringing back Ian Desmond. Has a smooth swing that leads to a bunch of line drives all over the diamond. Can hit for a good average right away. Power not developing yet and the ceiling seems limited here due to a downward swing. Greatest fantasy baseball strength will lie in the stolen base as Turner can really move. Looks like a guy who can bet 30 steals before too long. Average should check out as well.

ETA: April 2016

7. Nomar Mazara (OF-Rangers): Tall kid at 6-5 and has the look of a pure slugger as a major league player. Can fill out his frame more as he matures and the home runs are already flying out with regularity in the minor leagues. Like most young sluggers, strikeouts are an issue and that could lead to average troubles early on in his career. Still Mazara can hit 25 home runs in his sleep and takes enough walks to not be a tremendous liability in batting average.

ETA: September 2016

8. Orlando Arcia (SS-Brewers): Already looks like a future Gold Glove winner at shortstop. With Jean Segura coming off two down seasons, has a chance to be a factor in 2016. Reminds me a bit of Francisco Lindor, with his above-average speed and good contact skills. Not much in the way of power yet but that was the same knock on Lindor who wound up hitting a good amount of home runs as a rookie.

ETA: June 2016

9. Yoan Moncada (2B-Red Sox): Despite standing just 6-0, Moncada is built like a tank. Stands out physically and is a pure gym rat. Portends to some very good power numbers, with Fenway Park eventually helping with the process. Possesses good bat speed but strikes out a bit too much at this early stage. With Dustin Pedroia aging quickly, Moncada could get a look before the end of the 2016 season.

ETA: August 2016

10. Brad Zimmer (OF-Indians): Another big kid at 6-5 but so far without the natural power that Nomar Mazara possesses. Can run well despite the size, looking like a guy who can contribute 10-15 steals. Contact rate is good; swing is a bit long at times though. Needs to work on his approach a bit more before a promotion is warranted.

ETA: April 2017

THE REST

11. Jose Berrios (SP-Twins)

12. Rafael Devers (3B-Red Sox)

13. Alex Reyes (SP-Cardinals)

14. Jose De Leon (SP-Dodgers)

15. Robert Stephenson (SP-Reds)

16. Hector Olivera (2B-Dodgers)

17. Franklin Barreto (SS-A's)

18. Raul Mondesi (SS-Royals)

19. Gleyber Torres (SS-Cubs)

20. Nick Williams (OF-Rangers)

21. Dylan Bundy (SP-Orioles)

22. Josh Bell (Pirates)

23. Jose Peraza (Braves)

24. Brendan Rodgers (SS-Rockies)

25. Dansby Swanson (SS-Arizona)

26. Aaron Judge (OF-Yankees)

27. Sean Newcomb (SP-Los Angeles)

28. Alex Bregman (SS-Astros)

29. Austin Meadows (OF-Pirates)

30. Manuel Margot (OF-Red Sox)

31. Jesse Winker (OF-Reds)

32. Ozhaino Albies (SS-Braves)

2016 FANTASY BASEBALL TEN BURNING QUESTIONS

By Eric C. Wright

One of our more popular yearly features in the Fantasy Sports Boss Fantasy Baseball Draft Guide is our "Ten Burning Questions" section where we try to get some clarity on some of the more pressing issues surrounding the game going into the season. While we can surely sit here all day and answer unending questions about any player or particular subject, these are the topics that we fee need to be addressed the most as you prepare for your draft.

1. Q: It is Mike Trout first and everybody else comes after this season right?

A: Mike Trout as the number 1 pick in 2016 fantasy baseball is as close as you can get to a non-debate. While in the recent past a case could have been made for Miguel Cabrera being the top dog, Trout has clearly separated himself from the rest of the pack during the last two years. Other than maybe Bryce Harper, no one is even in the same area code as Trout.

2. Q: With Trout the obvious choice at number 1, who are the other 11 names that should make up Round 1 in a 2016 mixed ROTO league?

A: Once Trout hears his name called first, the next 11 guys who SHOULD be off the board in most leagues should include the following: Miguel Cabrera, Clayton Kershaw, Paul Goldschmidt, Jose Abreu, Nolan Arenado, Josh Donaldson, Andrew McCutchen, Giancarlo Stanton, Anthony Rizzo, Bryce Harper, and Manny Machado.

3. Q: Let's take this one step further. Who would make up the next 12 picks in Round 2?

A: The first two rounds are generally the cream of the crop among pitchers and hitters and some of these names are also worthy of going in Round 1 as well. They include the following: Nelson Cruz, Todd Frazier, Madison Bumgarner, Dee Gordon, Jose Altuve, Buster Posey, Adam Jones, Ryan Braun, Carlos Correa, Joey Votto, Justin Upton, and Carlos Gomez.

4. Q: Just how good is Carlos Correa?

A: I thought you would never ask. There is not a better young hitter in all of baseball than the Houston Astros dynamic shortstop. Not only is Correa a gem at the most shallow position in the game but his 5-tool ability puts him among the most talented players at any spot on the field. Consider that Correa already has 20/20 ability, with the chance to easily better that in his first full major league season in 2016. Despite only having a half-season of major league play under his belt, we already will proclaim Correa as the number 1 shortstop in fantasy baseball. The kid is that good.

5. Q: How about the sudden explosion of top-shelf third baseman?

A: And how. 2016 saw the previously shallow and injury-plagued third base position absolutely take off as five young thumpers put up some monster numbers. Joining American League MVP Josh Donaldson was Colorado's Nolan Arenado, Cincy's Todd Frazier, Baltimore's Manny Machado, and the Chicago Cubs' Kris Bryant to make third base suddenly one of the most potent spots on the diamond.

6. Q: How much better can Bryce Harper get after his MVP 2015?

A: Needless to say Harper was the epitome of a one-man offensive machine in 2015, hitting .330 with 42 home runs, 118 runs, and 99 RBI. When you consider that Harper is still just 23, one can make the case that he is the only possible challenger to Mike Trout as the number 1 overall player in the game. With such a dominant season in the books, it is tough to imagine Harper bettering that production in 2016 and beyond. However Harper cut his K rate from 26 to 20 percent over the last two years and that number can go lower. In addition, Harper won't reach his power prime for another three years which means 50 home runs is very possible. His biggest challenge other than health is that opposing pitchers will be much more careful around him this season and that alone could lessen the counting statistics a bit. Either way, Harper should go number 2 in all formats this season and is a monster bat even if he simply just repeats his 2016 production.

7. Q: What should be done with the "Wins" column in standard formats?

A: We have gone on record too many times to count in pushing for the elimination of the "Wins" category in standard league 5 x 5 ROTO fantasy baseball. There is not a more fluky statistic in the game and one only has to look at how Washington Nationals ace Max Scherzer tossed two no-hitters in 2016, registered a 2.79 ERA, but yet went only 14-12 with his record. Then there was the case of the Atlanta Braves' Shelby Miller who put up a terrific 3.02 ERA but went 6-17 due to a complete lack of run support from the team's woeful lineup. The fact of the matter is that the wins column should be replaced by the K/BB statistic which is totally in the pitcher's control. Guys who don't beat themselves with walks but yet strike batters out at a high clip should carry extra value in fantasy baseball and that is what this additional statistic does. No longer do you have to pull your hair out when a closer blows a dominant start from your pitcher or rue the fact you own a guy who is an ace hurler who operates on a horrific team and gets no support. Add K/BB to your scoring system and make things even more realistic.

8. Q: What big-name players should we be a bit wary of due to advancing age?

A: Age is the unavoidable factor that takes down every pitcher or hitter at some point. The effects can start as soon as a player reaches the age of 30 and its likelihood increases each year that goes by. Every season is littered with big-name players who fell off sharply due to getting up there in age and the negative effects on their value can be very tough to endure for his owners. This season should be no different of course and with that in mind we have identified a few names to be wary of during your draft. Be extra cautious around the following: Adam Wainwright, Russell Martin, Mark Teixeira, Joe Mauer, Ian Kinsler, Dustin Pedroia, Brandon Phillips, Hanley Ramirez, Jose Reyes, David Wright, Adrian Beltre, Jacoby Ellsbury, and Matt Holliday.

9. Q: Any catcher or shortstop sleepers who can help infuse the two shallowest positions on the diamond?

A: We are always on the lookout for fresh blood at these two spots and there are some newbie's to be aware of at your draft who could supply some very solid value. At catcher, you have a veteran comeback case in the Cleveland Indians' Yan Gomes. Gomes was a budding high-end catcher going into the 2015 season before an early six-week DL stint took him completely out of routine and had him out of sorts when he returned. With 20-home run power and the ability to hit for average, Gomes is a solid comeback candidate. As far as sleepers go, Miami's J.T.

Realmuto and Boston's Blake Swihart have hinted at top ten ability and both should be squarely on your late round radar.

As far as shortstop is concerned, we have a much tougher time identifying undervalued players. While Corey Seager will be the one upstart everyone wants, Trea Turner of the Washington Nationals looks like a better value since his name brand is not as established as his Los Angeles Dodgers counterpart.

10. Q: How does the Fantasy Sports Boss attack a draft again?

A: Our tried-and-true methods remain bronzed and pretty much goes as follows: by the end of Round 2, try your best to have a first baseman and a five-tool outfielder. Avoid catchers until the late middle rounds and the same goes for closers. Your first starting pitcher can be taken as late as Round 5 and eve as late as Round 6 given the massive depth among this group. Do your best to have your middle infielders (second base/shortstop) yield a high number of your stolen base and runs allocation, while your corner infielders (first and third base) should supply you with a major portion of your team's power. Finally your second outfielder should be a four-category guy (while trying to avoid poor batting averages) and your third either a power or speed specialist based on how your middle infield looks. If you have more power guys and are lighter on steals in the middle infield (think Robinson Cano/Jhonny Peralta), look for speed in that third outfielder spot. On the flip side, go with power for your outfielder 3 if your middle infield swipes a bunch of bags. While not an exact science, this is how we have won countless leagues for ourselves and hopefully for all of you.

THE TOMMY JOHN EPIDEMIC: WHICH PITCHERS ARE MOST AT RISK TO BECOME THE NEXT VICTIM?

By Michael E. Keneski

If you are a young and hard-throwing pitcher in today's major league baseball, you have been forewarned. Based on some very ugly recent trends, there is a very good chance you too will soon fall under the Tommy John knife at some point. With more pitchers (and even some position players) falling victim to the surgery over the last few years, some around the game think we are getting close to epidemic proportions. While no one has any one answer as far as how to remedy the issue, many have voiced their thoughts on how best to proceed. One of the smartest and more accurate statements that was spoken on the topic recently came from new Washington Nationals ace SP Max Scherzer who shared some views that make a ton of sense given what we have seen over the last few years. Scherzer, in angling for why he deserved a long-term contract as a free agent last offseason, argued that once a pitcher goes past the age of 27, he is pretty much in the clear for Tommy John. His argument was that pitchers under 27 are more susceptible to the procedure due to the fact that their arms and ligaments are still developing and thus they have to be managed more carefully in terms of workload. Based on the evidence, Scherzer seems dead on. You can count on one hand the amount of veteran starters who have had the surgery and there are clear trends that have emerged in terms of what type of pitchers more often than not wind up needing the procedure. The red warning flashes should be going off above the heads of starting pitchers who are under the age of 27 and who throw fastballs on average of 95 or greater. Under that premise, we have compiled a list of pitchers who fit this criteria heading into the 2016 season. While we are not suggesting you avoid these names altogether, we are advising you at least understand the risks associated with drafting such an hurler.

Yordano Ventura: I have spoken more than a few times about the very high risk Ventura brings due to his slight frame and full-out torque when he throws. Ventura had a Tommy John scare in 2014 when his elbow began to bark but at that point no structural issues were found. However that is the same schedule 2015 Tommy John victim Zack Wheeler of the New York Mets had when he too showed a clean MRI on his elbow the year prior. Tread carefully here.

Chris Sale: It is old news in saying that Chris Sale is injury prone and that was before he fractured his foot at the start of spring training last season. Sale has had shoulder or elbow trouble at least once from 2012 through 2014. While Sale's arm stayed sound throughout the 2015 season, his very awkward delivery has been blamed for his history of arm trouble. Remember too that Sale followed the Adam Wainwright bullpen to starter path and we all know how that turned out for the St. Louis veteran.

Madison Bumgarner: Bumgarner is very scary for a few reasons. The first is the insane amount of innings he tossed in 2014 during the San Francisco Giants' World Series championship run. The second is that Bumgarner is number 1 in all of baseball in pitches thrown by a starter who was 25 years old or younger over the last three seasons combined.

Sonny Gray: Gray is a lower risk as he is not a pure heat guy but he has thrown a lot of tough innings at a young age which is always risky.

Alex Wood: Nothing yet to suggest Wood will succumb to anything but I hate the starter-to-bullpen-to-starter path he traveled in 2014 and last season saw his numbers plummet when expectations were sizable. The last time someone did such a flip flop was Joba Chamberlain and he ended up needing the surgery.

Gerrit Cole: Cole already has dealt with shoulder trouble and pitching to compensate for that injury puts more stress on the elbow. Also Cole is near the top in all of major league baseball in terms of his average fastball velocity which adds to the red flags.

Andrew Cashner: Cashner has already had a few Tommy John scares and dealt with a slew of elbow/shoulder trouble since becoming a starter for the San Diego Padres. He too throws very hard and seems like a classic case waiting to happen.

Tyson Ross: Ross is incredible scary as he throws his elbow-killing slider over 40 percent of the time, no doubt an extreme red flag. There is only so much an elbow can take in terms of that stressful pitch.

Noah Syndegaard: The tall and lanky right-hander was in the top five in baseball when it came to average fastball velocity during his 2015 debut and Syndegaard also had a major scare late in 2014 while in the minors when his elbow began screaming. Slight frame and high velocity fastball often leads to trouble.

Jacob DeGrom: Just like with rotation mate Noah Syndegaard, Jacob DeGrom lingered in the top 5-7 starting pitchers in all of baseball in terms of average fastball velocity last season. DeGrom already has a Tommy John surgery under his belt which shows you how prone he could be to another procedure and the innings are really starting to pile up for him since becoming a Mets mainstay in 2014.

Carlos Martinez: The latest pitching gem to come out of the St. Louis Cardinals system, Carlos Martinez was as good as any other starter in the game in 2015, his first ever full season as a member of the team's rotation. Martinez is the personification of a power pitcher, unleashing a heater which stays in the 98-100 range consistently. He also has bounced around from the bullpen to the rotation which has been an avenue to Tommy John surgery for other young hurlers.

Jake Odorizzi: Last but not least we have a hard thrower in Odorizzi who is also quite young. Nothing has shown up yet but he is still in the infant stages of his development.

There you have it. While I wouldn't avoid all of these young and talented pitchers, I would particularly look to pass on Sale, Bumgarner, Cole, Ventura, and Ross who all look like the biggest injury risks. The ability is clearly there but so is the inherent risk in each.

2015 FANTASY SPORTS BOSS FANTASY BASEBALL POSITION RANKINGS AND PLAYER ANALYSIS

CATCHERS

Draft Strategy: Outside of maybe shortstop, there is not a position in all of fantasy baseball that causes more angst and frustration than catchers do. With the position already thinned out in recent years with former top tier bats like Joe Mauer, Mike Napoli, and Victor Martinez losing eligibility there, this already thin group was made even more barren with Carlos Santana and Evan Gattis leaving the position as well for 2016. Buster Posey is obviously the diamond in the rough here whose combination of high batting average and solid power perennially makes him a popular target in the early rounds of the draft but from that point on chaos reigns. With that said, we continue to espouse on our firm strategy of drafting catchers in the mid-to-late rounds, in particular looking for players that fit two different criteria. The first centers on veteran catchers who are coming off a down season that will result in a much more affordable draft price the following spring. Players who fall into this category for 2016 include Jonathan Lucroy, Yan Gomes, Devin Mesoraco, and Matt Wieters. The other grouping is to target young catchers who are on the verge of being promoted to the big leagues and who carry some decent sleeper value. Those who came through under this scenario with varying degrees of impact in 2015 included Kyle Schwarber, Stephen Vogt, Francisco Cervelli, J.T. Realmuto, Wellington Castillo, Derek Norris, Travis D'Arnaud (when he was on the field), and Yasmani Grandal. In fact we pushed both Vogt and Grandal heavily in last year's draft guide under this premise which worked out well for those who followed the advice.

In two-catcher formats you obviously have to move a bit sooner to get your first backstop but again we prefer passing on the big names early on as you instead fill out the rest of the roster with more stable players at other positions. In single-catcher leagues, wait until the middle-to-late round where you can find some significant value if you know where to look.

1. Buster Posey: Simply the best among all catchers once again, Buster Posey will remain a debate talking point in regards to whether or not it is smart to use a very early round pick on a catcher. On numbers alone, Posey makes the grade as he is the rare catcher who can hit for both average and power, coming in at 19/.318 in 2015. Now having logged four straight full seasons since his devastating broken leg in 2011, Posey's durability makes investing in him a bit less risky than it once was. In terms of the numbers, Posey is one of the best pure hitters in the game, having now logged 4 of his six major league seasons with an average north of .300. While his career-high in home runs is a modest 24, this is like 34 at the catcher spot. Still early in his prime at the age of 29, Posey incredibly stuck out in just 8.8 percent of his at-bats in 2015, while walking at a 9 percent clip, making a .300 average a lock when looking ahead to this season. While we still prefer looking for value in the middle rounds when it comes to addressing this position, Posey is so far ahead of the next catcher in fantasy baseball that he does qualify to be chosen so high.

2016 PROJECTION: .311 22 HR 93 RBI 73 R 1 SB

2. Kyle Schwarber: Meet the new "must have" fantasy baseball bat, as Chicago Cubs backstop/outfielder Kyle Schwarber became the latest prospect gem to become an instant impact player for the team in 2015. Evoking some memories of Mike Piazza, Schwarber showed instant massive power, while hitting over .300 his first two months in the majors in June and July. Schwarber's high strikeout rate was exploited from that point on though, as his 28.2 percent K rate caused his average to sink to a shaky .246 by the end of the season. We can chalk a lot of that up to Schwarber being a rookie but he did hit well over .300 in his final minor league season in 2014 which points to an expected improvement there as he continues to develop. The power is already here though (16 home runs in just 273 at-bats with the Cubs) and Schwarber seems like a lock to be a future 25-30 home run threat as soon as this season. Also carrying outfield eligibility, Schwarber is the new catching-eligible toy we all want to have. The price will be steep though given the lack of top-end options at catcher and the excitement Schwarber generated during his debut. However the upside is tremendous and the name Jim Thome has been mentioned as a power comparison.

2016 PROJECTION: .265 25 HR 77 RBI 84 R 5 SB

3. Brian McCann: With chaos once again enveloping the catcher fraternity in 2015 fantasy baseball, old reliable Brian McCann came through yet again with top 5 numbers at the position. Looking much more comfortable in his second season with the New York Yankees and in the American League, McCann smacked 26 home runs, drove in 94, and batted .232. Yes the average was ugly but McCann has been a liability there going back to 2012 so no surprise there. Instead embrace the power and runs batted in as McCann was as good as any catcher when you combine the two last season. While McCann is getting a bit long in the tooth at 32, his lefty swing is a perfect match for the short porch in rightfield at Yankee Stadium. That alone should keep him at or around top five numbers once again.

2016 PROJECTION: .239 25 HR 89 RBI 65 R 0 SB

4. Salvador Perez: A solid sleeper from behind the dish over the last few years, the Kansas City Royals' Salvador Perez finally put a full season together in 2015 when he hit a career-high 21 home runs and drove in 70. Over the last two years Perez has traded the .300 batting average he showed when he first debuted with the Royals for more power, making him more interesting to own in his present form. Turning 26 in May, we are likely at or near the standard allotment of numbers Perez will produce in his prime and that puts him among the top 4-6 catches this season. With a walk rate that would make Vladimir Guerrero proud (2.4 percent in 2015), Perez is swinging for the fences like never before. As long as he can keep down his history of injuries, Perez will supply the value anticipated.

2016 PROJECTION: .267 20 HR 71 RBI 55 R 1 SB

5. Jonathan Lucroy: Veteran Milwaukee Brewers backstop Jonathan Lucroy went down as yet another example of the risks in investing too high a draft pick on your fantasy baseball catcher. Coming off a terrific 2014 where Lucroy was the rare catcher who contributed across all five standard ROTO categories, the encore in 2015 was nothing short of a major letdown. While Lucroy's hitting rate statistics were well down across the board, injuries were the main factor in his rough season as he missed a month-and-a-half early on with a busted thumb and then saw his second half ruined by the effects of a concussion that lingered for weeks. In between, Lucroy was only able to hit .259 with 7 home runs and 41 RBI in 402 at-bats. Some negatives with regards to the bat was the fact Lucroy struck out at a 14.9 percent clip, his highest in that category since 2011. Turning 30-years-old in June, Lucroy wouldn't be the first backstop to see his numbers erode as he begins to age. Of course we can also give Lucroy a mulligan regarding last season's struggles due to all the health woes and at the very least a batting average rebound is likely since he has hit .320, .280, and .301 from 2012 through 2014. The draft price will be a bit cheaper this time around which is mildly attractive but Lucroy is starting to feel like old news to us.

2016 PROJECTION: .284 12 HR 71 RBI 67 R 2 SB

6. Stephen Vogt: After years of toiling in the minor leagues, Oakland A's catcher Stephen Vogt finally got his chance to be a starter as the 2015 season got underway. Having intriguing power and having come off a 2014 when he batted .279 in 287 at-bats, Vogt made our Sleeper list due to the upside he brought to the table. Needless to say, Vogt went nuts in the first half as he batted .287 and slammed 14 home runs in just 279 at-bats. On pace for a tremendous season, the wheels began to come off once the All-Star Game was in the books. In a likely case of fatigue due to having caught a major league season for the first time, Vogt sank all the way to a .217 average and only four home runs during the second half. Things got so bad that Vogt took a seat on the bench at times for the fresher Josh Phlegey. Ultimately though, Vogt had a successful year and staked his claim to the starting job for 2016. No doubt better prepared for the grueling length of the season given his 2015 experience, Vogt will likely be able to carry his numbers further into the summer. 20 home runs is not out of the question with a decent average as well. Better yet, Vogt's fade last season will help keep his draft price in check and thus make him a good value for the second year in a row. Go get him.

2016 PROJECTION: .275 19 HR 74 RBI 63 R 1 SB

7. Travis D'Arnaud: When you have been traded for two Cy Young Award winners, there is understandably a great deal of hype attached to your name. That is the narrative for New York Mets catcher Travis D'Arnaud who was considered a can't miss future star coming up the Toronto Blue Jays system. It was that hype which led to him being moved in separate deals for Roy Halladay and R.A. Dickey over the last few years. Unfortunately, a very bad run of injuries have stunted D'Arnaud's growth and led many to think he is nothing but a tease.

While that is an understandable thought given the frustrations of owning D'Arnaud the last two years, it also is showing itself to be a premature one. While D'Arnaud's first half of 2015 included two more DL stints, the second half of the season brought some encouraging signs. Altogether D'Arnaud hit 8 of his 12 home runs from that point onward, collecting 24 RBI in 168 at-bats. For a catcher, D'Arnaud has shown a better than average K rate and he draws walks as well at a decent clip. Combined together, D'Arnaud should be able to bat higher than last season's .268 as he further refines himself. There is still some ceiling left to D'Arnaud's game and if he can just scratch out 400-plus at-bats, 20 home runs and a .280 average are in the cards.

2016 PROJECTION: .277 17 HR 66 RBI 56 R 1 SB

8. Devin Mesoraco: Yeah so that breakout encore did not go over so well. Mesoraco was a fantasy baseball darling in 2014 as he finally unleashed the power potential he had hinted at previously but never was able to show under the veteran-loving stewardship of Dusty Baker. Mesoraco got a fresh start with Baker out of the picture to start the 2014 season and the results were immediate as he smacked 25 home runs, drove in 80, and batted .273. Those numbers sent Mesoraco's 2015 draft stock soaring as he went as high as the second catcher off the board in many leagues. Only 45 homerless at-bats later and Mesoraco was done for the year after being forced to undergo hip surgery. Mesoraco is expected to be fully healthy for the start of 2016 but hip surgery almost always results in a decrease in power, at least for the start of the next season which makes his immediate future a bit murky. In addition, Mesoraco's .273 average in 2014 was a bit misleading as he batted only .237 the second half of the season as opposing pitchers began to get a book on his tendencies. Overall there are quite a few red flags surrounding Mesoraco in 2016 but at least the draft price will be drastically reduced which is about the only positive thing we can say.

2016 PROJECTION: .262 17 HR 67 RBI 51 R 1 SB

9. Welington Castillo: It was a nice tour around baseball for Welington Castillo in 2015, as the backstop was traded twice in the span of a month. First the Chicago Cubs moved Castillo to the Seattle Mariners for pitcher Yoervis Medina, who then flipped him to the Arizona Diamondbacks in the Mark Trumbo deal. A late bloomer who turns 29 in April, Castillo was very productive with the

Diamondbacks as he smacked 17 home runs and batted .255 in just 274 at-bats. Overall Castillo put up a career-high 19 home runs and 57 RBI between his three MLB stops and his swing really seemed like a good fit in the offensive dimensions of Chase Field. Castillo goes into 2016 as the clear-cut starter for the first time in his career and 20 home runs seems very possible given how well he mashed in his new environment last season. What is doubly interesting here is the fact that Castillo's average should have been quite a bit higher. His .263 BABIP was very unlucky and Castillo has hit as high as .274 in the past, meaning there is room for improvement there. When you combine the 20 home run power and a better batting average in 2016, Castillo looks like a tremendous late-middle round pick who is the type of classic value play we always are searching for at catcher.

2016 PROJECTION: .258 20 HR 65 RBI 44 R 0 SB

10. Yan Gomes: It appeared as though the Cleveland Indians had a real find on their hands when it came to Brazilian catcher Yan Gomes. A previously unknown 10th round pick by the Toronto Blue Jays, Gomes broke through with the Indians in 2013 and immediately began opening eyes by hitting .294 with 11 home runs in just 293 at-bats. Showing that his debut performance was no fluke, Gomes hit another 21 home runs with a .278 average in 2014 to stamp himself as a future star at the always shallow catching position. Despite all the good vibes Gomes had previously, his 2015 season was an abomination as he went on the DL for six weeks at the start of the year and then batted a listless .231 in 363 at-bats afterwards. The 12 home runs show that Gomes still has some very good pop to offer his owners but he went backwards both in his K rate and his walk rate which caused the average to drop. Ultimately though, we can give Gomes a mulligan for 2015 as the injury so early in the season threw off the timing for a still developing hitter. Gomes is older then you may think as he turns 29 in July but he was a classic late bloomer who can threaten 20 home runs again with good health.

2016 PROJECTION: .275 19 HR 78 RBI 65 R 0 SB

11. J.T. Realmuto: The Miami Marlins are set on bestowing the starting catcher duties on former 2010 third round pick J.T. Realmuto after giving him a baptism by fire last season. With just 29 previous major league at-bats under his belt, Realmuto was given the starting nod right out of spring training with the Marlins having no other decent option to turn to. While there were some extended struggles along the way as one would expect from any young player, Realmuto acquitted himself quite nicely by hitting .259 with 8 home runs and 47 RBI in 441 at-bats. As an added bonus, Realmuto supplied a pleasant surprise in the form of 10 stolen bases. While Realmuto is not Jason Kendall when it comes to pilfering bags, he has good speed that could net a few more thefts in 2016 to go along with growth in the other categories. Realmuto has to show some more patience as his BB/9 was a rancid 4.1 percent but the flipside is that he makes good contact for a young player with just a 15.0 K/9. That means a push up in batting average is likely to go with some added pop as he further develops. The trends are all pointing in the direction you want them to be going in and the lack of focus on anything the Marlins do outside of Jose Fernandez and Giancarlo Stanton make Realmuto a very attractive upside pick.

2016 PROJECTION: .267 14 HR 54 RBI 55 R 10 SB

12. Blake Swihart: Sleeper alert! The Boston Red Sox are almost fully embracing a youth movement all over the diamond and that includes behind the dish in the form of top catching prospect Blake Swihart. The former 2011 first round pick (26th overall) left us wanting to see more last season as he hit 5 home runs and batted a very solid .274 in just 288 at-bats. While even the most hyped catchers tend to struggle early in their careers as they often get overwhelmed with handling a pitching staff and defensive duties, Swihart is the kind of classic sleeper that makes for a possibly tremendous middle round grab. While guys like Buster Posey, Carlos Santana, and Matt Wieters all came up with massive hype, Swihart is sort of flying a bit under the radar which makes him an even better buying option. The kid has a nice approach at the dish with developing power and even some speed. In 2014 at Double-A, Swihart batted .300 with 12 home runs and 7 stolen base, showing some very attractive potential numbers. Now Swihart won't come close to hitting .300 at the major league level yet due to a strikeout issue (24.9 percent with the Red Sox last season), but he could be a slightly better 2015 version of J.T. Realmuto. Upward and onward we go.

2016 PROJECTION: .278 11 HR 56 RBI 54 R 7 SB

13. Yadier Molina: We are well on the back nine in terms of the Hall of Fame-worthy career of St. Louis Cardinals backstop Yadier Molina. While still as good as it gets defensively, Molina has been leaking offensive numbers the last three years. In addition, all those years of catching is starting to catch up to Molina physically as he has dealt with serious injuries in each of the last two years. A torn thumb ligament was the latest health blow for Molina at the end of 2015 which required surgery but prior to that the 33-year-old was having his worst offensive season ever as he hit .270 with just 4 home runs in 488 at-bats. A clear trend is emerging with the home runs as over the last four seasons Molina's totals there have been 22, 12, 7, and now 4. The batting average has taken the same path, with Molina hitting .319 in 2013, .282 in 2014, followed by last season's 270. Even a fantasy baseball novice can see that Molina is becoming nothing but an empty bat and an injury-prone player as well. There is not much left to work with here as Molina is now more name brand than anything he can do on the field.

2016 PROJECTION: .275 5 HR 63 RBI 32 R 2 SB

14. Russell Martin: We all know the Toronto Blue Jays grossly overpaid for the services of aging catcher Russell Martin prior to the 2015 season but the intangibles were part of the equation such as leadership and calling a game. That has no bearing on those who evaluate him for fantasy baseball purposes but Martin was no slouch with the bat either last season as he hit a career-high 23 home runs and drove in 77 batters. Clearly Rogers Center helped boost the power for Martin and in turn helped ward off him being discarded for fantasy purposes. Things were quite ugly with the average though as Martin batted just .240 and that has been an annual negative with him for awhile now. In addition to the putrid average, Martin's speed is now almost completely evaporated as he turns 33 in February. Again the fact he can continue hitting in Rogers Center half of the season should help keep Martin useable for another season or two but you would surely like some more upside if you can from somewhere else.

2016 PROJECTION: .245 19 HR 74 RBI 75 R 3 SB

15. Matt Wieters: After being the rare hitter forced to undergo Tommy John elbow surgery, catcher Matt Wieters was pretty much a forgotten man going into the 2015 season. A puzzling development in that Wieters had already proven himself to be a 20-plus home run catcher who wouldn't kill you in batting average either; which is nothing to sneeze at when it comes to this always volatile group. Once Wieters finally made his return in mid-June, he looked like his old self in cracking 9 home runs and batting .267 in just 258 at-bats. While Wieters did strike out a bit more than usual (23.8 percent), a lot of that could be chalked up to rust. With another year removed from the surgery and still young at the age of 30, Wieters is shaping up as a very good value play that can be had in the late rounds of the draft as he remains in a prime hitter's park after accepting Baltimore's $15.8 million qualifying offer.

2016 PROJECTION: .263 17 HR 74 RBI 59 R 0 SB

16. Yasmani Grandal: Last season at this time we included Los Angeles Dodgers catcher Yasmani Grandal in our "Sleepers" section due to our steady belief in his hitting skills despite getting caught up in the Biogenesis mess. A former top catching prospect when coming up the San Diego Padres system on the strength of some terrific batting averages but with some mediocre pop, Grandal has reversed those tendencies since getting to the majors. That continued on in his first full season with the Dodgers in 2015 as Grandal hit 15 home runs but batted just .234 in 355 at-bats. It actually started looking like Grandal was headed for a tremendous season when he went into the All-Star break with a .282 average and 14 of those 16 home runs. The bottom completely fell out during the second half though as Grandal was benched often for backup A.J. Ellis. While Grandal clearly possesses very good power, the hacking approach has him above the 20 percent mark in K rate which is not where you want a hitter to be. Over the last three seasons now, Grandal has batted just .216, .225, and .234, meaning he has to hit at least 15 home runs to be worth your time in fantasy baseball. With Ellis playing more than a true backup, that could be tough to reach.

2016 PROJECTION: .244 17 HR 54 RBI 50 R 3 SB

17. Nick Hundley: When we advise you to avoid drafting your fantasy baseball catcher in the early rounds of yearly drafts, our counter argument is to look for upside later on. While we like to check out prospects on the cusp of the majors here, more often it is the undervalued veteran backstops that supply the most value. One such example of the latter in 2015 was Colorado Rockies catcher Nick Hundley. After failing to do much of anything during his time with the San Diego Padres, Hundley latched onto an ideal hitting situation with the Colorado Rockies going into 2015. Coors Field is always a ballpark that makes any hitter operating there interesting and Hundley did his part by batting a career-high .301, while also swatting 10 home runs and posting another career-high in RBI with 45 before going on the shelf for good in early September with a neck strain. While those numbers won' blow you away, Hundley was quite useful in two-catcher formats and even worked as a short-to-moderate injury fill-in in single-catcher leagues. At 33-years-old, Hundley will not do any better than what he supplied in 2015 and in fact a slight step back in numbers would not be a shock. His .356 BABIP was extremely lucky which means a drop in batting average is a guarantee. Best if used in two-catcher formats.

2016 PROJECTION: .284 9 HR 44 RBI 41 R 2 SB

18. Derek Norris: While he didn't elicit the same type of hype that Justin Upton, Matt Kemp, or James Shields carried, catcher Derek Norris was part of the massive overhaul undertaken by the San Diego Padres leading up to the 2015 season. Norris was acquired from the Oakland A's to be the team's everyday backstop and he impressed by hitting 11 home runs during the first half of the season, albeit with an ugly .233 batting average. Norris reversed those numbers during an injury-marred second half, hitting .278 with just 3 long balls. While the overall line was a bit underwhelming, Norris yielded some good value in two catcher formats. Norris has now hit .250 or worse in three of his four major league seasons though and the 14 home runs he hit in 2015 were his high thus far. Throw in the awful home ballpark and Norris remains best left as the second catcher in formats that play two.

2016 PROJECTION: .254 16 HR 65 RBI 63 R 3 SB

19. Wilson Ramos: Having carried sleeper value that was always undermined by injuries over the last few seasons, Wilson Ramos burned through any remaining goodwill left prior to 2015. While he finally did manage to stay healthy in accumulating by far a career-high of 475 at-bats, Ramos' average sank badly to a horrid .229. The 15 home runs were all right but Ramos had done that twice before with less than 400 at-bats, meaning he was on a firm decline on a per game basis in that statistic last season. With Ramos being an injury waiting to happen and having shown underwhelming numbers when he finally stayed healthy, it is now time to look for a new upside play.

2016 PROJECTION: .253 16 HR 67 RBI 48 R 2 SB

20. Francisco Cervelli: Having finally been given a chance to be a starting catcher after years of minor league and backup duty with the New York Yankees, Francisco Cervelli went into the solid but unspectacular bin last season. After hitting .301 in part-time duty with the Yankees in 2014, Cervelli batted .295 with the Pittsburgh Pirates last season, lending credence to him being a good average bet at a position filled with .250 hitters. Cervelli doesn't offer much in the power department though, collecting just 7 home runs in 451 at-bats. In addition, Cervelli has quite a checkered injury history which means he should be just a very late round pick in two catcher formats.

2016 PROJECTION: .286 8 HR 48 RBI 59 R 1 SB

21. Miguel Montero: While the Chicago Cubs will say that they were happy with the production of veteran catcher Miguel Montero last season, they surely had to have regrets for dealing away Wellington Castillo who took off immediately after he was moved to the Seattle Mariners (and later Arizona Diamondbacks). While we will take 15 home runs from our fantasy baseball catcher, Montero combined that with a ugly .248 average. Now turning 33 and three full seasons removed from even a decent batting average, the falloff could come sharply for Montero going forward. Be sure not to make the same mistake the Cubs made in sticking with an aging veteran.

2016 PROJECTION: .249 14 HR 57 RBI 46 R 1 SB

THE REST

22. John Jaso: Veteran catcher John Jaso is an interesting player in that he doesn't fit the classic mold of a hitter who also dons the tools of ignorance. Having on-base ability that is very rare at the position, Jaso has held down the leadoff spot at times in his career, primarily with the Tampa Bay Rays who he reunited with last season. There is very little in the way of power with Jaso, as he has reached double-digits in home runs once in his six-year career. On the flip side, he makes up for that with a decent .263 average for a catcher. A free agent as of this writing at the advancing age of 32, Jaso needs to find another starting job somewhere to stay relevant in either AL or NL-only formats.

23. James McCann: Along the same lines of Blake Swihart and J.T. Realmuto, Detroit Tigers 2011 second round pick James McCann seems primed to be part of the next generation of solid offensive catchers. With Alex Avila looking completely finished, McCann took advantage of the chance to stick with the team in 2015 by hitting .264 with 7 home runs and 41 RBI in 425 at-bats. The Tigers will likely open up the starting job to McCann for 2016 as well and the kid has some very appealing upside as a late round pick. McCann also has a bit of speed as he stole some bases in the minor leagues which could be an added bonus as well. It won't cost hardly anything to check McCann out and the payoff could be decent.

24. Robinson Chirinos: The Texas Rangers have gotten some positive usage out of veteran catcher Robinson Chirinos over the last two years, getting a total of 23 home runs in 593 at-bats. Another catcher who took awhile to stick in the majors, Chirinos will already turn 32 in June. Chirinos has yet to hit even .240 in his career and he possesses only moderate power. Just a smidge of value in AL-only formats.

25. Cameron Rupp: The Philadelphia Phillies completely ushered in their youth movement in 2015 and that included moving away from perennial backstop Carlos Ruiz. With Ruiz on fumes, the Phillies inserted the hulking Cameron Rupp and immediately were rewarded with 9 home runs in only 270 at-bats. At 6-2 and 258, Rupp looks like your classic slugger and his expected starting assignment in 2016 means he should easily move into the mid-teens in the home run category. The batting average is another story though as Rupp strikes out way too much (23.7 percent) to be anything better than a .250 guy at best. If you are looking for a slight upside play for your second catcher in two backstop formats, Rupp is your guy.

26. Carlos Perez: With the Los Angeles Angles getting absolutely horrendous offensive production from their catchers over the last five years, it made sense they decided to take a look at prospect Carlos Perez at the beginning of May last season. Perez earned the promotion by hitting a scorching .361 in 79 at-bats at Triple-A. While Perez wound up hitting just .250 and 4 home runs in his 86 game trial run with the Angels, he likely earned himself the inside track to the starting spot for 2016. Perez has a nice hitting approach as he makes good contact to the tune of a 17.3 percent K rate which points to a batting average improvement going forward. While there is not a lot of power here even going back to his Triple-A run, Perez has enough upside to be worth using in two catcher formats.

27. Curt Casali: Always on the lookout for emerging catchers who can handle the bat, the Tampa Bay Rays might have found someone there in the form of Curt Casali. A late bloomer who didn't make his major league debut until he was 25, Casali hit 10 home runs in only 101 at-bats in 2015 which earned him the starting catching job during the second half of the season. Unfortunately like many catchers, the average was an issue as Casali hit only .238. Casali strikes out a ton (30.01 percent in 2015) which will make hitting north of .250 a challenge but the power is interesting enough in two catcher setups. Overall Casali has very limited upside but he should at least get a bunch of at-bats as the starter for the Rays next season.

28. Jason Castro: We never bought into the so-called "breakout" year that Jason Castro had with the Houston Astros back in 2013 when he hit 18 home runs and batted .257 for the team. Instead we correctly pointed out the two major red flags with Castro, with the first being his high strikeout rate that kept opposing pitchers from giving him anything to drive and the second being his persistent injury woes that annually stunt his growth. Both issues took center stage for Castro the last two seasons as he has hit a terrible .222 and .211 during those campaigns and he also dealt with more knee problems. There is no good reason for you to want any part of this mess.

29. Caleb Joseph: A backup to Matt Wieters the last two seasons, Joseph picked up a bunch of unexpected playing time when his counterpart missed large chunks during both of those campaigns due to Tommy John elbow surgery. As a result, Joseph showed some very good power potential, cracking 20 home runs total in a combined 566 at-bats. While that was no doubt solid production, Joseph will once again back up a healthy Wieters from the start of 2016. That means he pretty much has no value unless Wieters gets injured again.

30. Tyler Flowers: It was a fairly typical 2015 season for Chicago White Sox catcher Tyler Flowers. Having logged his 7th consecutive season with the team, Flowers hit some home runs (9) and did nothing else as he batted just .239, while also failing to reach the 40 mark in both runs and RBI. You really have to be a big White Sox junkie to even think of owning Flowers in AL-only formats.

31. Kurt Suzuki: The recent trend of Minnesota Twins catcher Kurt Suzuki alternating a good batting average season to a horrific one continued in 2015 as his number there sank to a terrible .240 after he batted a surprisingly good .288 the year prior. Having been selected to the All-Star Game due more to his skills calling a game and defensively, Suzuki offers very little from the offensive side at this late stage of his career. At the advancing age of 32, Suzuki's utter lack of pop (5 home runs in 476 at-bats last season) make him barely even worth owning in AL-only setups.

32. Hank Conger: A first round draft pick going all the way back to 2005, Hank Conger has failed to live up to initial expectations of him developing into an above-average catcher as he made his way through the Los Angeles Angels organization and more recently with the Houston Astros. Showing horrific contact skills from the start, Conger is just a .225 career hitter who has never even received 250 at-bats during any one season due to his terrible performances. While Conger did hit a career-best 11 home runs in 2015, he has shown himself to be nothing but waiver junk in all formats.

33. Dioneer Navarro: It is tough to carve out any sort of impact season when you are backing up a freshly signed Russell Martin when it came to the 2015 Toronto Blue Jays. While Dioneer Navarro has been a useful player as recently as 2013 and 2014 (a combined 25 home runs to go with .300 and .274 batting averages, Navarro needs to get himself back into a starting spot in order for him to have any semblance of value. As he begins to age at 32, Navarro is looking like old news.

34. Josh Phegley: The very rough finish to Stephen Vogt's season in 2015 opened the door to some playing time for backup catcher Josh Phegley. While Phegley did a decent enough job with 9 home runs in only 225 at-bats, he is just a career .227 hitter in parts of three seasons and is nothing more than a backup on his own squad.

35. John Ryan Murphy: The Yankees have a new intriguing backup catcher on their hands after shipping out Francisco Cervelli prior to the start of the 2015 season. In Cervelli's place went John Ryan Murphy who had a reputation of being a good defensive catcher but who struggled with the bat. The latter projection was not accurate as Murphy wound up hitting .277 with 3 home runs in just 155 at-bats. The Yankees even had Murphy get some work at first base down the stretch of the season when Mark Teixeira went out injured. Still Murphy has zero value unless he gets moved prior to 2016, a distinct possibility since the Yankees have Gary Sanchez next up for promotion.

36. Alex Avila: By now it is obvious that the very productive 2011 season by Alex Avila for the Detroit Tigers (.295/19 HR/82 RBI) was a gigantic outlier campaign. Over the next four seasons, Avila hit a grand total of 35 home runs and wound up batting no better than .243 as his strikeout rates were hideous. In addition to the awful offensive numbers, Avila was a physical mess who missed large chunks of games. With the Tigers now turning to the much younger and more interesting James McCann, it is likely Avila's days being a starting catcher are through.

37. Christian Bethancourt: The Atlanta Braves tried to give catching prospect Christian Bethancourt a chance to stake his claim to the starting job as the team began their complete roster overhaul last season but the kid failed to do so by hitting just .200 with 2 home runs in his 155 at-bats. Bethancourt at least deserves another shot since he was hitting .327 at Triple-A prior to his promotion by the Braves but there are question marks about how high the upside is. You don't want to wait around to find out.

38. Mike Zunino: On a per game basis last season, there may not have been a worse major league hitter than Seattle Mariners backstop Mike Zunino. The Mariners stayed very patient through Zunino's struggles but eventually sent him back to Triple-A in late August in order to revamp his ugly swing. The previous results were staggeringly bad as Zunino went into the demotion hitting only .174 in 350 at-bats with 11 home runs and 28 RBI. No that is not a misprint. Neither was Zunino's unfathomable 34.2 percent K rate in 2015. There is not a hitter on the planet that can hold down a major league job with numbers that hideous and Zunino's once-intriguing potential looks now like a complete joke. Even in AL-only leagues, Zunino doesn't warrant your attention.

FIRST BASEMAN

Draft Strategy: Once again first base is Ground Zero when it comes to collecting a bunch of your team's power numbers (home runs, RBI) and in actuality, it is a great idea for you to get your CI or UTIL bat from this group as well. First base is annually the deepest position in fantasy baseball as almost every major league team sticks their best power hitter there and it is from this group that we strongly suggest you spend one of your first two picks on. Unlike with catcher or shortstop, there should be no panning for value in the middle rounds here as you want to have that power anchor for your team right off the bat in your drafts. We still strongly suggest using your first two picks on a five-tool outfielder and a slugging first baseman who is both solid in the power and average categories. Accomplish that feat and you are on your way to constructing a very solid hitting team. And then be sure to come back here in the early middle rounds for your CI or UTIL bat.

1. Paul Goldschmidt: Just when you thought Paul Goldschmidt couldn't get any better, he goes out and does just that in a truly remarkable 2015 season. Putting himself right at the top of the fantasy baseball MVP talk, Goldschmidt hit a career-high .321 to go with another best in the stolen base category with 21. Of course power is Goldschmidt's calling card as he hit 33 home runs and collected 110 RBI. Also crossing the 100 mark in runs scored with 103, Goldschmidt became the incredibly rare five-category stud that has him in the discussion for the number 3 spot overall behind Mike Trout and Bryce Harper. Just the fact that Goldschmidt steals 21 bases while manning first base is ridiculous in and of itself when combined with the awesome power and batting title-worthy average. It made our debate column between Goldschmidt and the Chicago White Sox' Jose Abreu prior to last season laughable. In fact Goldschmidt is now the clear standard bearer at the potent first base position and he absolutely should be under strong consideration as the number 3 pick in any draft.

2016 PROJECTION: .315 35 HR 114 RBI 107 R 19 SB

2. Miguel Cabrera: It was another batting title season for Detroit Tigers first baseman Miguel Cabrera in 2015, an achievement that reaffirmed his status as a top five player regardless of position in fantasy baseball after a somewhat disappointing year by his lofty standards in 2014. By now it is stating the obvious that Cabrera is one of the greatest hitters ever when you combine average and power in the modern era but turning 33 in June, you have to wonder how much longer he will be able to maintain his lofty numbers. There is some concern over the fact Cabrera has dealt with some more than minor injuries over the last two years, with 2015 being more adversely affected as he accumulated just 429 at-bats. In addition, Cabrera's home run rates have slipped during that span as well, coming in with 25 and 18 long balls the last two seasons after going for 40-plus the two years prior. While Cabrera still showed that at least in the average department he is at the height of his abilities, we have to accept that his days of 40 home runs and 120 RBI could be finished. Right now the best case scenario is that Cabrera remains relatively healthy in 2016, which should guarantee a trip back to 30 home runs and 100-plus RBI/runs to go with the dominant average. We will gladly sign up for that sometime in the middle of Round 1. Just keep in mind that Cabrera is now completely free of third base eligibility in all leagues.

2016 PROJECTION: .329 29 HR 98 RBI 104 R 1 SB

3. Anthony Rizzo: The 2015 season for Chicago Cubs first baseman Anthony Rizzo was all about validating his terrific 2014 breakout campaign (.286/32 HR/78 RBI) but the fantasy baseball community was clearly sold on the slugger as his ADP rose to the second round of most drafts. Well those who took such an early plunge on Rizzo made a great investment as he hit 31 home runs, batted .278, and went past the 100-RBI mark for the first time in his career with 101. Needless to say, Rizzo has fully graduated into a top five overall first baseman and he also is knocking on the door to late first round consideration for 2016. We haven't even mentioned the fact that Rizzo became a five-tool Paul Goldschmidt-lite first baseman last season on the incredible bonus of 17 stolen bases to go with all the power. Rizzo has good speed for a big man and he is fully capable of reaching another double-digit number in steals again this season. At this point the only thing left debating over is whether or not Rizzo can reach the 40 home run plateau for the first time in his career. Even if Rizzo stays in the 30 ballpark, he remains a slam dunk top tier first baseman who can anchor your home run and RBI numbers. With a K rate that came in at a career-low 15 percent in 2015, Rizzo could even push the average to the .290 range which would be icing on his five-category cake.

2016 PROJECTION: .286 34 HR 104 RBI 95 R 14 SB

4. Jose Abreu: The hype machine almost broke down entirely prior to last season when it came to Chicago White Sox Cuban first baseman Jose Abreu. Coming off what was considered one of the greatest rookie debuts in modern baseball history (.317/36 HR/107 RBI), Abreu was drafted in the top five-to-seven players in almost all fantasy baseball leagues. The early returns were not promising though as Abreu hit under .300 in each of the first two months of the season and hit a total of just 8 home runs. However Abreu eventually got into his standard groove and went ballistic the rest of the way to finish with 30 home runs, 101 RBI, and a .290 average. While Abreu did not graduate to the 40-home run penthouse that we all thought he would reach as (he actually lost six from the season prior), we can chalk a lot of that up to pitchers being much more careful when dealing with him at the dish in 2015. Other then drawing slightly fewer walks, the rest of Abreu's hitting trends were almost equal to his smashing debut. As a result, Abreu should be a lock to be in the same neighborhood in terms of numbers from his first two seasons and that has him once again worthy of a mid-first round pick.

2016 PROJECTION: .299 32 HR 105 RBI 86 R 0 SB

5. Joey Votto: Heading into the 2015 fantasy baseball season, one of the more debated players in the game was Cincinnati Reds first baseman Joey Votto. A stalwart first round pick as recently as 2013, Votto struggled through two seasons of depressed numbers and some serious injury issues that included a potentially chronic knee problem. As a result of these questions, Votto's stock took a hit in drafts last spring, with some potentially significant value to be had if he could morph back into his former top tier self. As it turns out, Votto was able to do just that and more as he put together an MVP-type campaign, hitting .314 with 29 home runs and 80 RBI. With 95 runs scored and 11 stolen bases, Votto put himself right back into the top 5-7 tier of first baseman leading into 2016. Long considered one of the best pure hitters in the game, Votto's very high walk rates (20.6 percent last season) makes hitting .300 a lock. While some say his tremendous patience have hurt his potential power output, Votto made that a moot point in 2015 by tying for his second-best high in home runs. Still young at

32, Votto staying healthy last season reinforces his standing as a very good early round investment.

2016 PROJECTION: .310 27 HR 90 RBI 96 R 10 SB

6. Edwin Encarnacion: We have been saying in these pages the last two seasons that Toronto Blue Jays 1B Edwin Encarnacion is well worth using a first round draft pick on, a point that brought on somewhat of a debate. Our argument centered on the high level of power Encarnacion brings to the table in an era where home runs are becoming more and more scarce. Of course Encarnacion was making us look bad early on for the second season in a row in 2015, as he came out of April hitting just .205 and with just 4 home runs. Encarnacion was similarly brutal the previous April as well so his reputation as a slow starter became burnished even more. Encarnacion was just fine from that point onward though, slamming 35 home runs the last five months of the season to finish one shy of 40. His 39 long balls were his most since he had 42 in 2012 and it showed that Encarnacion was still in his power prime despite the fact he turns 33 in January. In addition, Encarnacion scores a lot of runs for a first baseman, going for over 90 in three of the last four seasons. A couple of things need to be noted though as we look toward 2016, with the first being that Encarnacion's K rate is staring to climb which could hurt the average moving forward. The second point is that Encarnacion has always been a guy prone to being beat up, an issue that will only get more pronounced as he continues to age. However Encarnacion will once again be able to take aim at the short outfield walls of Rogers Center and be surrounded by the best lineup of power hitters in the game. We think he has another big season ready to go before the inevitable slide does its thing.

2016 PROJECTION: .275 35 HR 108 RBI 90 R 4 SB

7. Adrian Gonzalez: We have been saying for years now that it can be argued Los Angeles Dodgers first baseman Adrian Gonzalez is quite possible the best value among the top ten at his position in fantasy baseball. While guys like Paul Goldschmidt, Miguel Cabrera, and Jose Abreu cost and arm and a leg to own, Gonzalez can be had as late as the fourth round in mixed leagues. When you consider that Gonzalez is almost a lock to give you 25 home runs, 100-plus RBI, and a solid average, that is terrific value relative to draft spot. 2015 was no exception as Gonzalez hit his most home runs since 2010 with 28, while driving in

90 with a .276 average. By now we should know that Gonzalez's days of 35-plus home runs are never coming back but his amazing durability and consistency count for something extra at the draft table. He will be 34 in May which is getting a tad up there but sluggers can hold their power into their late 30's as we have seen with guys like David Ortiz. The rate stats all check out as well, with Gonzalez lowering his K/9 and improving his BB/9 from 2014. There are no signs of a drop in production just yet which means Gonzalez is set to be another great place to put your draft money.

2016 PROJECTION: .278 27 HR 98 RBI 77 R 1 SB

8. Eric Hosmer: Joining Mike Moustakas and Lorenzo Cain, Kansas City Royals first baseman Eric Hosmer posted a career season in 2015 which helped put the organization back into the playoffs for the second year in a row. While Hosmer had previously gone bust amid high expectations both in 2012 and 2014, something clearly clicked last season as he hit 18 home runs, collected a career-high 93 RBI, and batted .297. Now 26-years-old, Hosmer is reaching his prime years, which means he has just a tiny bit of upside window left to his name. Really what we are talking about here is whether or not Hosmer can reach the 20 home run mark or if he will be more Billy Butler (the Royals version) with the ability to steal some bases. Right now Hosmer works as a very low-end first baseman in fantasy baseball due to his power shortcomings and ideally you want him in your UTIL or CI slot if at all possible. At the very least we can count on a .300 average, around 10 steals, and good counting stats in runs and RBI. The home runs are always the big question mark but Hosmer seems to be establishing his baseline in the 17-20 range which is solid but not great.

2016 PROJECTION: .304 19 HR 96 RBI 104 R 9 SB

9. Freddie Freeman: Long one of our favorite young hitters here at the Fantasy Sports Boss, we had a bit of hesitancy when it came to investing in Atlanta Braves first baseman Freddie Freeman for 2015. The most interesting part of that assessment was that it had nothing to do with what Freeman himself could do with a bat in his hands. Instead we were leery of the fact the Braves almost complete tore apart the batting order in an attempt to clear salary to gear up for a buying spree to coincide with the opening of their new ballpark in a few years. Hence there was valid concern regarding if Freeman would get any kind of protection in the order and if he would be able to drive in anybody when he delivered hits. Considered a can't miss prospect from the moment he was selected by the Braves in the second round of the 2007 draft, Freeman seemed to put it all together in 2013 when he clubbed 23 home runs, drove in 109 batters, and batted .319. Alas 2014 turned into somewhat of a disappointment as Freeman hit just 18 home runs, drove in only 78 batters, and saw his average dip to .288. Combine the drop in numbers to the lack of order protection entering into the minds of draftees as 2015 dawned and it was clear to see why one would be nervous about an investment in Freeman. Ultimately we were proven spot as Freeman saw a sizable drop in his numbers across the board for the second season in a row. While Freeman matched his 2014 total in home runs with 18 (still a disappointing number from a guy who we thought would be a perennial 25 homer guy), he managed to drive in a woeful 66 batters, and saw yet another dip in average to .278 (in fact the average should have even been worse due to a lucky .322 BABIP). If the name "Freeman" was not attached to the back of the jersey, you would have thought you were looking at a Billy Butler or a Garret Jones. And again some of the blame goes to the Braves for giving Freeman zero protection in the lineup. With a dearth of runners on base, Freeman's drastically lowered RBI total was not shocking. Also opposing pitchers carefully threw around Freeman last season, forcing him to chase at times which helped knock the average down. So where are we now with Freeman as he reaches his prime at 26? Needless to say the situation is still muddled in terms of the Braves lineup. Without an infusion of even competent major league bats, expecting Freeman to reach 80 RBI is foolhardy. In addition, Freeman has been at 20 percent in his K rate the last two years as he is a bit of hacker, making batting .300 dicey. When you put it all together, Freeman looks like a guy who is toward the back half of starting first baseman in 12-team mixed setups. We still like the potential here but Freeman needs more help to achieve it.

2016 PROJECTION: .281 19 HR 79 RBI 82 R 5 SB

10. Prince Fielder: When it came to the discussion regarding the AL Comeback Player of the Year Award, Texas Rangers first baseman Prince Fielder certainly deserved some consideration. While he didn't win, Fielder engineered a nice comeback season of his own in 2015 when he returned from 2014 neck surgery that cost him almost the entire year. Having reported to spring training fully healthy, Fielder hit a scorching .339 in the first half of the season, which included a .377 month of May. Throw in 14 home runs during that span and Fielder seemed primed to make good on all the hype he had the year prior when he landed in the offensive haven that is Texas after coming over from Detroit via a trade. Of course Fielder cooled off during the second half as expected, hitting just .264 with 9 home runs the rest of the way but he more than reestablished himself as a starting fantasy baseball first baseman. When you look at the overall numbers, Fielder's .305 average, 23 home runs, and 98 RBI were very good numbers but they still represent a sizable drop from even his Detroit days. We are talking primarily about the home runs as Fielder has not hit 30 since 2012. The fact that Fielder did not boost himself back up to that mark while playing half of his game in the launching pad in Texas means he is now simply a 25-home run guy and nothing more at this stage of the game. While Fielder only turns 32 in May, he no longer is that must-have big bat that showed up in the first two rounds of drafts.

2016 PROJECTION: .308 25 HR 97 RBI 86 RBI 0 SB

11. David Ortiz: For what seemed like the 7th or 8th straight season where we were all ready to bury David Ortiz once and for all due a slump or because of injury, the ageless slugging first baseman/DH got the last laugh yet again in 2015. Rallying back from an ugly first half that brought forth the latest "he is finished" talk, Ortiz would rally to finish with 37 home runs, drove in 108, and batted a decent .273. Number accomplished at the advanced age of 39. As Ortiz gets ready for his age-40 and final MLB season, we have more than learned never to doubt the guy under any circumstance. In fact the 35 and 37 home runs Ortiz has hit the last two seasons were both his highest totals there since 2007, showing just how the guy is aging like a fine wine. With a K rate that was still a very solid 15.5 percent and a walk rate of 12.5 that was right around his career norms, Ortiz once again makes for a very good UTIL or CI power bat. Since no one ever wants to own Ortiz, the payoff should be good yet again.

2016 PROJECTION: .266 32 HR 107 RBI 74 R 0 SB

12. Chris Davis: While we admittedly have not been big boosters of slugging first baseman Chris Davis, we will concede that there is not a better pure home run hitter in the game. Davis reinforced his standing as a monster power producer in

2015, slamming 47 long balls and reaching the 100 mark in both runs (100) and RBI (117). The counting stats are obviously tremendous and when combined with the extreme power, Davis has put himself back into early round consideration after his awful 2014 campaign (marred by terrible numbers and a 25-game PED suspension). The downside with Davis though is that he can really hurt you with the batting average as we saw when he hit just .196 in 2014. With a K rate that has been over 30 percent four of the last 5 years, Davis is always going to be a liability there. Despite all the whiffs, Davis hit a very solid for him .262 last season and he has been above that number in four of the last five years as well. His 10-plus BB/9 rate helps there and shows that Davis is not a total "grip it and rip it" slugger. As long as Davis can hit .260 again in 2016, his extreme power output and 100-plus numbers in the counting runs and RBI columns make him one of the first options to possibly come off the draft board once the top tier guys are selected. Keep in mind though that Davis is just first base-eligible this season as he lost third base in 2015 due to Manny Machado's presence.

2016 PROJECTION: .257 42 HR 108 RBI 106 R 2 SB

13. Buster Posey:*******SEE CATCHER RANKINGS******

14. Albert Pujols: After hearing endless talk about how he was on the fast track to retirement going into 2015, Los Angeles Angels first baseman Albert Pujols unleashed a vintage power season that brought back memories of his St. Louis Cardinals heyday. Having some truly remarkable stretches where he seemed to hit a home run every game, Pujols would finished with 40 long balls and 95 RBI. The 40 homers were Pujols' most since 2010 with the Cards and even more encouraging, he stayed healthy to the point of accumulating 602 at-bats. Of course Pujols did show his age in one way and that was with his ugly .244 batting average. That was the worst full-season average for Pujols in his entire major league career and it brought to 8 straight years his streak of losing points in that category which is more than a trend. As he turns 36 in January, Pujols is now a pure hacking slugger all the way, right on down to the poor average. While Pujols' K rate has remained relatively steady, he is not drawing many walks anymore, seeing his BB/9 drop to a very low 7.6 percent. Unfortunately the injury bug bit Pujols again in November as he was forced to undergo another foot procedure that will keep him out until mid-April. That will chop a few home runs and RBI from his ledger. This is also a reminder of the injury risk Pujols brings to the table.

2016 PROJECTION: .254 28 HR 93 RBI 84 R 6 SB

15. Mark Teixeira: Heading into the New York Yankees' game on August 17th, first baseman Mark Teixeira was in the home stretch of a tremendous comeback season that had him in the conversation for American League MVP. Flashing his best power and long ball rate since 2005, Teixeira was sitting on 31 home runs and 79 RBI as he suited up for that late summer game. It was at that moment when Teixeira once again lost his ongoing battle with injury as he fouled a ball off his shin that shelved him for a week. After coming back to make one more start, Teixeira went right back on the shelf with ongoing pain in the shin which led to the testing that discovered a season-ending fracture. The real shame of it all is that the injury will surely overshadow the terrific work Teixeira did leading up to the misfortune. That is somewhat understandable though as Teixeira has been a physical mess over the last five years, with the shin fracture joining the tendon sheath injury that marred his 2013, and numerous leg injuries that impacted multiple other seasons. Moving back to the numbers, Teixeira obviously can still hit for major power and at this late stage of his career, home runs and RBI are the only categories he can make an impact in with regards to fantasy baseball. Teixeira began his transition to a pure home run swinger soon after his arrival with the Yankees in 2009 when he batted .292. From that point on through the next six seasons, Teixeira has hit .256, .248, .251, .151, .216, and .255 which means the hurt he puts on your average category takes away some of the shine from the power. Ultimately Teixeira is a very limited player and one who at the age of 36 is as big an injury risk as you can get.   2015 could very well be a last hurrah.

2015 PROJECTION: .253 26 HR 86 RBI 66 R 0 SB

16. Kendrys Morales: We have admittedly been among the biggest Kendrys Morales apologists in the industry, going back to his early monster days with the Los Angeles Angels. There was a sense of connection with Morales after we had him as a prime sleeper entering into the 2009 season when he wound up slamming 34 home runs and driving in 108 to put himself in the conversation as one of the best young first base sluggers in all of baseball.   Unfortunately fate intervened when Morales suffered the now infamous broken leg in very next May while jumping on home plate after a walk-off bomb. After missing all of 2011, Morales returned the next season to post a solid 22 home runs and .273 average. The home run rate was down quite a bit from his pre-injury form and the Angels moved on at the end of the year. Morales then began a two-season odyssey that took him to the Seattle Mariners twice and the Minnesota Twins where he hit a grand total of 31 home runs, while seeing his average go from .277 to a woeful .218. It seemed Morales was on his last legs as a major leaguer, with fantasy baseball usage not even in the conversation. The always budget-conscious Kansas City Royals gave him one last shot for 2015 and needless to say the results were spectacular. While Morales stayed at his post-broken leg home run rates with a modest 22, he became a huge force in the RBI department with 106 (two shy of his 2009 total). Morales also batted .290 which became his highest mark since 2010. With 81 runs scores, Morales was a contributor to four ROTO categories for the price of a very late round pick or even a free agent add. He is back with the Royals for 2016 and thus will be in the middle of another potent lineup. Repeat his 2015 numbers and enjoy one of the best UTIL or CI bats out there.

2016 PROJECTION: .286 23 HR 98 RBI 80 R 1 SB

17. Mitch Moreland: After waiting for what seemed like ten years for Texas Rangers first baseman Mitch Moreland to make good on his power potential, the post-POST-hype season arrived in 2015 when he cracked 23 home runs and recorded career-highs in RBI (85) and batting average (.278). A clear veteran in his prime at the age of 30, it took Moreland quite a long time to find his major league footing. What primarily helped Moreland post such a nice breakthrough season was the fact he lowered his K rate a bit (almost 2 K's per nine from the year prior) but he has to prove he can repeat things again in 2016. The Rangers will trot Moreland out there at DH and first base for a majority of the upcoming season given what they got in 2015 and his draft price remains dirt cheap given how many people he has burned in the past. As a result, Moreland is a very solid late-round grab for your UTIL or CI slot.

2016 PROJECTION: .265 22 HR 88 RBI 56 R 1 SB

18. Lucas Duda: It was a big "prove it" season for New York Mets first baseman Lucas Duda as 2015 got underway, due to the fact it would serve as confirmation whether his tremendous breakout the year prior was legit or a fluke. After smacking 30 home runs and driving in 92 on an ascending Mets team in 2014, many expected some more improvement as Duda continued to move into his prime years. Unfortunately Duda only proved to still be a bit rough around the edges. Blessed with terrific natural power, Duda still hit an impressive 27 home runs but they still came up short from the 30 he smacked in 2014. In addition, Duda saw an uptick in his K rate (22.7 to 24.9) which took a toll on his batting average (dropping from .253 to .244). While Duda did perform better against lefties which were a major issue previously, he seems incapable of getting past the high strikeout tendency that hurts his average on a yearly basis. Turning 30 in February, we might already have seen the best Duda has to offer which makes him more valuable in a CI or UTIL spot.

2016 PROJECTION: .257 28 HR 86 RBI 75 RBI 1 SB

19. C.J. Cron: Putting a young player on a team managed by the veteran-loving Mike Scoscia is not the best way for your sleeper picks to develop based on recent history. Taking a clear page out of the Dusty Baker handbook, Scoscia stubbornly refused to play budding first baseman/DH C.J. Cron more than a handful of times before finally jettisoning him back to the minor leagues in June. The demotion was quite harsh as Cron was not horrible as he batted .269 with 5 home runs in the first half but he clearly could not get into a groove due to inconsistent playing time that resulted in just 145 at-bats during that span. Cron was soon brought back by the team once the Josh Hamilton saga was put to rest with the latter being dealt to the Texas Rangers. Given another chance to show what he could do, Cron impressed with 11 second half home runs and 47 RBI in 340 at-bats. While Cron's season numbers of 16 home runs and a .262 average was a bit underwhelming, understanding the context of his season would lead you to correctly view his 2015 was better than it seemed. As the 2016 season approaches, Cron is now firmly in the Los Angeles Angels' everyday plans at either DH or first base and that should ensure at the very least 20 home runs and 70 RBI to go with a useful average. Remember that Cron was a first round pick (11th overall) in 2011 by the team so there is good pedigree here. Cron has a smooth swing that could make him a .280 hitter with those 20 home runs as soon as this season and he could even have a bit more upside then that since he is still just 26. For the second season in a row, Cron is a solid sleeper bat.

2106 PROJECTION: .280 23 HR 67 RBI 59 R 4 SB

20. Carlos Santana: When Carlos Santana loses catcher eligibility for 2016, a lot of his value went right out the window. The fact of the matter is that while Santana also qualified at first and third base last season, catcher is where you wanted to stash him due to his above-average offensive production at the position. While Santana has his warts which are mainly centered around his ugly batting averages (.231 each of the last two seasons), his 66 home runs over the last three years put him in the top tier among all catchers. With that eligibility now a thing of the past, Santana becomes much more of a shaky investment for first or third base. Turning 30 in April, Santana is now well into his prime and thus won't be improving any of his numbers going forward. As a result, what you now see is what you get, starting with the ugly average hurt by a K rate that has been historically around 18-20 percent. Now on the flip side, Santana does draw a bunch of walks (17 and 16 percent the last two seasons) which you would think would help the average more than it has. That has not been the case though as Santana is not going to be anything better than a .260 batter based on historic trends and even that could be optimistic. The power is very solid here, with Santana having reached 20 or more home runs three times in his six-year career. Throw in 80-plus RBI and 70-plus runs and you have a bat that can help in your CI or UTIL slot. Without having his old catcher eligibility however, Santana is not starting material at either first or third base.

2016 PROJECTION: .253 21 HR 88 RBI 74 R 8 SB

21. Adam Lind: We are always on the lookout for cheap power and Milwaukee Brewers first baseman Adam Lind has been very obliging in that venture over the last few years. Having been held unfairly to his monster 2009 (35 HR/114 RBI/93 RBI/.305) with the Toronto Blue Jays, massive struggles against lefties and a home run rate that went back to his normal levels pushed Lind to the netherworld of the fantasy baseball world. A 23-home run 2013 campaign when Lind batted .288 put him back on the map though and his 2015 season was also quite solid with 20 home runs and a .277 average. Lind will never go near the 30-home run mark as that was a clear outlier in his career and he almost always sits against lefties which hurts his counting stats due to so many missed games. However on the plus side, the fact Lind sits against lefties is a help to his batting average and on a per game basis, his power is solidly above-average. Lind is a terrific late round investment as you can move his 20-25 home run bat into your UTIL or CI slot when needed and his average is not a hindrance either like with similarly priced players such as Brandon Moss or Ryan Howard.

2016 PROJECTION: .276 22 HR 84 RBI 77 R 0 SB

22. Pedro Alvarez: The transition of Pittsburgh Pirates slugger Pedro Alvarez from a full-time third baseman to the team's everyday first baseman was completed in 2015 but his offensive numbers remained relatively unchanged. That is not such a good thing as Alvarez solidified his reputation of being a home run asset but at the same time a batting average liability. There is no denying the power that Alvarez brings to the table as he has smashed as many as 36 home runs in a season. While that is a very impressive total, Alvarez has come under the 30 mark the last two years, hitting 18 and 27 respectively. There are some glaring holes in Alvarez' swing as his K rate has been north of 25 percent in every single year of his major league career. The result has been some truly ugly batting averages, with Alvarez having hit .245 or worse four years running. When Alvarez did have third base eligibility, he was much more valuable given the lack of depth there. However with first base-only for 2016, you would be hurting yourself by having him as your starter there.

2016 PROJECTION: .243 26 HR 84 RBI 65 R 5 SB

23. Ryan Zimmerman: If there were an All-Injury Prone Team in existence when it comes to fantasy baseball, the Washington Nationals' Ryan Zimmerman would be holding down the first base spot for sure. It was his fragile body after all that forced Zimmerman to move from his natural third base position (he will lose eligibility at that more valuable spot for 2016) to first base full-time entering into 2015 with the idea of preserving his health. That plan really didn't work out too well as Zimmerman spent on time on the DL during the summer with plantar fasciitis in his foot and then saw his season end early in September with a strained oblique. While still technically young at 31, Zimmerman has the body of someone much older which makes him a tremendous injury risk to invest in. The real shame of it all is that when he is in the lineup, Zimmerman can still hit the ball very hard as evidenced by his 16 home runs in only 346 at-bats last season. Alas, Zimmerman's batting average plummeted to an ugly .246, helped along though by an unlucky .268 BABIP. Expect the average to come up some in 2016 and if Zimmerman can somehow put together 500 at-bats, he could get back to the 25-home run range which is still a very impressive number in today's game. The fact of the matter is that Zimmerman just can't stay healthy and a DL stint or two has to be factored into whatever you pay for him at the draft table. The injury threat will only get worse as he continues to age and Zimmerman is also starting to strike out at a higher clip since reaching 30 as well. One of the most frustrating players to own in all of fantasy baseball due to the constant injuries, Zimmerman is someone you want to do your best to stay clear of.

2016 PROJECTION: .265 20 HR 75 RBI 62 R 0 SB

24. Brandon Belt: It was another season filled with promising offensive results and injury interruptions for San Francisco Giants first baseman Brandon Belt. The rare player who has been hanging around the sleeper realm for the last four years, Belt continues to hint at big-time potential with the bat when he put up career-high numbers in both the home run and RBI columns with 18 and 68 respectively during the 2015 season. Belt even threw in 9 stolen bases which made him the rare first base-eligible player who can help some in the speed column. The flip side is that Belt couldn't maximize his counting stats as he accumulated only 492 plate appearances due to more injury woes. During the first half of the season it was a groin issue that cropped up, while in the second half Belt was shut down early with a concussion. Now turning 28 in April, Belt is right into his prime years, which means he should no longer qualify as a sleeper. The caveat is that if Belt can somehow carve out 550 at-bats, he could put himself close to 25 home runs and 80 RBI with a solid average. When Belt was coming up the San Francisco system, he was lauded for his natural hitting ability and athleticism. As a major leaguer, Belt has struck out more than expected (26.4 percent in 2015) but he helps offset that with a nice 10.1 BB rate. His .363 BABIP from a year ago means Belt will be giving back some of the .280 average but otherwise he remains an affordable and useful CI/UTIL option with a bit more ceiling left to his game.

2016 PROJECTION: .271 21 HR 77 RBI 79 R 10 SB

25. Victor Martinez: Two major Fantasy Sports Boss Draft sacraments read like the following: 1.) Never draft a hitter or pitcher off a career-season unless the price is decent. 2.) Absolutely never buy in on an "outlier" campaign. Both of these labels were affixed to the fantasy baseball stock of Detroit Tigers 1B/DH Victor Martinez entering into the 2015 season. Despite being in his mid-30's, Martinez somehow experienced both a career and outlier season at the same time in 2014 when he slammed 32 home runs and drove in 103 batters while hitting .335. It was an incredible display from Martinez who was always considered one of the better pure hitters in the game. However the power was beyond off the charts from Martinez whose previous high was the 25 he swatted way back in 2007. Coincidence that this output came when Martinez was a pending free agent? In the interest of not going all Oliver Stone with any conspiracy theories, Martinez' 2014 numbers were looking quite fluky to even the most novice fantasy baseball player. As a result Martinez highlighted our 2015 All-Bust Team in our Draft Guide last season and he quickly went to work proving us spot on by tearing the meniscus in his knee right at the start of spring training which needed surgery. While Martinez did make it back for the opener, he proceeded to go out and bat a woeful .231 in April and then followed that up with a more putrid .196 May before needed to go on the DL for a month with yet another knee injury. Even upon his July return, Martinez had really no consistent stretches of hitting that helped his unfortunate owners, finishing up with a .245 average, 11 home runs, and 64 RBI in 440 at-bats. Oh and Martinez got hurt again the last week of the season with soreness in his quad. Needless to say, Martinez' 2014 output could join Chris Davis' 2013 home run binge, and Jose Reyes' batting title as recent major outliers. About the only positive thing we could say about Martinez' 2015 was that his .253 BABIP was very unlucky which means he was more of a .275 hitter or better. Martinez's average though was his one constant but now everything is in full flux as we look ahead toward the 2016 season. Having turned 37, having lost catcher eligibility, and with his body betraying him, Martinez is almost worthless.

2016 PROJECTION: .288 15 HR 86 RBI 71 R 0 SB

26. Justin Bohr: Leave it to the Miami Marlins to continually uncover hidden gems and value players regardless of the position. With the team always looking to save money and give jobs to cheaper prospects, immense (6-4/250-pound) first baseman Justin Bohr got his first extended look in the major leagues last season. With his size correctly giving off the impression he could hit for power, Bohr opened some eyes by cracking 23 home runs in just 446 at-bats, while also driving in 73 batters. We also liked the fact that Bohr was solid in the strikeout department for such a raw player and one that swings primarily for the fences. His 22.6 K rate kept the average competitive at .262 and portends to some improvement in the latter category as he further develops. The Marlins will give Bohr the inside track on the starting first base job for 2015 and he could end up being among the cheapest 25 home run bats in the game. We sign on fully toward using a late round pick for Bohr to fill your UTIL or CI slot.

2016 PROJECTION: .273 25 HR 79 RBI 56 R 0 SB

27. Greg Bird: Tough case here as top New York Yankees first base prospect Greg Bird proved to already be worth the hype after he was an instant impact hitter during his two month debut with the team in 2015. During the heat of a playoff race, Bird took over as the team's everyday first baseman when Mark Teixeira was lost for the season with a fracture in his shin and proceeded to swat 11 home runs in just 157 at-bats. Toss in a solid .261 average and Bird shapes up as one of the more exciting sleepers for the 2016 season. The power is big-time here with Bird already showed but the 23-year-old needs polish as he struck out in a ridiculous 29.8 percent of his at-bats. Despite all the potential Bird carries, his status is based solely on what transpires with Teixeira. According to GM Brian Cashman, Teixeira is the team's starter at first base for 2016 and with no openings at DH which is manned by Alex Rodriguez, Bird has no position to play. Cashman said under that scenario, Bird would begin the 2016 season in the minors and get promoted again if injuries strike. Given the extremely brittle nature of both Teixeira and Rodriguez, count on that happening at some point. However Bird's price tag figures to be high at the draft table given the nice debut he had in 2015 and the New York Yankees tag. With no guaranteed spot to start, Bird figures on be overpriced.

2016 PROJECTION: .257 19 HR 65 RBI 56 R 0 SB

28. Chris Colabello: While not a main component, first baseman Chris Colabello more than did share as part of a record-setting Toronto Blue Jays lineup. After two ugly seasons to begin his career with the Minnesota Twins when he batted .194 and .229 respectively, Colabello suddenly turned into Tony Gwynn overnight as he sprayed line drives all over the ballpark. In the batting title hunt for a big chunk of the season, Colabello finished with an excellent .321 average. In addition, Colabello collected 15 home runs and drove in 54 in just 360 at-bats. Needless to say, the Blue Jays made out like gangbusters on their tiny investment in Colabello. Now let's tear things apart here and change the narrative a bit. Just as impressive as the batting average turned out to be, what could be considered more surprising was the incredibly lucky .411 BABIP. Seeing a BABIP over .400 is like seeing Haley's Comet and it is doubly rare to see it from someone who doesn't possess top-end speed. When you consider that a neutral BABIP is .300, you can accurately determine that Colabello was not as good a hitter as the average showed. Remember this is the same guy who couldn't even hit .230 during his first two MLB seasons and his 26.7 percent K Rate a year ago is another major red flag going forward. Everything about Colabello's season screams out "fluke" and he stands to be a solid bust candidate based on the fallacy his average suggested.

2016 PROJECTION: .277 16 HR 61 RBI 62 R 2 SB

29. Mark Trumbo: Already a guy who had some pronounced negatives (such as an annually ugly average), Mark Trumbo saw his shaky fantasy baseball value plummet into the gutter when the Arizona Diamondbacks dealt him away to the Seattle Mariners early in the 2015 season. As a result of the move, Trumbo went from one of the best home run parks in the majors to one of the worst. With home runs and RBI being pretty much the only attractive qualities about Trumbo, going to Seattle buttressed those numbers to the point he was barely worth owning. As a result, Trumbo hit just .262 for the season with 22 home runs and 64 RBI. No longer qualifying at third base or the outfield, Trumbo's previously interesting eligibility is now a moot point. A full season with the Mariners in 2016 is not a recipe for success for a slugger like Trumbo and the damage he will do to your average is not going to be offset enough by the home runs. Avoid him altogether.

2016 PROJECTION: .257 24 HR 79 RBI 74 R 1 SB

30. Matt Adams: For the second consecutive season, St. Louis Cardinals first baseman Matt Adams went bust, further pushing him to the brink of ownership levels. Despite having a classic slugger's build at 6-3 and 260, Adams has not translated that size into power at the major league level, with his career high in home runs just a modest 17 through four years in the league. The disappointment started in 2014 when Adams recorded just a 15-homer campaign in 563 at-bats and it continued on into 2015 when massive injuries allowed him to play in only 60 games. While we can sort of throw out the 5 home runs and .240 average Adams had due to the injuries, we still are openly questioning how much power he can supply given the meager rates we have seen thus far. Ultimately Adams could be another Billy Butler-type, with a .280 average combined with 15-20 home runs. That could help you in a CI or UTIL spot but the once solid sleeper spotlight Adams carried is now nothing but a flicker.

2016 PROJECTION: .278 17 HR 73 RBI 59 R 3 SB

31. Logan Morrison: When you are known more for what you do on social media than anything you accomplish with a bat in your hands, you have problems. That is what has enveloped the stalled career of Tampa Bay Rays 1B/outfielder Logan Morrison as he entered into the 2015 season. A once promising power hitter coming up the Miami Marlins system, Morrison bombed out of that locale with a bad attitude and ugly offensive results. The Mariners took a cheap gamble on Morrison though and they were encouraged enough with his 2014 results (.262/11 HR in 365 at-bats) to give him another shot in 2015. Actually batting leadoff for a time, Morrison was not terrible as he hit 17 home runs and even stole 8 bases. However his average remained a big problem as he batted just .225. Some of the blame for that falls on a very unlucky .238 BABIP and in actuality Morrison is more of a .260 guy which we can live with. There is no guarantee Morrison will have a starting spot to his own when the 2016 season begins but he has 20 home run power if all breaks right. As Morrison turns 29 in June, it is clear that he is close to running out of chances. The Mariners quickly dealt him to the Rays days after the World Series which is another reminder of his disappointing play. Ignore the guy unless he grabs another starting spot somewhere.

2016 PROJECTION: .259 15 HR 53 RBI 46 R 5 SB

32. Chris Carter: Chris Carter must be a big fan of retired slugger Adam Dunn as he pretty much did a carbon copy performance of the guy's past baseline numbers in 2015 but only to a point. The .199 average surely was around what we saw from Dunn in his later years but the 24 home runs came up quite a bit short from his former counterpart's massive power numbers. Flat out, it was a complete disaster of a season for Carter who opposing pitchers didn't fear much at all last season. With a strikeout rate that can only be described as hideous (over 30 percent each of the last four seasons), Carter was not being given much of anything to drive as pitchers made him chase outside the zone which he more than obliged. Thus with Carter not hitting at least 30 home runs, the guy was pretty much useless to his owners. We always avoid guys like Carter due to the immense damage his average does on your overall number in that category for standard ROTO formats. Again if he is not doing at least 30 home run damage, Carter is not worth even carrying on your roster. The guy is a pure one-trick pony who by last year's numbers was not even great at that one skill.

2016 PROJECTION: .215 28 HR 79 RBI 65 R 2 SB

33. Adam LaRoche: There was at least some mild interest when it came to veteran first baseman Adam LaRoche as the 2015 season approached after the second-half warrior signed as a free agent with the Chicago White Sox. With LaRoche moving from one of the worst power parks in the majors to one of the best, it was expected that he could supply one or two more solid seasons as the White Sox' primary DH. Instead LaRoche looked completely shot almost overnight as he hit .207 with 12 home runs and 44 RBI. In fact it was a downright putrid performance from LaRoche who could be finished skills-wise at the age of 36. The fact LaRoche was so bad in an offensive park and only DH-ing most of the time was very telling and it makes him completely impossible to own for 2016. Forget his annual second half uprising, LaRoche is not looking like he will come back to do much of anything anymore no matter what part of the season it is.

2016 PROJECTION: .227 14 HR 57 RBI 46 R 1 SB

34. Billy Butler: There may not be a more boring player to talk about in today's fantasy baseball than Oakland A's first baseman Billy Butler. Now a veteran who turns 30 in April, Butler's career has been very disappointing in terms of never developing the power we expected outside of one gigantic outlier 29-home run season in 2013. Even without the power, at one time we were able to bank on a .300 average and around 100 RBI from Butler when he was with the Kansas City Royals early in his career. Even that has become an issue, with Butler seeing his average drop each of the last four seasons, all the way down to a shoddy .251 in

2015. The RBI? Butler didn't even reach the 70 mark in each of the last two seasons. With Butler operating in a horrible offensive park in Oakland and having little protection in the barren lineup, he is now moving to belonging more on the waiver wire then on a fantasy baseball roster.

2016 PROJECTION: .263 14 HR 67 RBI 65 R 0 SB

35. Joe Mauer: Even when he was catcher-eligible, Joe Mauer was often grossly overrated and that was even more so after his extreme outlier of a 2009 season when he smacked 28 home runs and batted .365. While no one can ever knock Mauer's pure hitting ability early in his career, the power that season was an absolute fluke as he has not topped 11 in any year since. In addition, Mauer's average is leaking badly due to an increasing K rate (16 percent or higher in three straight seasons after never touching that mark previously) and injuries adding to the problem. As a result, Mauer has batted just .277 and .265 the last two seasons and with a grand total of 14 home runs in that same span. With Mauer only being first base eligible as he turns 33 in April, there is pretty much zero value left to be had. In fact the only thing that seems to get Mauer drafted now is his name itself, as the numbers show nothing but a waiver wire bat. It is looking like a very ugly end to what was once looking like a Hall of Fame career.

2016 PROJECTION: .275 9 HR 67 RBI 73 R 3 SB

36. Brandon Moss: After years of trade rumors, the Oakland A's finally unloaded powerful first baseman Brandon Moss to the Cleveland Indians during the 2015 season. Having swatted 30 and 25 home runs in 2013 and 2014, Moss had solidified a reputation as a very underrated power hitter. A career-long high strikeout rate made Moss a batting average liability but when it came to the power alone, he was always a good guy to have on your bench or to play in spurts when he was hot. Alas the 2015 season was quite ugly for Moss as the average sank to a horrid .226 and the power slipped under the 20 mark with 19. At the age of 32, Moss is in search for a starting spot somewhere with no guarantee he will find one. With the K rate now in the mid-20's and an average that may not go above the .250 mark ever again, Moss is a guy who offers little to no upside at this stage of his career.

2016 PROJECTION: .239 22 HR 63 RBI 55 R 2 SB

37. Mike Napoli: The post-catcher phase of Mike Napoli's career has been nothing short of disappointing, with the 2015 season reaffirming this undeniable fact. While Napoli at one time was a top-five fantasy baseball catcher due to his above-average power, his struggles in the batting average department made him that much more of a liability to own when the homers began to fall off. After six straight seasons hitting 20 or more home runs, Napoli has come under that number the last two years despite playing most of that time with the Boston Red Sox in the power-haven that is Fenway Park. Having turned and aging 34 and with a K rate that has been 25 percent or worse the last five years, Napoli is barely worth talking about no matter where he ends up for 2016.

2016 PROJECTION: .226 16 HR 48 RBI 44 R 1 SB

38. Yonder Alonso: When it comes to empty batting averages at first base, San Diego Padres first baseman Yonder Alonso is the poster child. Prior to having his season end early due to a stress reaction in his back, Alonso batted a decent .282 but with a grand total of just 5 home runs in 354 at-bats. Now turning 29-years-old, Alonso is pretty much who he is in terms of being a very mediocre player when it comes to offensive numbers. The lack of home runs is a major turnoff, especially for a guy who is eligible at the power-packed first base position.

2016 PROJECTION: .280 10 HR 55 RBI 48 R 5 SB

39. Ryan Howard: Age and poor health continue to destroy what little value former MVP Ryan Howard currently has. Howard was not able to finish the 2015 season, playing his last game September 14th due to a bruised knee that wouldn't respond to treatment. That is a clear product of age as big-bodied players like Howard break down physically at a quicker rate that others given the stress on joints from carrying such high weight and muscle. Howard also has been a strikeout machine at the dish, hitting only .229 in 2015 with a laughable 27.4 K rate. Now 36-years-old and on his last legs, Howard is only capable of another 20 home runs or so with 70-80 RBI. That could work in short spurts in NL-only formats but that is as far as his value goes.

2016 PROJECTION: .227 21 HR 74 RBI 51 R 0 SB

THE REST

40. Justin Smoak: We are well past the point now where Justin Smoak can be considered anything but a bust considering he was once a first round pick in 2008 (11th overall) and was the main piece the Seattle Mariners got back for Cliff Lee in that much-ballyhooed trade with the Texas Rangers. While there is no doubting the power Smoak possesses, his utter lack of hitting skills is apparent now six seasons into his major league tenure. Just a .224 career hitter with massive holes in his swing, Smoak couldn't even make it as an everyday bat in Rogers Center with the Toronto Blue Jays last season. His 2015 was typical Smoak, what with the ugly 26.2 K rate and horrific .226 average. While the 18 home runs were decent, Smoak should not be on any fantasy baseball roster that wants to be competitive.

41. Ben Paulsen: Whenever a hitter is promoted from the Colorado Rockies system, we must always pay attention given the offensive haven that is Coors Field. The Rockies have been on the lookout for stability at first base ever since Todd Helton retired and in 2015 they gave Ben Paulsen a look-see in order to find out if he could be a part of the future. Paulsen performed well enough by hitting .277 with 11 home runs in 325 at-bats and that performance likely earned him the inside track to the starting first base job for 2016. Paulsen still is anything but a sure thing as he took a long time to make it to the majors as he turned 28 in October. He did however hit .290 or better at Triple-A both in the 2013 and 2014 seasons and the average should be decent enough given the home park. What is up for debate is how much power there is and we should get a better read on that in 2016. With Justin Morneau out of the picture after his option was not picked up, the opportunity will be there for Paulsen to make a name for himself.

42. Travis Shaw: Those who were still paying attention during the late summer when it came to their fantasy baseball teams could have given themselves a boost when the Boston Red Sox gave first base prospect Travis Shaw the majority of playing time at the position. While Shaw was doing poorly at Triple-A (.249/5 HR in322 at-bats), the Red Sox needed a body and handed it to their former 2009 9th round pick. Not considered a top prospect by anyone in baseball, Shaw actually did a nice job in cracking 13 home runs, driving in 36, and batting a solid .274. Shaw likely took advantage of the fact opposing pitchers had no previous film on him which is why he got so many good fastballs to hit. There is a very good chance Shaw fades back into oblivion as pitchers will now have a plan of attack on him for 2016 and even with his good amount of initial success last season, a K rate of 23 percent spells trouble. Some upside but go with Shaw only one your terms.

43. James Loney: Veteran first baseman James Loney has had a pretty decent career as a professional hitter who works the count and gets on base. However Loney's numbers have never translated to the world of fantasy baseball, with his severe lack of power being a major drawback at first base. Since you want to get at least 25 home runs from your first baseman, Loney doesn't make the grade as his career-high there is just 15 way back in 2009. On the positive side, Loney is a terrific pure hitter who possesses a career average of .285. Turning only 32 in May, Loney figures to have another few seasons left to help you in NL or AL-only formats due to the positive average and solid counting numbers in runs and RBI.

44. Mark Canha: The Oakland A's gave power-hitting first baseman Mark Canha his first crack at the majors in 2015 as part of their ongoing lineup reconstruction and the guy didn't embarrass himself by smacking 16 home runs in 485 at-bats. In addition, Canha collected 70 RBI and even stole 7 bases to help a bit across the board. That is with the exception of batting average as Canha put up just a .254 mark due to a high 19.8 K rate. Canha looks like a pure slugger who fits the classic low average/decent home run total profile many guys put forth. The steals are a bonus and at the very least make Canha a last 2-3 round grab to see if he can improve. Keep in mind though Canha will already turn 27 in February.

45. Justin Morneau: The end is near for former MVP first baseman Justin Morneau. A two-year stint in the hitting haven of Coors Field with the Colorado Rockies failed to delay the rapid decline we have seen from Morneau over the last three seasons. Age and ongoing problems with concussions put Morneau on the brink last season as he hit just three home runs in 182 at-bats. While .310 Morneau hit was very good, the veteran has clearly lost most of his power. Now at the age of 35 this May, Morneau doesn't even make for a good a decent bench bat.

46. Wilin Rosario: What was at one time looking like a very promising hitting career for catcher/first baseman Wilin Rosario, has now devolved into nothing but a lamentation about what might have been. Rosario certainly seemed on the fast track to being a very good major league hitter after he cracked 28 home runs with catcher eligibility for the Rockies in 2012. However ongoing problems with the responsibilities of playing catcher and some less than exemplary work habits put Rosario on the fast track to the team's doghouse. Things have gotten so bad that Rosario has now spent time at Triple-A in each of the last two years, with nothing but a backup catcher/first baseman's role with the Rockies when summoned. While Rosario's aversion to walks and annually high strikeout rates are well known, a fresh start with another team would make him somewhat interesting again due to the fact he is still just 27. Until that happens though, Rosario can be ignored.

47. Steve Pearce: Sometimes an outlier season can be very obvious and to the point that even unseasoned fantasy baseball players can spot it a mile away. This was the case when it came to the 2014 career-year of Baltimore Orioles 1B/outfielder Steve Pearce. After seven years of being a backup journeyman player on five teams, Pearce took advantage of unexpected playing time that season to belt 21 home runs and bat .293 in just 338 at-bats. Consider that Pearce had never so much as reached double-digits in home runs previously, nor hit anywhere near that batting average since he was a rookie which put fluke spotlight squarely onto his shoulders. As a result we told you in these pages as year ago to avoid Steve Pearce altogether and we made sure to include him on our BUST list to further make the point. Well it took Pearce all of two months to prove our prediction right as he failed to hit .200 in both April and May. The bottom would completely fall out in a .203 second half of the season that put the ugly finishing touches on a .218/15-HR campaign. The 15 home runs were actually not terrible in that Pearce collected them in just 294 at-bats but clearly he went right back to his backup/journeyman performances that dotted the first seven years of his career. With the Orioles not even wanting Pearce to play during the second half of the year, his standing with both the team and in terms of netting a starting spot somewhere else is in doubt.

48. Kennys Vargas: After a somewhat decent debut in 2014 (9 home runs and a .274 average in 234 at-bats), Minnesota Twins first base prospect Kennys Vargas was a complete non-factor in his follow-up 2015 campaign. Opposing pitchers found some major holes in Vargas' swing which they took advantage of fully. The result was a poor 20.3 percent K rate, an ugly .240 average, and just 5 home runs in 184 at-bats. Likely will get a look in spring training but Vargas will be nothing but a bench bat on the Twins this season.

49. Mike Morse: While Mike Morse had a brief but very impressive run as a power hitter from 2010 through 2012, he is now firmly into a journeyman finish to his career that centers on mostly backup duty. Injuries continue to dog Morse which has hurt his ability to possibly claim a starting spot somewhere and his .231 average and only 5 home runs in 256 at-bats last season show a guy on fumes. Turning 34 in March, Morse will likely need a minor-league deal to stick in the majors. Nothing to see here.

50. Mark Reynolds: The home run specialist that is Mark Reynolds continued on in 2015 as he found some decent playing time with the St. Louis Cardinals who needed a replacement for injured first baseman Matt Adams. We have seen some tremendous power seasons from Reynolds in the past during his days with the Arizona Diamondbacks and Milwaukee Brewers but currently he is just a backup first baseman/third baseman who can sneak into playing time due to injuries like he did last season. Reynolds still can hit the baseball a mile but his .230 average in 2015 was his highest since 2009 which is quite telling. No reason to get involved here outside of AL or NL-only formats.

51. Darin Ruf: Twice in the last three seasons, Darin Ruf has taken advantage of some playing time on an out-of-contention Philadelphia Phillies team to hit some home runs and possibly position himself for more playing time moving forward. Last season was such a situation as Ruf played more as the year went on and as the Phillies sank to being one of the worst teams in baseball. Ruf would hit 14 home runs in just 268 at-bats but the average was once again very ugly at .235. For his three-plus year career, Ruf is just a .245 hitter and is pretty much a home run asset in NL-only formats.

52. Nick Swisher: It looks like the end is approaching for the always colorful Nick Swisher. The quote machine and excitable first baseman looked finished in 2015 as injuries and awful numbers seemed be push him to the edge of his career. After batting a terrible .198 with 2 home runs in 30 games with the Cleveland Indians, the team gave him away to the Atlanta Braves who were looking for a few warm bodies to fill out their lineups in a complete abomination of a season for them. Swisher's run with the Braves was not much better as he stayed under the .200 mark with a .195 average and just 4 home runs. It is very doubtful Swisher will get anything other than a minor-league invite to camp as he is now

35 and with a quiet bat. His days of offering cheap power are through and the average is as hideous as ever. The media will miss him.

53. Clint Robinson: With all of the injuries afflicting the Washington Nationals last season, Clint Robinson got a chance to play some outfield and first base for the team. Robinson acquitted himself well by hitting 10 home runs and posting a .272 average in his 352 at-bats but he figures to be back in the minors to begin 2016. Has some NL-only appeal down the road if injuries open up more playing time but for now Robinson has zero value.

54. Kyle Blanks: We are always intrigued by the power of Kyle Blanks but the guy remains a perennial tease who can't seem to stick with a major league team. Last season Blanks had a stint with the Texas Rangers that amounted to just 67 at-bats where he put up a .313 average and swatted 3 home runs. A nice bit of hitting in a very small sample size but the dye was cast long ago on Blanks as a high-strikeout underachiever. Has mild appeal in AL or NL-only formats if he works his way into another opportunity but that even could be asking a lot.

55. Jesus Montero: The Seattle Mariners continue to try and get something out of failed catcher/first base prospect Jesus Montero who was acquired by the team prior to 2012 for Michael Pineda. Since that time, Montero has done next-to-nothing with the Mariners except get busted for PED's and posting some ghastly batting averages. Things got so bad that Montero spent a large amount of time back in the minor leagues, with only a cursory opportunity in 38 games with the team to show he should still be counted on as a potential bat. Instead Montero hit just .223 with 5 home runs in 112 at-bats. A complete bust of a prospect that has no business on any fantasy baseball roster.

56. Brett Wallace: Yes Brett Wallace is still around. Finding his way back to the majors with the San Diego Padres for 107 at-bats in 2015, Wallace batted .305 with 5 home runs. The only reason Wallace got that shot was due to injuries impacting the Padres during the second half of the season and honestly there is nothing left to talk about here that hasn't already been discussed with regards to him being a gigantic bust as a former 2008 first round pick. All Wallace does now is bring back bad memories when discussing what he could have been.

57. Jon Singleton: The hype has almost completely died down when it comes to the power-hitting Singleton due to the Grand Canyon-sized holes in his swing.

The Astros only were able to stomach 44 at-bats from Singleton in 2015 when he hit all of 1 home run with an ugly .205 average; a performance that got him sent down to the minors for nearly the rest of the season. When you strike out in almost 40 percent of your at-bats, you have no place on both a major league and a fantasy baseball roster.

58. Ike Davis: The disintegration of Ike Davis' once-promising career continues as he couldn't even carve out more than a backup first base role on the woeful Oakland A's in 2015. It seems like nothing but a rumor that Davis once hit 32 home runs in a season. In fact since that all-time outlier campaign in 2012, Davis has hit a grand total of just 23 home runs in the three seasons since, hitting under .230 overall in that time period. Could be out of the game real soon and obviously shouldn't be discussed in terms of fantasy baseball usage.

SECOND BASEMAN

Draft Strategy: Finally for the first time in years, we no longer have to tell advise you all about the fact drafting Robinson Cano in the first round is foolish. With Cano becoming a clear victim of Safeco Field, second base should not have one single member of their fraternity seeing their name in the first round of drafts. Despite this, there is a very nice batch of impact youth in this group, mainly centering on Jose Altuve, Jason Kipnis, Brian Dozier, Kolten Wong, and Mookie Betts. Feel free to tab your second baseman in Round 3 at the earliest (this would require passing on Jose Altuve as you follow our advice of going outfield/first base during the first two rounds) or even somewhere in the 4-6 range if you wait a bit longer. Second base is almost a carbon copy of third base regarding the infusion of youth propping up the impact of the position and pushing down the aging veterans.

1. **Jose Altuve:** One of the main talking points going into the 2015 fantasy baseball season was whether or not Houston Astros second baseman Jose Altuve was fully worthy of being a first round pick. After an MVP-type 2014 campaign that included blockbuster numbers in stolen bases (56) and average (batting title-winning .341 mark) Altuve was among the most impactful players in fantasy baseball. As a result, Altuve moved to late first round territory for the 2015 season which opened up a debate about whether or not he was deserving of such a lofty spot. In the end, Altuve did show he was well-worth a first round pick, as he reached double-digits in home runs for the first time in his career with 15, while continuing to excel in steals (38) and batting average (.313). Hitting leadoff or in the third spot for a vastly improved Astros lineup, Altuve should once again pace the second base position for 2016 as he contributes in all five standard ROTO categories. While he stands just 5-6, Altuve is now growing into some power as he moves closer to his prime in turning 25 in May. The added home runs are like an exclamation point to what already was a monstrous set of numbers for Altuve and he should be also be able to pass the 90 run mark for the first time in his career in 2016 due to better bats hitting behind him. While the .341 average looks like an outlier (as it would be for anyone), Altuve is here to stay as a blockbuster fantasy baseball second baseman who has only added distance between himself and most other hitters.

(2) 20
Dee Gordon

2016 PROJECTION: .323 14 HR 67 RBI 95 R 43 SB

2. Robinson Cano: It certainly appeared as though signing that blockbuster free agent contract with the Seattle Mariners prior to the 2014 season was turning out to be nothing short of a disaster for second baseman Robinson Cano, a talking point backed up by depressed offensive numbers during his first two years in that locale. While it was expected Cano would lose some home runs going from Yankee Stadium to Safeco Field, the 14 long balls he hit in 2014 went even lower than anticipated. With the Mariners having a terrible lineup surrounding him, Cano also sank in the RBI and runs department which called into question his first round value going forward. Just when it appeared things couldn't get any worse, Cano went out and looked completely listless at the dish the first half of 2015, hitting just .251 and swatting only 6 home runs in 346 at-bats. It was at this point where Cano reported he was dealing with an ongoing stomach ailment going back to the previous season which many chalked up as a cheap excuse. However Cano immediately began hitting ropes once the All-Star Game was in the books, putting up a scorching .331 average and upping the power dramatically by hitting 15 home runs in 278 at-bats. That second half run was vintage Cano and reminds us that few hitters are more dangerous when locked in. Perhaps a diagnosed sports hernia impacted Cano early on as well, which was surgically repaired last October. So as we look toward 2016, which Cano will his fantasy owners get? The 2014 dud or the monster 2015 second half star? Cano is aging a bit as he turned 33 last October and his advanced metrics are starting to go in the wrong direction. For one, Cano's walk rate tumbled to 6.4 percent in 2015, down from being above 9.0 both in 2013 and 2014. In addition, Cano's K rate is rising as he struck out at a career-high rate of 15.9 percent. Age has to be considered part of the equation there and into the future and the ballpark is still a drag no matter how great Nelson Cruz' numbers look. It is always dicey investing in "name brand" guys like Cano who are past the age of 32 due to the historical declining trends. No longer a first round star, we would sign off on a third round spot for Cano and nothing earlier.

2016 PROJECTION: .300 22 HR 80 RBI 84 RBI 4 SB

3. Brian Dozier: 28 home runs is a tremendous show of power no matter the position but when it comes at the shallow second base spot, the value goes through the roof. Such was the 2015 case of still-developing Minnesota Twins second baseman Brian Dozier who cracked those 28 home runs, collected 77 RBI and scored 101 runs in a terrific overall performance. The burst in power brought to four the number of seasons with increased home run totals which is no small feat. As impressive as those numbers are, we have to be wary of expecting another jump in production in 2016 due to the fact Dozier turns 29 in May. That is prime territory, with ceiling seasons ending around the age of 27. Even if there is simply a repeat of 2015, Dozier is a slam dunk top five option among second baseman when you consider he excels in home runs, RBI, and runs near the top of the Twins batting order. While Dozier's stolen bases dropped off a bit from 21 to 12, he remains a help there which checks off the box regarding getting speed from your middle infielders. As tremendous a player as Dozier has turned out to be, there is a bad side to the drafting him. Primarily speaking, Dozier is a big batting average liability to the tune of a horrific .240 lifetime average in four MLB seasons. There was hope Dozier would improve there last season but instead he went even lower by batting .236, after putting up a .244 mark in 2014. Dozier strikes out a ton, as his 21 percent mark was a career-worst last season and thus expecting anything north of .250 is asking a ton. Also the ebb in Dozier's steals could mean he is staring to lose interest there as well. Project Dozier for three category help and consider the steals and any average improvement a nice bonus.

2016 PROJECTION: .248 29 HR 79 RBI 104 R 14 SB

4. Ian Kinsler: Veteran Detroit Tigers second baseman Ian Kinsler continued chugging along in 2015, putting up another top 5-7 season at second base despite his statistics being moved around a bit. Having seen his speed and power slip to career-low levels in both categories last season, Kinsler kept himself viable by hitting .296 (getting some .323 BABIP helped though), his best mark there since all the way back in 2008. In addition, Kinsler scored 94 runs after going for 100 the year prior. Finally, Kinsler has been one of the best RBI guys at second base the last two seasons, coming in with 92 and 73 respectively. Clearly Kinsler is not anywhere near as exciting to own at this stage of the game, what with his two 30/30 seasons nothing but a fading memory. However there is something to be said for Kinsler reinventing himself as he ages and another bonus is his recent ability to stay healthy which of course was a major challenge for him during his early years. Kinsler will turn 34 in June which is getting quite a bit up there for a second baseman with a ton of mileage but the guy still leads off or bats second for one of the best lineups in baseball. Give him one more season before age invariably does its irreversible thing.

2016 PROJECTION: .280 12 HR 75 RBI 95 R 14 SB

5. Jason Kipnis: The burgeoning career of Cleveland Indians second baseman Jason Kipnis got back on track in 2015 after a disastrous 2014 campaign that called into question whether or not he could be a top second base option for fantasy baseball purposes. After two straight 30-plus steal seasons and a home run tally that rose to 17 from 2012-13, Kipnis shot up to as high as a mid-second round pick once 2014 drafts came around. With visions of five-tool production dancing his owners' heads, Kipnis instead fell flat on his face as the average cratered to a ghastly .240, he hit just 6 home runs, and saw a drop in stolen bases with 17. Kipnis did fight through injuries for a good portion of the season however but the fantasy baseball community was now leery of going back to the well here for 2015 based on a lowered ADP. With full health going into the season, Kipnis began the task of reestablishing himself as a prime player, sitting near the top of the batting race during the first half of the year when he hit .323 and collected 6 home runs. The average was in outlier territory though which made it a non-surprise when Kipnis hit just .271 the rest of the way. The final tally of a .303 average was a career-best which was encouraging; not so nice were the modest 9 home runs and very disappointing 12 stolen bases. Now fully in his prime as he turns 29 in April, Kipnis is still a tough guy to get a read on. It appears as though Kipnis is losing interest in stealing bases, with a total of 34 the last two years after he went for over 30 from 2012-13. In addition, Kipnis' power has not developed adequately enough, with his output now entrenched in the mediocre 10-15 range. Finally, Kipnis won't go near .300 again this season as he got a big boost from an incredibly lucky .356 BABIP to help him get there. With a K rate that remains above 16.0 percent, Kipnis is more of a .280 hitter than one who bats .300. Overall we are leery here given the outlier average and shaky counting statistics in home runs and stolen bases. More stable options are the better way to go and they also are more cheaply priced.

2016 PROJECTION: .284 11 HR 67 RBI 88 R 16 SB

6. Rougned Odor: Add Rougned Odor's name to the recent growing list of prospects that began to take off after having gone through an early season demotion back to the minors. The Texas Rangers had no choice but to send Odor back to the farm after he opened up with a .147 April and .137 May. When Odor was brought back up in June, he looked like a completely different player as the hits began to pile up. After smacking just four home runs during the first half of the year, Odor slammed 12 long balls in the second half as the whole narrative of his season changed for the better. While the composite .261 average needs work, Odor is still ridiculously young at 22 and already is a very solid player. The signs are mainly positive here as Odor's 16.8 percent K rate is a good number for such a young player and his unlucky .283 BABIP shows the average should have been better than it was. There are future 25-home run seasons in Odor's bat and he also has the speed to swipe 10-15 bases. Throw in the launching pad ballpark and Odor is a must have sleeper who could be an All-Star as soon as this season.

2016 PROJECTION: .276 19 HR 77 RBI 63 R 9 SB

7. Kolten Wong: A lot was expected out of St. Louis Cardinals second baseman Kolten Wong for the 2015 season, especially after he came back from an early demotion the year prior to finish in a very impressive manner. As the team's first round pick in 2011, there were already optimistic projections for Wong and the tools checked out as he possessed above-average speed and some developing power. Just like in 2014 however, Wong failed to put a whole season together. This time around the opposite was in play as Wong posted a big first half (.280/9 HR/10 SB) and followed that up with an ugly second (.238/2 HR/5 SB). With two seasons of 400-plus at-bats in the book, some themes are starting to emerge. The first is that Wong is very prone to prolonged slumps, like the kind that got him demoted in 2014 and through his ugly second half last season. In addition, Wong does not draw walks at all (4.8 and 5.9 percent the last two years) which hurts him in the average department. Ultimately the tools are still attractive as Wong could put it all together and go 20/20 which would surprise no one. However Wong is a bit rough around the edges in the average and patience department which could hold him back from a possible leadoff spot which is where he would achieve his best value.

2016 PROJECTION: .273 14 HR 65 RBI 77 R 16 SB

8. Daniel Murphy: While Daniel Murphy went nuts with the bat once the postseason arrived, his numbers that counted during the 2015 fantasy baseball regular season went into the good but not great classification. After two seasons of quietly solid five category production (22 home runs and 36 stolen bases from 2013-14), Murphy changed his statistical spreadsheet last year. On the positive side, Murphy hit a career-high 14 home runs (and again went crazy in the postseason) which is a solid number for a second baseman but nothing otherworldly by any means. He also batted .281 which became his fifth straight season over the .280 mark. Alas Murphy's brief two-season run where he figured out mid-career how to steal some bases appear to be over. Murphy stole only 2 bags in 538 at-bats and at the age of 31 in April, he very well could be finished as a base runner. When you look at the whole picture of Daniel Murphy, you understand that the guy is a better real-life player than a fantasy one but he can still help you quite a bit.

2016 PROJECTION: .284 11 HR 75 RBI 65 R 4 SB

9. Brandon Phillips: Sometimes we wonder if players read the critiques and criticisms we place on them each and every season and react accordingly. After bashing Cincinnati Reds second baseman Brandon Phillips leading into both the 2013 and 2014 seasons due to our strong belief he was shot as a daily fantasy baseball option, the veteran came back and stuck it to the critical masses with a terrific comeback campaign in 2015. While we didn't so much attack Phillips' power or RBI numbers, it was his massive drop in stolen bases that made him a shell of his former 20/20, top tier second base self. Well Phillips seemed determined to re-write that analysis, stealing 23 bases which turned out to be his most there since 2009. This after Phillips stole a grand total of 7 bases in 2013 and 2014 combined. It was downright shocking to see Phillips run that much and when combined with a .294 average (his highest since 2011) and 12 home runs, the end result was a top five performance at the position. Of course we have seen late career jumps before, only to be followed by a crash back to a level that more reflects an aging player's adequate rates. As a result we have to consider Phillips' 2015 numbers as an outlier and instead grade him on his 2013-14 haul. Turning 35 in June, Phillips could fall off completely at a moment's notice and you never want to invest in players who have the double whammy of age and a fluky looking late career burst.

2016 PROJECTION: .273 14 HR 78 RBI 74 R 10 SB

10. Dustin Pedroia: Another prominent name on our 2014 BUST list was Boston Red Sox second baseman and former MVP Dustin Pedroia. This one was an easy call for us as Pedroia looks like another in a sizable-line of smallish second baseman who began to decline early. Like Carlos Baerga and Juan Samuel before him, the extreme wear and tear of playing second base on a 5-8 body have caused Pedroia to move to the bottom of daily mixed league usage status in 12-team leagues. For one thing, Pedroia's speed is completely shot as he stole only two bases last season. Also since stealing 20 bags in 2012, Pedroia has gone for 17, 6, and those 2 the last three years. Pedroia also is losing the battle to the injury bug, as he registered just 425 at-bats in 2015. Finally, Pedroia has now had a K rate of over 12 percent each of the last two seasons. Consider that he never topped that mark in his other 8 major league seasons, which shows how Pedroia's hitting skills are also hurting. Turning 33 in August, Pedroia is still capable of being a top 12 option but he also stands just as good a chance of having an injury-marred and statistically declining season.

2016 PROJECTION: .288 11 HR 77 R 43 RBI 5 SB

11. Howie Kendrick: Productive but always undervalued Howie Kendrick continued to do his thing in 2015 for the Los Angeles Dodgers in terms of helping in all five ROTO categories but not excelling in any of them. While Kendrick never lived up to the initial hype of being a possible future batting champion, he has hit over .290 the last three seasons and for his career has a .293 average. Kendrick is a strange hitter in that he is seemingly allergic to walks (5.5 percent) but he always seems to post useful numbers in the average department despite this. Outside of the average, Kendrick has also proven that he can crack between 8-12 home runs, score 60-80 runs, and steals 10-14 bases. Again nothing that will wow anyone but Kendrick's extreme durability and annually cheap draft price makes him a tremendous late round investment if you choose to pass on selecting your second baseman early.

2016 PROJECTION: .296 10 HR 59 RBI 67 R 11 SB

12. Joe Panik: The smooth-swinging second baseman first put himself on the map by hitting ropes all over the field during the San Francisco Giants' run to the World Series during the 2014 season. Still Panik had little to no buzz surrounding his name going into 2015 due to the fact he has previously shown himself to be an empty .300-plus batting average guy with no power and speed. While Panik will never be confused with Jason Kipnis in the steals department, he did however show some power last season by cracking 8 home runs in 382 at-bats and hitting for his customary .300 average (.312). Panik is quickly earning a reputation as one of the better pure hitters in baseball, with a minuscule K Rate of only 9.7 percent last season showing how good his batting eye is. Things didn't end well though for Panik as he hardly played in the second half of the season due to a persistent back issue. Overall we can accept the slight power growth from Panik as he begins to move closer to his prime years. Paired with the .300 average and decent run/RBI counting statistics, Panik has put himself toward the edge of daily usage in 12-team mixed formats.

2016 PROJECTION: .308 11 HR 59 RBI 84 R 5 SB

13. Jung Ho Kang: No one had any clue what to expect out of Korean shortstop import Jung Ho Kang heading into the 2015 fantasy baseball season. With Kang's Korean League being compared to the type of competition seen in A-Ball, the tremendous power numbers he put up in his final season in the Far East were universally taken with a grain of salt. A steep learning curve against major league pitching was expected, with Kang's propensity for striking out possibly being a major drag on his batting average. Well Kang wound up proving to be more than up to the task of being a major league hitter, getting better as the season went on. While Kang did strike out at a high 21.2 percent clip, he showed off the power stick that got everyone's attention in the first place by hitting 15 home runs and collecting 58 RBI in only 467 at-bats; also contributing a better than expected .287 average. Of course a lucky .344 BABIP helped Kang post the useful average which and that means he could sink to the .265-ish range in 2016 when the luck regresses to the mean. On the positive side, Kang is just getting started as a major league hitter and more power should be in the offing this season as he continues to mature. A torn left ACL and fractured tibia was a very tough way to end his rookie season but Kang is expected to be 100 percent healthy for the start of spring training. 20 home runs is not out of the question here.

2016 PROJECTION: .272 19 HR 73 RBI 67 R 6 SB

14. **DJ LeMathieu:** After seeing glimpses of solid play out of infielder DJ LeMathieu for a couple of seasons, the Colorado Rockies finally gave him a starting job entering the 2015 season. The Rockies were rewarded with an All-Star campaign from LeMathieu as he hit .301, scored 85 runs, and stole 23 bases batting at or near the top of the lineup. An uptick in walks helped LeMathieu get on base more and see better pitches which boosted the average to a career-best number. LeMathieu also became an adept base stealer, as he also netted a career-high there. Don't look for much power though as LeMathieu won't reach double-figures even in the thin air but instead embrace the speed/average game at a shallow position. While you can do better, LeMathieu is a cost-effective second base option.

2016 PROJECTION: .297 8 HR 88 R 63 R 25 SB

15. **Devon Travis:** For one fleeting month, it appeared as though the Toronto Blue Jays' Devon Travis was the next big power/speed star at the very shallow second base position. After staking his claim to the second base job out of camp, Travis looked like an instant star as he batted .325 with 6 home runs and a stolen base in April. A left shoulder injury eventually cropped up at the start of May, which coincided with Travis suddenly not being able to hit a lick and eventually be placed on the disabled list. What originally looked like a short DL stay grew to so much more as Travis eventually made it back in late June. While Travis did flash back to his April performance by batting .313 in his five June games and .368 in 21 July contests, he went back on the DL with renewed soreness in the shoulder which eventually led to exploratory surgery. After a few failed rehab stints, threw in the towel on the rest of his 2015 campaign. Now when you look at the 238 at-bat small sample size of numbers, Travis was pretty darn good with a cumulative .304 average with 8 home runs and 3 stolen bases. With hitting haven Rogers Center as his home park and still possessing intriguing power/speed/average ability, Travis should be on your second base sleeper list for the second year in a row. At the age of only 24, Travis has some years left before he reaches his prime which adds to the intrigue. A .347 BABIP means there will be some average give back for Travis in 2016 but otherwise he could come close to or better a 15/15 season if he can stay on the field. Alas yet another shoulder surgery muddies the picture again.

PROJECTION: .288 15 HR 61 RBI 75 R 11 SB

16. Neil Walker: Sort of along the same lines as Howie Kendrick, Pittsburgh Pirates second baseman Neil Walker seemingly is always there for you in the last few rounds of the draft or when needed during the season off the waiver wire. While Walker has had a nice career, fantasy baseball players always seem to want more out him. The 2015 season brought forth a jog back in the power department, as Walker's 23 home runs from the year prior went into the outlier file. Still Walker's 16 home runs checked out nicely at the shallow second base position and his average (like the .269 he batted last season) never seems to ever hurt you. Walker has driven in over 70 runs each of the last two years which is another positive and the runs usually come in around the high-60's which is workable. If it sounds like we are making excuses for Walker, we are not. Instead we are simply pointing out the fact that Walker's numbers each season almost always are better then you thought they were.

2016 PROJECTION: .267 15 HR 74 RBI 73 R 3 SB

17. Ben Zobrist: The offensive numbers continued to leak air for veteran second baseman Ben Zobrist during the 2015 season. Still a very valuable player (a point reinforced when up to a dozen teams inquired about his services leading up to the July 31 trade deadline), Zobrist has now ceded to age the stolen base part of his game after he took just three last season. Zobrist was still able to hit 13 home runs and bat a respectable .276 in a year split between the Oakland A's and Kansas City Royals, while also having solid enough numbers in runs (76) and RBI (56). More of a better real-life player than a fantasy baseball one, there is no reason to invest in a guy who will be 35 in May and whose offensive numbers are fading.

2016 PROJECTION: .273 14 HR 57 RBI 79 R 5 SB

18. Starlin Castro: The Chicago Cubs moved around their middle infielders in 2015, with incumbent shortstop Starlin Castro eventually taking over at second base during the second half of the season. Top shortstop prospect Addison Russell is now here to stay with the team, which means Castro will likely open up 2016 at second base once again while still retaining shortstop eligibility. Obviously you want to play Castro in your shortstop spot one last time given the more pronounced lack of depth but at either position his numbers are not overly impressive. After looking like a future star when he hit 10 home runs, stole 22 bases, and batted .307 his second year in the league in 2011, Castro has been chasing those numbers ever since. Annually having one of the worst walk rates in the majors, Castro has hit under .270 in two of the last three years and he also has remained stuck in the 10-14 home run range despite reaching his power prime. Additionally, Castro doesn't steal bases anymore as he has just 9 altogether the last two seasons. While Castro has lowered his strikeout rate, he is a completely undisciplined hitter whose career has stalled badly as he turns 26 in March. Again play Castro at shortstop if you draft him but it is starting to really look like his career will fall into the "what might have been" category.

2016 PROJECTION: .266 14 HR 65 RBI 56 R 6 SB

19. Javier Baez: 2016 will be a very crucial season in the development of top Chicago Cubs infield prospect Javier Baez. While other top prospects in the organization have taken off right away (Kris Bryant, Kyle Schwarber, Addison Russell), Baez has gone back-and-forth from the majors to the minors over the last two years due to an unfathomable K rate that is threatening to short-circuit what was looking like a very promising career. The former 9th overall pick in the 2011 draft, Baez didn't even make the Cubs out of spring training prior to last season due to his ridiculous K rate and he wouldn't make it back until September after also enduring a broken hand along the way. Now going back to Baez' 2014 debut, both sides of the statistical equation were at hand. On the plus side, Baez smacked 9 home runs and stolen 5 bases in just 229 at-bats. However he somehow managed to strike out in 41.5 percent of his at-bats that led to a .169 average. Both of those numbers are beyond hideous and speak to the big issues standing in Baez' way. Back in Triple-A last season however, Baez crushed minor league pitching by batting .324 with a 13/17 HR/SB ratio which engendered some Quad-A discussion. As soon as the Cubs brought him back for September, the strikeouts piled up again at a 30 percent clip. Perhaps more troubling, the Cubs infield is quite crowded going into 2016 as Russell is now the starting shortstop and Starlin Castro is manning second base unless a trade sends him out of town. That means Baez might need to play another position to stick with the team and at the same time show some semblance of a positive hitting approach. No one questions the terrific tools Baez possesses in both power and speed but there is a big question as to whether he can ever hit major league pitching. We always avoid average crushers like this no matter how much potential they bring and in the case of Baez, that once positive outlook has been dulled.

2016 PROJECTION: .234 14 HR 45 RBI 54 R 9 SB

20. Logan Forsythe: Even the Tampa Bay Rays had to be shocked at the unexpectedly good season posted by second baseman Logan Forsythe in 2015. After flaming out in the San Diego Padres organization, the Rays used Forsythe mostly in backup duty in 2014 when he batted an ugly .223. As a result it was doubly surprising when the Rays gave Forsythe a chance to man second base as the starter early in the 2015 season. As often happens with this organization though, things came up smelling like roses. Showing power he never hinted at before, Forsythe cracked 17 home runs and drove in 68 runners. Even more surprising, Forsythe batted .281 after failing to hit even .225 in three of his previous four MLB seasons. Throw in 9 stolen bases and Forsythe was a very nice free agent find. Of course whenever an out-of-the-blue performance like this comes forth, we have to look with a wary eye. We would not count on Forsythe to be your team's starting second baseman and instead you should pick him as a backup in order to cover yourself. If Forsythe further develops, it a win-win under that scenario but more likely he will go back to being a fringe MLB player.

2016 PROJECTION: .263 14 HR 57 RBI 75 R 7 SB

21. Jonathan Schoop: Yet another underrated Baltimore Orioles performance in 2015 came from second baseman Jonathan Schoop when he hit 15 home runs and batted .279 in just 321 at-bats. Seemingly always on the fringe of starting or backing up, Schoop has now hit 31 home runs over the last two years. A longtime Orioles property, Schoop figures to be in the lead for the starting second base job for 2016. While his .209 average in 2014 was very disturbing, Schoop has hit better than .275 in the two seasons surrounding that campaign. There is also no speed to speak of here as Schoop has never stolen more than two bases in a season, a solid negative since you want to have help in that category from your middle infielders. Still if you have an outfield that is adept at picking up steals, Schoop can work well enough as your starting second baseman in deeper mixed formats.

2016 PROJECTION: .257 14 HR 44 RBI 37 R 1 SB

22. Cesar Hernandez: With the Philadelphia Phillies immersed in a massive rebuild in 2015, youth was fully served. On such player who got an opportunity to play was speedy infielder Cesar Hernandez who mostly was a backup to second baseman Chase Utley in 2013 and 2014. With Utley spending time on the DL with injury and then eventually being dealt away, Hernandez did his best to stake his claim to be the second baseman for Opening Day 2016 by hitting a solid .272 with 57 runs scored and 19 stolen bases. Speed and versatility are the themes here as Hernandez has zero power but he can certainly help in the runs and stolen base columns. There is also the chance for a solid batting averages well but Hernandez has to answer to a .342 BABIP that was in the lucky tier. At a still young 25-years-old, Hernandez could work out well enough in NL-only formats and maybe make his way into mixed league consideration during the season.

2016 PROJECTION: .266 1 HR 39 RBI 65 R 23 SB   *Mets*

23. Danny Espinosa: When you are known more for your extravagant mustache than anything you do on the field with the bat, your name must be Washington Nationals infielder Danny Espinosa. Having had a fleeting two seasons of interesting fantasy baseball appeal due to nice power/speed combo's in 2011 and 2012, Espinosa from that point on has been a colossal average liability and a complete health mess. A .230 career hitter, Espinosa strikes out like he is the second base version of Mark Reynolds. While he still cracked 13 home runs last season and can run a bit despite turning 29 in April, Espinosa is only someone to turn to when an injury strikes down your starter. Even that would be pushing the limits of his usage though.

2016 PROJECTION: .235 12 HR 43 RBI 59 R 7 SB

THE REST

24. Jace Peterson: Getting his first crack at being an everyday player in 2015, there was the expected ups and down from Atlanta Braves second baseman Jace Peterson. After a very rough first half that almost cost him the job outright, Peterson got going during the summer as he ran more and started collecting hits. The final tally of a .239 average was ugly but Peterson also was able to hit 6 home runs and steal 12 bases. Ultimately though much more was anticipated when it came to Peterson and the running game; he was not good enough to where the

Braves wouldn't look for an upgrade there. Just not enough numbers for us to be intrigued.

25. Jimmy Paredes: The Baltimore Orioles have had a knack for uncovering useful hitters during the Buck Showalter era and that continued on in 2015 in the form of infielder/outfielder Jimmy Paredes. He would put himself squarely on the fantasy baseball map by hitting 10 first half home runs while carrying eligibility at second base. A .299 average during the first three months further rose the interest meter on Paredes despite his utter lack of a previous track record. As often happens with stories like this, Paredes cooled off dramatically during the second half, as he batted a terrible .218 from the All-Star Break onward. Things got so bad that Showalter benched Paredes starting in mid-August and ignored him the rest of the way. Already 27 and having shown that his first half of 2015 was somewhat of a fluke, Paredes may not even start in 2016. A 28.9 K rate shows the gigantic holes in his swing and when Showalter gives up on you, that's saying a bunch.

26. Cory Spangenberg: The San Diego Padres seem ready to ride with infield prospect Cory Spangenberg, who was once a 2011 first round pick of the team back in 2011. In his first extended look in the majors , Spangenberg was a late-season boost to both his real and fantasy baseball teams by hitting .271 with 4 home runs and 9 stolen bases in 345 at-bats last season. Showing good on-base skills and a decent enough K rate for a young hitter, Spangenberg looks like a future help in runs scored, steals, and batting average. There is very little power to speak of here so Spangenberg is just a three-category guy at a shallow infield spot. Worth a late round gamble given the position he plays.

27. Dustin Ackley: After four-and-a-half years of completely bottoming out in the Seattle Mariners organization after he became the team's number 2 overall pick in the 2009 draft, Dustin Ackley was pretty much given away to the New York Yankees at the trade deadline last season. When Ackley first arrived in Seattle, he was tabbed as a possible future batting champion and a top-end infield prospect. Unfortunately Ackley simply could not hit major league pitching, with his average habitually falling in the .230-.240 range. The Yankees were a decent landing spot for Ackley however as the team had a need at second base after losing Stephen Drew to a concussion. After a quick DL stint with the team, Ackley returned and proceeded to hit some home runs and become a spark for the Yankees down the stretch. As 2016 arrives, Ackley will battle with infield prospect Rob Refsnyder for the staring second base spot. If Ackley wins, the move to an offensive park at Yankee Stadium could make him relevant again in deeper formats and especially in AL-only leagues.

28. Yangervis Solarte: While Yangervis Solarte has turned out to be a solid late-bloomer infielder, he simply comes up short outside of maybe NL-only formats when it comes to fantasy baseball numbers. Yes the 14 home runs were nice but Solarte is mediocre to poor everywhere else.

29. Scooter Gennett: While the name is cool, Scooter Gennett comes up short everywhere else in terms of fantasy baseball. Nothing but a stopgap second baseman for the Milwaukee Brewers until they find someone better, Gennett could post another solid batting average and nothing more in 2016.

30. Rob Refsnyder: While no one doubts the hitting ability of Rob Refsnyder, the New York Yankees have been lukewarm about his prospects of being the team's everyday second baseman. Even with Stephen Drew struggling as much as he did last season, Refsnyder didn't get much of a chance to show what he could do. Refsnyder is capable of a .280-plus batting average and around 15 home runs but he is not much of a story unless the Yankees finally give him a look.

31. Derek Dietrich: The Miami Marlins gave some more at-bats to infielder Derek Dietrich in 2015, with underwhelming results once again. While the 10 home runs were all right, Dietrich doesn't do any one thing that stands out and has hit just .228 and .256 the last two seasons. When you are known more for getting into it with the team's coaching staff (Dietrich had a run-in with Tino Martinez in 2014), you pretty much are a non-factor in fantasy baseball.

32. Eduardo Escobar: Somehow Eduardo Escobar fell into 12 home runs last season but the backup Minnesota Twins infielder should not be finding a bunch of playing time in 2016 or on your fantasy baseball roster.

33. Aaron Hill: When it comes to career volatility, few can match the massive swings in performance seen from infielder Aaron Hill over the last 7 seasons. From a high of hitting 36 home runs with the Toronto Blue Jays, to batting just 205 the following season, Hill has been all over the statistical map. The last two seasons have been very ugly however, will Hill losing his starting second base spot in 2015 after he hit just .230 with 6 home runs in 353 at-bats. With just a total of 16 home runs over the last two seasons despite operating in Chase Field, Hill looks cooked as he turns 34 in March. No longer a story worth reading.

34. Elian Herrera: Getting a shot to play somewhat regularly during the second half of 2015 as the Milwaukee Brewers hit rock bottom, Elian Herrera played decently with 7 home runs and 3 stolen bases in 277 at-bats. The .242 average was hideous though and Herrera's 26 percent K rate shows nothing more than the bench/injury league replacement that the already 31-year-old has always been.

35. Jedd Gyorko: Briefly interesting due to his power bat, the first three seasons in the major leagues for San Diego Padres infielder Jeff Gyorko have included a failure to hit above .250 and a yo-yoing back and forth from the minors. With holes as big as the Grand Canyon in his swing, Gyorko is a strikeout waiting to happen. Since he offers nothing in the stolen base department, Gyorko doesn't offer enough numbers elsewhere to make up for the hit there and in the average department. 16 home runs in 458 at-bats last season is very good indeed for a second baseman but a lot of shine comes off those numbers when you factor in the horrible average. Not a chance.

36. Arismendy Alcantara: With the massive infusion of top-end prospects arriving with the Chicago Cubs over the last two years, someone had to be squeezed out of a roster spot. That person was Cuban second baseman/outfielder Arismendy Alcantara who got only 26 at-bats with team in 2015, where he registered just 2 hits. The problem with Alcantara.....and it is a big one....is his propensity to strike out which makes him a major batting average liability. Even at Triple-A last season, Alcantara struck out in a ridiculous 25 percent of his at-bats which showed in an ugly .231 average. While Alcantara did post a somewhat interesting 12/16 home run/stolen base split at Triple-A, the kid simply can't hit enough to be anything more than a bench guy for the Cubs and worth zero in fantasy baseball.

37. Stephen Drew: When you have hit .162 and .201 the last two seasons, there is little reason to discuss you game much. Veteran second baseman Stephen Drew was the owner of those pathetic averages, despite the fact he did crack 17 home runs last season in just 428 at-bats. Drew took full advantage of his ballpark in Yankee Stadium to boost up the power numbers but the team is expected to let him walk in free agency. Aging as he turns 33 in March, Drew is pretty much worthless even though he plays a shallow position.

38. Chase Utley: At the age of 37 and no longer a starting-caliber player, Chase Utley's retirement is very close. When the most notable thing you did in 2015 was break an opposing player's leg on a takeout slide at second base, it might be time to hang them up. While Utley has had a terrific career as a former fantasy baseball first round pick, the guy should not be even mentioned in our fake game ever again.

39. Ruben Tejada: Now six seasons into his disappointing major league career, New York Mets infielder Ruben Tejada simply can't hit even remotely enough to be interesting in fantasy baseball. While his glove is excellent, Tejada has never hit more than 5 home runs in a season and his average continually stays in the mediocre .250-.260 range.

SHORTSTOP

Draft Strategy: The shortstop position in fantasy baseball remained a massive train wreck in 2015 as big-name guys such as Ian Desmond, Jimmy Rollins, Starlin Castro, Elvis Andrus, and Alexei Ramirez all went bust. Throw in an offensively reduced Troy Tulowitzki and there was almost complete carnage among this group. Luckily the arrival of Carlos Correa and to a lesser extent Francisco Lindor helped infuse some much-needed impact youth to the position but overall this is a group you want to wait until the middle rounds to address in looking for a value play like you would with catcher. The only exception we will make here is with Correa who is the one guy at any position we would sign off on using a second round pick on and thus breaking up the 1B-OF combo we always preach. Correa's upside is extremely high and ultimately he has the chance to have a Mike Trout-like impact when you consider how shallow shortstop remains. While the position did lose perennial top 2 star Hanley Ramirez, those who have 5 games started as the benchmark for eligibility gain a monster superstar in Manny Machado. The fact Machado had a truly epic five-category season at third base for the Baltimore Orioles that launched him into first round territory, make it icing on the cake that he now has gained shortstop eligibility in some leagues.

1. Carlos Correa: Other than when Mike Trout first debuted, there may not have been a more smashing instant success story at the major league level than what we saw out of Houston Astros shortstop Carlos Correa in 2015. Universally acclaimed as one of the top 1-3 prospects in all of baseball, Correa was considered a can't miss five-tool star. From the moment he was called up in June, Correa was a fantasy baseball monster as he slammed 22 home runs, stole 14 bases, and batted .279 in 432 at-bats. Comparisons to a young Hanley Ramirez appear to be spot on and at only 21-years-old, it is staggering to think how great of a player he can. Only a few special players can go from being a rookie to a slam-dunk first round fantasy baseball draft pick in one season and that is exactly what will transpire with Correa. Given how shortstop has very little depth to it, Correa's extreme five-tool ability is that much more valuable. His 18.1 K rate as a rookie was tremendous given his age and his 9.3 BB rate was also very impressive. 30 home runs seems a given in short order, with 20-plus steals and a .300 average also included. We are running out of positive things to say about Correa and fully endorse him as a late first round pick. The kid is scary good.

2016 PROJECTION: .294 27 HR 83 RBI 75 R 19 SB

2. Manny Machado:*******SEE THIRD BASE RANKINGS*****

3. Troy Tulowitzki: In last season's draft guide, we had shortstop Troy Tulowitzki included in our "Busts" section for the third straight year. While the overall narrative was similar, our reasoning in advising you to once again avoid Tulowitzki was a bit different this time around. Historically speaking, the book on Tulowitzki has always been of a guy who is a supreme and sometimes dominant hitting superstar who gets undermined almost every season by one or more injury issues that cost him a large portion of games. What we were concerned about in a slightly different way going into 2015 was the fact Tulowitzki was coming into the season off major hip surgery that historically derails power output. While Tulowitzki was scheduled to start the season on time, we advised avoiding him altogether due to our expectation his power numbers would trend downward by more than a bit. And down Tulowitzki's offensive numbers went, especially the first half of 2015 as he went into the All-Star break with just 10 home runs and 49 RBI. In addition, Tulowitzki once again showed a sharp split in terms of being a force at home (.283/11 HR) to less than that on the road (.272/6 HR). Despite the ugly first half, Tulowitzki was staying healthy which led to the Toronto Blue Jays finally being the team that acquired him in a trade after months of rumors that included up to ten different possible destinations. While having to give up Coors Field as a home park would ordinarily be looked at as a major negative, Rogers Center has actually been a better power ballpark going back to 2014 which kept Tulowitzki in an ideal hitting situation. Unfortunately Tulowitzki didn't get the memo as he hit a woeful .232 north of the border with just 5 home runs in 155 at-bats. In addition, the inevitable injury hit in early September as Tulowitzki suffered a fractured scapula in his shoulder while colliding with teammate Kevin Pillar chasing a fly ball that ended his regular season early. In the end Tulowitzki had his worst offensive season in terms of games played since 2008, finishing with a composite total of 17 home runs and a .278 average. Now 31-years-old, still as injury-prone as ever, and showcasing sliding offensive numbers, there is not a whole lot to get excited about anymore regarding Tulowitzki. A full season in

Rogers Center is as good as it gets for any hitter and Tulowitzki still grades out as a top shortstop given how shallow the position is. The headaches associated with drafting Tulowitzki are just too great to make him worth your time.

2016 PROJECTION: .302 22 HR 83 RBI 86 R 2 SB

4. Francisco Lindor: For all the well-deserved hype and accolades that Houston Astros rookie shortstop Carlos Correa received last season, the debut of Francisco Lindor with the Cleveland Indians was also very impressive to say the least. When Lindor was promoted early in the 2015 season, initially he was expected to help in the average, runs, and steals department, while also flashing a top-notch glove. Power was not yet supposed to be part of the equation, especially after Lindor hit all of 2 home runs in 262 Triple-A at-bats prior to his arrival. As often happens though with top prospects once they get to the majors, the full unleashing of their abilities get released. Such was the case for Lindor who did in fact supply the good batting average (.313), and stolen bases (12) in his 438 at-bats. However Lindor also cracked 12 home runs to change the entire narrative for the better when it came to his 2015 campaign and his overall outlook going forward. Already possessing a terrific K rate for a young hitter at 15.8 percent and a walk rate that will only go up as he sees more pitches from major league hurlers, Lindor could be encroaching on a 15/20-plus season in 2016 if all breaks right. At the very least, Lindor's advanced hitting approach will once again ensure good totals in runs and steals, in addition to a very useful average. Last year's power we think is repeatable as well since Lindor will continue to grow physically. Only 22-years-old, Lindor has a good 4-5 years of ceiling left which is very tantalizing indeed. While he is not in Carlos Correa's class, Lindor may not be as far behind his counterpart as many might think.

2016 PROJECTION: .308 14 HR 67 RBI 77 R 19 SB

5. Jose Reyes: The slow fade of Colorado Rockies shortstop Jose Reyes continued on during the 2015 season, a campaign that included being dealt away from the Toronto Blue Jays in the Troy Tulowitzki deal. A one time a slam-dunk early first round pick when he was in his early days with the New York Mets, Reyes is a vastly stripped-down version of his old self these days. Still one of the most frustrating players to own due to his massive injury history, Reyes is three seasons removed from stealing 40 bases. The batting average is also starting to slip as

Reyes has gone from .296 to .287 to .274 the last three years. Never one to take walks in the first place, Reyes is as impatient as ever after posting walks rates under 6.00 each of the last two years after being in the 8-plus range for awhile. Turning 34 in June, Reyes is still an injury waiting to happen and his sliding numbers are a major red flag. The fact Reyes saw his statistics decline across the board last season after playing in two of the best hitting parks in the game is telling. We have been on record for two straight seasons now in suggesting you stay far away from Reyes. This makes it three straight.

2016 PROJECTION: .275 8 HR 53 RBI 79 R 22 SB

6. Corey Seager: The Los Angeles Dodgers ushered in a big part of their youth during the second half of the 2015 season when they pushed washed-up shortstop Jimmy Rollins aside to make room for top prospect Corey Seager. The team's 18th overall pick in the 2012 draft, Seager immediately began to impress when he hit a scorching .337 with 4 home runs in 113 at-bats in the heat of a pennant race. His stint with the Dodgers completed the hat trick for Seager last season in terms of playing in Double-A, Triple-A, and eventually the Nationals. In terms of the offensive profile, Seager has burgeoning power that should eventually have him in the 20-plus home run range to go along with a useful batting average. What is really impressive about Seager is the fact that he walks at a very high rate for a young hitter (12.4 percent with the Dodgers) and he also doesn't strike out a ton which will help in the average department right away. While he doesn't have classic middle infielder speed, Seager is capable of swiping around 10 bags or so. The upside here is tremendous and Seager should be on all sleepers lists for 2016. Primed to join Carlos Correa as the new generation of top shortstops.

2016 PROJECTION: .288 14 HR 65 RBI 67 R 9 SB

7. Addison Russell: The Chicago Cubs redefined what it means to have a fertile minor league system, as universally acclaimed top shortstop prospect Addison Russell made his way to the team during the 2015 season. The Cubs acquired Russell from the Oakland A's in the Jeff Samardzjia deal and needless to say, they likely have their shortstop for the next decade. While Russell struggled at times during his rookie campaign, he still showed more than enough flashes to uphold his standing as a future high-impact player by hitting 13 home runs and driving in

54 batters while hitting at the bottom of the team's lineup for most of the season. Keep in mind that Russell in incredibly young as he turns just 22 in January and that means some extra patience is required through any struggles. Russell is still growing into his body, which means the power is a work in progress. He does looks like a future 20-25 home run bat but that may not come until 2017. There also is a lack of speed here as Russell has not reached double-digits in steals since doing it way back in A-Ball. The 28.5 K rate in 2015 is very ugly but again hitting at the bottom of a National League lineup at the age of 21 is an incredibly tough chore for anyone. While Russell may not light things up in 2016, he still is too talented to not be in the conversation as a top ten shortstop this season.

2016 PROJECTION: .263 17 HR 65 RBI 67 R 8 SB

8. Ian Desmond: A walk year for most hitters or pitchers usually elicits the best performance/numbers for that given player due to the motivation of the payday at hand. In some rare cases though, the pressure sometimes leads to a busted campaign such as what we saw out of shortstop Ian Desmond with the Washington Nationals in 2015. After posting three straight 20/20 seasons at the shallow shortstop position, Desmond was arguably one of the worst performing hitters in the game during the first half of the year. Desmond went into the All-Star Break with a miserable .211 average, to go with 7 home runs and just 2 stolen bases. He would rebound to post a decent .262 average in the second half with 12 more home runs but the damage was already done. For the year, Desmond's 19 home runs were very good for sure but his 13 steals and .233 average were quite ugly. Desmond has now finished a two-season run where his K rate has been over 28 percent in each; a big red flag for his batting average. Just to show it more clearly, Desmond batted a very good .292 in 2012 and .280 in 2013 with K rates under 23 percent in each. The last two years not so good with the .255 and .233 averages as the K rate has gotten out of hand. In addition, Desmond's drop in steals is a big negative since much of his past allure was tied to the power/speed ability. Often though we see players begin to lose some steals when they reach the age 30 and that could be what is going on with Desmond. While Desmond is still hitting for power, the eroding numbers elsewhere make us very leery of trying him out again unless the price checks out.

2016 PROJECTION: .253 20 HR 75 RBI 76 R 14 SB

9. Alcides Escobar: Over the last few years, there was never any reason to select Elvis Andrus in the early middle rounds of your draft due to the fact you could get the very similar Alcides Escobar about ten rounds later. Escobar's calling card has always been in the stolen base and runs category, while also sometimes helping in average. Having stolen 30 or more bags in two of the previous three seasons coming into 2015, Escobar was looking like a very good value again in a run-heavy Kansas City Royals lineup. Escobar had somewhat of a down year though, stealing just 17 bases and batting a listless .257 while battling some injuries. We can probably chalk it up to simply being a poor season from Escobar due to the fact he is still early in his prime years at the age of 29. The Royals are always about stealing bases and scoring runs and that should put Escobar in play as another very affordable shortstop option. With a very low K rate of 11.3 percent last season and with a somewhat unlucky .286 BABIP helping to depress the average a bit, we think there is a very good rebound chance here.

2016 PROJECTION: .277 3 HR 52 RBI 75 R 19 SB

10. Marcus Semien: Having been the highlight piece that that Oakland A's acquired in trading Jeff Samardzjia, the team wasted no time throwing shortstop prospect Marcus Semien into the deep end of the major league pool to begin 2015. Semien seemed up to the task as he batted over .280 in each of the first two months of the season, with 6 home runs and 7 stolen bases total. While opposing pitchers began to adjust in a difficult June (.213), Semien would up adjusting himself to actually hit for a slightly higher average the second half of the season compared to the first. Overall Semien put up a 15/11 split in the power/speed game which looks very nice at shortstop and there is still some solid room for growth here as he goes into the 2016 season just 25-years-old. We like seeing the fact Semien lowered his K rate from 2014 to 2015 and that points to a young player who is starting to come into his own as a hitter. While the ballpark is a drag, we could be looking at a breakout season for a cheap draft rate in 2016.

2016 PROJECTION: .263 17 HR 55 RBI 74 R 14 SB

11. Elvis Andrus: It appears as though the fantasy baseball community finally got in line when it came to our firmly stated opinion on how vastly overrated Texas Rangers shortstop Elvis Andrus has been for a few seasons now. Even when Andrus held his highest draft value, he was pretty much a statistical fraud in that he was an asset only in steals and runs, while mediocre to very poor in the other three categories. The last two seasons have now seen Andrus begin to slip in the runs and stolen base categories as well which has pushed him to the edge of daily usage. He comes off a 2015 season where he posted a career-worst .258 average and his 25 stolen bases were his second-fewest yearly haul as well. With little power to speak of and sliding numbers in his only positive categories, Andrus is a complete waste of time.

2016 PROJECTION: .260 5 HR 59 RBI 66 R 23 SB

12. Jhonny Peralta: The 50-game Biogenesis ban that veteran shortstop Jhonny Peralta endured in 2014 did little to prevent his strong rebound last season after signing a sizable free agent deal with the St. Louis Cardinals for 2015. Showing his customary above-average power at a home run-starved position, Peralta hit 17 long balls, drove in 71, and batted .275. Peralta has now reached double-digits in home runs for 11 straight seasons and he also continues to hit for average despite the fact he turns 34 in May. While we respect what Peralta brings to the table, we have never been a big booster of his due to a complete lack of speed. Again you want your middle infielders to supply a high percentage of your team stolen bases and Peralta simply is not the guy to do it with. If you have speed at other spots than by all means give Peralta a look. With consistent numbers and good durability, Peralta at least gives you comfort in knowing what you will get with your investment.

2016 PROJECTION: .272 16 HR 77 RBI 67 R 2 SB

13. Brandon Crawford: Meet the new J.J. Hardy. While the aging Baltimore Orioles shortstop is quickly fading into oblivion due to a persistent back problem, his clone is beginning to emerge in San Francisco in the form of Brandon Crawford. Just like with Hardy, Crawford has top-end power for the shortstop position, while also having little speed and a somewhat ugly batting average. Crawford stormed out of the gates in 2015, hitting 12 first half home runs with a .262 average. The average cooled a bit in the second half as expected but the power remained steady. For the season, Crawford posted career-highs with 21 home runs, collecting 84 RBI, and batting .256. With a K rate of 21.2 percent, Crawford will always be a rough batting average guy and with only 6 steals in 561 at-bats in 2015, he won't help you in the stolen base department either. This is a pure power grab at a weak position only and nothing more. Again if you have steals covered at second base or elsewhere, by all means. Just be aware of a possible outlier campaign as it was far-and-away Crawford's best ever season.

2016 PROJECTION: .253 19 HR 73 RBI 63 R 4 SB

14. Asdrubal Cabrera: None of us ever want to own Asdrubal Cabrera but since he still operates in the major leagues as a starting shortstop, we are obligated to discuss him. While it seems like he has been around forever, Cabrera turned just 30 in November. His career year in 2011 while with the Cleveland Indians is now nothing but a rumor though and since that time the numbers have been quite mediocre. On the plus side, Cabrera has kept himself viable by hitting 14 or 15 home runs and stealing between 6 and 10 bases each of the last three years. On the negative side, the average has tumbled under the .260 range in two of the last three years as the K rate is pushing up against the 20.0 mark. There is enough juice left in the power/speed categories to stay involved in AL or NL-only formats but in mixed league you only want to go here if an injury takes out your starter.

2016 PROJECTION: .258 14 HR 53 RBI 70 R 8 SB

15. Alexei Ramirez: While a 10/17 season is nothing to sneeze at when it comes from a shortstop in fantasy baseball, there is a good deal of offensive erosion taking place when it comes to the Chicago White Sox' Alexei Ramirez. During the 2015 season, Ramirez wound up losing 5 home runs and 4 steals from the year prior and the average tumbled all the way down to .249 after habitually being between .265 and .300 throughout his career. An unlucky .264 BABIP had a lot to do with the latter, as a neutral mark there would have had Ramirez back in his customary average range but the slip in the power/speed categories bears watching. Ramirez is now and aging 34 and his best days are clearly in the past. Again you want to avoid aging players that are 34 or older given the unlikelihood they can maintain their status quo numbers. This is especially true for middle infielders who tend to lose their numbers faster than their corner and outfield counterparts.

2016 PROJECTION: .263 11 HR 59 RBI 65 R 15 SB

16. Erick Aybar: The consistently boring career of Atlanta Braves shortstop Erick Aybar continued on in 2015, as he recorded his tenth season with the team.

During that time period, Aybar has been a good but not very impactful hitter who can add some numbers in all five standard categories. Unfortunately Aybar doesn't make any of those categories his own in terms of high-impact statistics which make him a borderline guy to own in fantasy baseball. You can pretty much write in ink what you will get out of Aybar as he has hit in the .270 range in four of the last five years and only once in those ten years with the Angels has he reached the double-digit mark in home runs. Even the stolen bases, where Aybar has made his biggest contribution, have slipped as he has been in the mid-teen area code lately after going for 20 or more from 2010-12. You really only want to have a stake in Aybar in NL-only formats, with maybe stretching things a bit to include him being a backup in mixed setups.

2016 PROJECTION: .267 7 HR 46 RBI 74 R 14 SB

17. Jean Segura: Having had to endure a season that no one would want to go through in 2014, Milwaukee Brewers shortstop Jean Segura posted a mini-comeback campaign in 2015. Using his speed more to steal 25 bases, Segura made an attempt to get back toward the top of the team's lineup. However the .257 average remained shaky and Segura has now only hit 5 and 6 home runs the last two seasons. Clearly the terrific first half of 2013 will go down in the outlier bin for Segura and since that time he has performed on the edge of the starter/bench line. A 2.2 percent walk rate just won't cut it at the major league level and that alone makes hitting better than .270 unlikely. If Segura is not swiping over 30 bags, he has little to no value.

2016 PROJECTION: .255 5 HR 43 RBI 59 R 27 SB

18. Brock Holt: The Boston Red Sox have gotten good use out of do-everything utility king Brock Holt over the last two years. The 2015 All-Star played his most games for the team in the infield between shortstop and second base and his high-walk/high-contact approach netted a .281 average which was a smidge over the .280 mark from the year before. The fact of the matter though is that Holt is another one of those guys who is a better real-life player then a fantasy baseball one due to his complete lack of power (2 home runs in 509 at-bats in 2015) and only average speed (20 steals the last two seasons). We like Holt in a bench capacity for your team due to the fact his eligibility everywhere allows you to plug him in on light schedule days or when injuries hit. That is as far as the value goes however as Holt is quite limited overall.

2016 PROJECTION: .282 3 HR 46 RBI 59 R 10 SB

19. Didi Gregorious: No one had a tougher chore heading into the 2015 season then shortstop Didi Gregorious who had the unenviable task of replacing New York Yankees icon Derek Jeter at the position. Having come over to the Yanks in a three-way deal with the Arizona Diamondbacks and the Detroit Tigers, Gregorious was more of a project than anything given his lackluster early numbers out West. It seemed early on that GM Brian Cashman made a brutal error in tabbing Gregorious as Jeter's replacement, with his new shortstop hitting a listless .238 during the first half of the season and fielding the position terribly. Eventually though Gregorious found his comfort zone and began lacing ropes all over the field. Gregorious looked like a potential future asset at shortstop as he hit .294 in his big second half, scoring a bunch of runs in process. What makes one optimistic about Gregorious is that his approach has shown major signs of progress, with his K rate being lowered to a career-low 14.7 percent last season. While you want Gregorious to walk more to help the average a bit better, he does possess very good speed that could result in a stolen base boost soon. With 9 home runs in 578 at-bats, there also could be a bit of a power improvement as well. The arrow is pointing upwards here and in deeper formats, Gregorious could be a terrific value. In 12-teams or fewer, he is more of an upside bench guy.

2016 PROJECTION: .271 12 HR 59 RBI 75 R 11 SB

20. Yunel Escobar: After a string of very disappointing seasons got him run out of Atlanta, Tampa Bay, and Toronto, it appeared as though shortstop Yunel Escobar finally got serious about being a major league player in 2015. With a reputation for being a less-than-stellar teammate or worker, Escobar was almost completely ignored when drafts got underway prior to last season. Escobar got another shot with the Washington Nationals who needed a placeholder for Trea Turner and they wound up getting a surprisingly good year out of him. After spending a large portion of the season in the batting title race, Escobar wound up with a .314 average to go along with 9 home runs in 591 at-bats. Having never approached such an average since 2009, there was some expected BABIP help there as Escobar posted a very lucky .347 mark. When you take away the average, Escobar was still pretty mediocre with just 2 stolen bases to go with the middling power. While the 75 runs were nice, Escobar still is a fringe guy for 2016 when you put it all together. With the average expected to slip when the BABIP luck corrects itself this season, there won't be a lot of useful numbers left over. If you benefitted at all from the 2015 version of Escobar, you did well. It was likely just a one-year blip however.

2016 PROJECTION: .286 8 HR 53 RBI 65 R 4 SB

21. Eugenio Suarez: There is always a bunch of excitement and attention paid to any young shortstop that comes up and starts hitting at a high level. That grows even more pronounced if this player can continue doing so deeper into the season. A scenario like that unfolded in the middle of 2015 when the Cincinnati Reds promoted Eugenio Suarez to take over the shortstop spot once Zach Cozart was lost to injury. Instantly Suarez began to hit for both power and average and he wound up becoming a decent impact player during the second half for those who decided to take him out for a spin. Suarez would hit 13 home runs and drove in 48 batters in just 398 at-bats, clearly putting himself on the fantasy baseball landscape. Add in a useful .280 average and Suarez merits a closer look for 2016. Having failed to hook on previously as a member of the Detroit Tigers organization, Suarez only has to beat out the often overmatched Cozart for playing time in 2016. Alas there is strong evidence that Suarez will fade right back into oblivion. First of all, Suarez' .341 BABIP was extremely lucky last season which means his average should have been quite a bit lower. In 277 at-bats in his debut with the Tigers in 2014, Suarez batted just .242 with another lucky but lower BABIP of .314. When the BABIP comes back closer to .300 this season, his average will drop accordingly and maybe by a wide margin. In addition, Suarez only walked in 4.3 percent of his at-bats last season while striking out at a high 23.6 clip which shows some red flags in his approach. As a result, you need to make sure not to overhype Suarez' 2015 production since a lot of the numbers don't look repeatable. A strong flash in the pan candidate.

2016 PROJECTION: .255 11 HR 48 RBI 43 R 2 SB

22. Adeiny Hechavarria: The always frugal Miami Marlins continue to entrust the team's starting shortstop job to Adeiny Hechavarria, who coming into the 2015 season had done a whole bunch of nothing during his first two years in the league. Having little power and speed that doesn't translate into stolen bases, Hechavarria really offered little from a fantasy baseball angle in the first place. A hot start to the 2015 season however got Hechavarria back onto the radar and he would finish with a very solid .281 batting average. Unfortunately the average came with little to no impact in the juice categories of home runs (5) and stolen bases (7). With a classic empty average that could slide when his lucky .325 BABIP normalizes in 2016, Hechavarria has just minimal value even in NL-only setups.

2016 PROJECTION: .266 6 HR 45 RBI 56 R 8 SB

23. J.J. Hardy: Age is taking firm hold of Baltimore Orioles shortstop J.J. Hardy, with a decline physically helping to hurt his offensive numbers significantly. With absolutely no speed to his name, the only reason you ever owned Hardy in the past was due to his rare power at the shortstop position.. With a back that seems to be perpetually sore, Hardy has hit just 9 and 8 home runs the last two years. Perhaps most alarming was the .219 average last season which could be the white flag waving on Hardy's career. Now an old 33 and with his the power vanishing quick, Hardy pretty much has nothing left to hang his hat on.

2016 PROJECTION: .244 14 HR 48 RBI 56 R 0 SB

24. Chris Owings: The Arizona Diamondbacks continue to give opportunities to infielder Chris Owings with varying degrees of results to this point in his still young career. Owings wound up with his most at-bats ever in 2015 but the results were not very good as he batted just .227 due to a very ugly 26.1 K rate. When your K rate is that high, you better walk at a high clip which is something Owings has failed to do as well which speaks to his very murky outlook. There is a smidge power/speed potential here as Owings went 4/16 last season but the persistent contact problems means he is barely worth owning as anything more than a backup in mixed formats.

2016 PROJECTION: .248 7 HR 44 RBI 65 R 17 SB

25. Zack Cozart: After years of failing to meet expectations with the Cincinnati Reds after coming up as a decent shortstop prospect, it appeared as though the light bulb finally went on for Zack Cozart in 2015. Cozart came out of the gates fast by hitting 4 home runs in April and notching a .280 batting average. From that point on through May and into June, Cozart began leaking statistical air and started regressing back to the very mediocre hitter he had previously been. The bottom completely fell out on June 10th when Cozart tore ligaments and tendons in his right knee that required immediate surgery. Needless to say Cozart was done for 2015 and overall was given a nine-month recovery period. That would put Cozart close to being ready for Opening Day but you really don't want to bother here unless you are in a very deep NL-only league. Even accounting for how shallow shortstop remains, Cozart is just a .238 career hitter versus righties and .245 overall. No thank you.

2016 PROJECTION: .255 10 HR 57 RBI 61 R 4 SB

THE REST

26. Jose Iglesias: It was a successful season for Detroit Tigers shortstop Jose Iglesias just on the fact that he played in the majors after he missed all of 2014 with injured shins. Iglesias also was successful in showing he was more than simply a smooth-fielding shortstop, hitting for average at .300, while also showing some speed with 11 stolen bases in 454 at-bats. Ultimately though, Iglesias is a very limited offensive player, with no power to speak of. In addition, that .300 average has to be taken with a big of a grain of salt due to his quite lucky .330 BABIP. You can do much better, even at the very shallow position of shortstop.

28. Brad Miller: A spring training curiosity both in 2013 and 2014, the major league performance thus far from Seattle Mariners infielder Brad Miller has been quite shaky. While Miller has continually ripped minor league pitching with a string of top batting averages, he has been a shell of that player with the M's since his 2013 debut. After a complete bomb of a 2014 season, Miller did come back in 2015 with a somewhat decent performance as he hit 11 home runs, stole 13 bases, and batted .258. However Miller tends to strike out too much and his ceiling is not looking as impressive as it once seemed to be. Think a younger version of Asdrubal Cabrera which certainly doesn't make you run out to get him. A fresh start in Tampa Bay is at least is encouraging in a sense that sometimes a new environment can help kick start a young career.

29. Jimmy Rollins: It was fun while it lasted. The end is here now for veteran shortstop Jimmy Rollins after he was benched outright during the second half of last season by the Los Angeles Dodgers. It was an understandable move as Rollins lost what little he had left as far as his offensive numbers were concerned. Whereas Rollins was still holding onto some speed and power the last couple of years while at the same time losing his already ugly batting average completely, everything went into the gutter in 2015. Hitting just .224 for the season, Rollins stole only 12 bases which turned out to be less than half the 28 he had the year before. Rollins did manage to hit 13 home runs but that was the only positive in a complete abomination of a season. Now a very old 37, Rollins is no longer worth using in any format.

30. Jose Ramirez: The Cleveland Indians were fooling themselves when they went into the 2015 season endorsing Jose Ramirez as their starting shortstop. Everyone knew it was only a matter of time before top prospect Francisco Lindor would be promoted and that happened early in the season when Ramirez had a tough time hitting his weight. Once Lindor was with the Indians, Ramirez was a non-factor the rest of the way as the average tumbled to the ghastly .221 mark. While Ramirez has good speed and a bit of pop, he doesn't have a starting spot at the moment as we look toward 2016. We should point out that a .232 BABIP was incredibly unlucky which explains the low average from a guy who batted .262 in 2014 and again Ramirez could steal some bases with some playing time this season. Ultimately though, this is a story only if an injury gets him another long look.

31. Andrelton Simmons: There was some hope that maybe Atlanta Braves top defensive shortstop Andrelton Simmons could develop some offensive skill in 2015 but it simply didn't happen. While no one is better with the glove, Simmons continued struggling with the bat as he hit just .265 and smacked all of 4 home runs in 583 at-bats. While Simmons has very good speed, he managed just 5 stolen bases last season, showing how quickness alone doesn't guarantee a player being a weapon on the base paths. As a result, there is almost nothing to go on here when it comes to possible fantasy baseball usage. The Braves also threw in the towel here when they dealt Simmons to the Los Angeles Angels during the Winter Meetings. With Simmons having to adjust to a new league, his mediocre numbers could get even worse.

32. Jordy Mercer: With veteran second baseman Neil Walker and upstart Korean import Jung-Ho Kang firmly in the picture, there is not likely to be any consistent playing time in 2015 for Jordy Mercer. Already a low-impact hitter, Mercer has pretty much zero value even in NL-only formats.

33. Nick Ahmed: After the Arizona Diamondbacks traded away Didi Gregorious to the New York Yankees and then saw his replacement Chris Owings get injured, the team turned to former Atlanta Braves 2011 second round pick Nick Ahmed to handle the shortstop assignment. Known more for his glove than anything he did with the bat, Ahmed hit just .226 as he struck out 81 times in 421 at-bats. However Ahmed showed a bit of pop with 9 home runs and he even chucked in 4 steals. The D-Backs will want to do better here and that means Ahmed may not even start on his own team.

THIRD BASEMAN

Draft Strategy: There was no other position that saw an arrival of top-notch offensive talent than what took place among the third base fraternity in 2015. Our spring training 2015 AL MVP pick of the Toronto Blue Jays' Josh Donaldson was spot on but offering up numbers not far off their counterpart in engineering mammoth seasons of their own were the Colorado Rockies' Nolan Arenado, the Cincinnati Reds' Todd Frazier, and the Baltimore Orioles' Manny Machado. Throw in the most hyped hitting prospect since Mike Trout in the Chicago Cubs' Kris Bryant and you have a position that will hear a slew of names being called in the first three rounds. This is a big help since both Miguel Cabrera and Chris Davis lose eligibility there for the 2016 season, while guys like David Wright and Adrian Beltre are fading fast. Ultimately what we suggest you do here is to spend one of your top two picks among this group if a five-tool outfielder is no longer available. If you still go outfield-first base, then Round 3 is when you strike with your third baseman. The competition figures to be fierce at the top of this tier however.

David Wright: Age is never kind to any professional athlete but David Wright's body took it to a whole other level in 2015. After playing just a week's worth of games to start the year, Wright hit the DL with a strained hamstring that was supposed to keep him out for just 15 days. Soon Wright began complaining of back pain, leading to the testing that revealed the dreaded spinal stenosis diagnosis. There was a tremendous amount of initial fear due to the fact spinal stenosis is the same type of injury that caused sudden retirements in some recent NFL football players. While Wright doesn't take the hits that his counterparts in the NFL suffer through, the fact of the matter was that it was open for discussion whether Wright's back could handle the extreme torque from swinging a bat countless times during a given season. Wright wound up missing more than 4 months as he worked his way back from the spinal stenosis but he finally returned to the field in late August to help the New York Mets win the NL East. In fact Wright performed better than expected by batting .277 and hitting 4 home runs in 119 at-bats down the stretch of the season and that sparked at least some mild future optimism. Still as we look ahead to the 2016 season, Wright's standing in the fantasy baseball community couldn't be any lower. Wright is now an "old" 33-years-old and he has now suffered serious injury in three of the last four seasons. The spinal stenosis will never go away and has to be managed on a daily basis as well, which means the Mets will likely sit Wright every three or four games which will hurt his counting numbers. A setback could occur at a moment's notice that would send Wright back to the DL as well which adds to the stress of owning the guy. Finally, it is a big question mark regarding how much power Wright can still hit for with his back in less than ideal shape. Remember that Don Mattingly was once a big power bat on the New York Yankees during his early-to-mid-portion of his career before a serious back problem sapped his strength. We are not saying this is Wright's destiny but his days of 20-plus home runs are likely gone for good. In addition, Wright won't be stealing many bases anymore in order to not add unnecessary strain to the back. So in essence what we are now looking at from the former first round star of the early 2000's is a guy whose power will be down, who is about as big an injury risk as you can get, and who will no longer steal bases. Even with the downright dirt cheap draft price Wright now carries, we would still suggest avoiding this potential mess.

2016 PROJECTION: .284 17 HR 86 RBI 84 R 5 SB

1. Josh Donaldson: Already a very good top tier third baseman going into the 2014 offseason, Josh Donaldson saw his value spike to the upper levels of the game when the Oakland A's moved him to the Toronto Blue Jays during the Hot Stove portion of the winter. You couldn't ask for a better ballpark improvement for a hitter than what we saw with Donaldson trading in spacious O.Co Coliseum for the power haven that is Rogers Center. Right on schedule Donaldson posted an MVP season by hitting 41 home runs, driving in 123, and batting a respectable .274. For good measure Donaldson compiled a mammoth 122 runs scored. Whereas we all suggested Donaldson would reach the 30-homer mark for the first time in his young career after the trade, he took it a step further by going past 40. Now a firm veteran at the age of 30, what we saw from Donaldson in 2015 was likely the best case scenario going forward and maybe a slight dip backwards is more likely for this season. Still other than a high 19.1 K rate, Donaldson is as good as any power hitter in the game. One who should hear his name called late in Round 1 or early in Round 2.

2016 PROJECTION: .277 38 HR 12 116 RBI 123 R 5 SB

2. Manny Machado: While Bryce Harper was the unanimous 2015 fantasy baseball MVP, a top runner-up would be Baltimore Orioles third baseman Manny Machado who made good on his top prospect status in a monstrous way. After having his first few years interrupted by two serious knee injuries that called into question if Machado could ever be as good as once predicted, he left no doubt last season that he already should be considered one of the top players in the game. Only 22-years-old at the start of the year, Machado went nuclear on opposing pitchers as he swatted 35 home runs, stole 20 bases, and batted .286. Machado also excelled in the other two standard categories as he drove in 86 batters and scored 102 runs, with the latter getting a boost after being moved into the leadoff spot early in the season. Simply put, Machado was the pure definition of a five-category stud in 2015 and as the ultimate topper, he picked up shortstop eligibility late in the year for those who use a 5-game benchmark to add a new position. Whether at shortstop (where he has more value due to the lack of depth there) or at third base, Machado is a certain mid-first round selection in 2016 fantasy baseball with no questions asked. It is amazing to think that Machado will turn only 24 in July, so advanced is his development. It is open for debate whether the Orioles will keep him at leadoff but if moved down the order, the loss of some runs and steals will be made up for in the RBI department. Many will wonder if Machado was performing over his head in 2015 but digging into the numbers deeper supports what he ultimately accomplished. For one, Machado lowered his K rate from 2014's 19.2 to last year's 15.6. That is a big drop and it speaks to the recognition of pitches and improved plate discipline of Machado. In addition, Machado boosted his walk rate to 9.8 percent (up from 2014's 5.6). Again, a tremendous jump which points to how massive the development Machado has undergone. There is nothing not to like here as Machado stayed healthy for all of 2015 which quieted the early injury-prone chatter. Get him everywhere you can.

2016 PROJECTION: .288 33 HR 96 RBI 100 R 19 SB

3. Nolan Arenado: There was not a fantasy baseball player alive prior to the 2015 season that didn't want Colorado Rockies third baseman Nolan Arenado on their teams. Oozing obvious potential due to both burgeoning power and the terrific ballpark environment, Arenado shot way up draft boards to the early rounds despite having just two partial MLB seasons under his belt which included home runs totals that did not reach the 20 range in each. Needless to say, even the most optimistic Arenado fan couldn't envision the incredible 42 home runs and 130 RBI he collected last season. We are talking about power that is in very short supply in today's game and Arenado combined that with a very good .287 average and 97 runs scored as well. The only thing you don't get here is stolen bases but who cares? Arenado is legit folks as the ballpark and his natural strength will combine for another extreme home run/RBI campaign in 2016 which necessitates a mid-first round pick. Turning just 25 in April, Arenado is already as good as hitter as there is in baseball even outside of power, showcasing a very low 14.7 percent K Rate for a guy who is considered a slugger. Feel free to tab Arenado over both Josh Donaldson and Manny Machado. No one will argue with you.

2015 PROJECTION: .290 39 HR 119 RBI 100 R 4 SB

4. Kris Bryant: Rarely have we seen the type of hype that attached itself to Chicago Cubs top third base prospect Kris Bryant going into the 2015 season. It was more than understandable since Bryant was considered the slam-dunk number 1 prospect in all of baseball and who was coming off a remarkable 2014 season in the minors where he put up video game numbers (43 HR/118 RBI/15 SB). While the Cubs stashed Bryant in the minors until late April due to the arbitration clock, they refused to wait any longer to unleash their Paul Bunyon-esqe third baseman. While Bryant went through some typical rookie cold spells and struggles, he still managed to hit 26 home runs and drive in 99 batters in 650 at-bats. With light tower power, Bryant is only scratching the surface of what he could do in the home run category. It is almost a certainty that Bryant will be a 40-home run star real soon, with the 2016 season very much in play for that kind of production. Adding even more juice to his stock, Bryant stole 13 bases last season as he made it a point to show off all of his vast talent. Many forget that Bryant turns only 24 in January, so poised he already is as a major league hitter. Now there are some warts that need to be worked out such as a very ugly 30.6 percent K rate that makes hitting for average very unlikely for now but nothing major by any means. Yes Bryant was able to post a respectable .275 average as a rookie but his BABIP was one of the luckiest in all of baseball at a ridiculous .378. With his type of K rate and with the BABIP no doubt moving toward he mean in 2016, Bryant may not hit .265 this season. Of course Bryant will more than make up for this with the power and with the hype already at insane levels, Bryant could even find his way into the late first round of drafts this season. While that may be stretching it a bit this early in his career, there is little debate about the fact Bryant will be an early round fixture for the next decade.

2016 PROJECTION: .263 38 HR 123 RBI 114 R 16 SB

5. Todd Frazier: After a full breakout season in 2014 when he slammed 29 home runs, stole 20 bases, and collected 80 RBI, there were questions about whether or not Cincinnati Reds third baseman Todd Frazier was really in fact as good as the numbers indicated. Well Frazier answered that question in the affirmative in 2015 when he hit an even better 35 homers, drove in even more batters with 89, while at the same time still collecting a decent amount of stolen bases with 13. Clearly the power is of the extreme variety in today's game when it comes to Frazier's fantasy baseball calling card and that figures to remain his strength going into 2016 as well. With a great home run park at his disposal, the easiest part of projecting Frazier is with his power numbers as he should stay in the 30-35 home run range, while collecting his 80-90 RBI. What is more up for discussion is the batting average which fell off last season to .255 after a solid enough .273 mark in 2014. That .273 average is so far the outlier for Frazier, which becomes more clear when you consider he is still just a .257 hitter through five MLB seasons. Frazier strikes out at a high clip (over 20 percent K rate each year of his career), which make hitting for a good average unlikely. A .271 BABIP last season was on the unlucky side though so an uptick to the .265 range sounds more likely. Then there are the stolen bases from Frazier which are quite valuable at speed-deprived third base. Like with the average in 2014 though, the 20 steals Frazier collected that season scream "outlier" as well. Frazier has some good speed but he is far from a burner and ultimately he needs to have catchers napping in order to swipe some bases. Another 10-15 is in the realm of possibility for 2016 but don't project Frazier for anything than that. Despite all this, Frazier is once again knocking on the late first round door in fantasy baseball this season but ideally he makes for a better investment in the middle of the second.

2016 PROJECTION: .265 32 HR 93 RBI 86 R 11 SB

6. Anthony Rendon: Consider the draft price, there was not a bigger bust in all of fantasy baseball for the 2015 season than Washington Nationals third baseman

Anthony Rendon. Expectations were understandably sky-high for Rendon heading into the year after he posted a tremendous breakout campaign in 2014; a season where he hit 21 home runs, drove in 111, swiped 17 bases, and hit .287. What was really exciting about that campaign for Rendon was the boost in power as he didn't show much of it while coming up the minor league ladder. Instead Rendon was lauded for his terrific pure hitting skills which pointed him as a perennial .300 batting average guy for years to come. When the power was paired with the average (and also supported by another surprise in the stolen base department), Rendon was the "must have" new toy in fantasy baseball prior to last season. Unfortunately Rendon became a complete abomination due mainly to an injury run that was so bad, he wound up logging just 80 games and 255 at-bats for the club. Even in part-time duty, Rendon was not productive as he hit just 5 home runs, stole all of one base, and struggled to a .264 average. Pretty much anything that could have gone wrong did and so now we have to pick up the pieces in order to try and figure out what to do from here. The scars are very deep and fresh for those who owned shares of Rendon last season and no doubt those same owners will stay far away from him in 2016. That will help push Rendon past the first two rounds of drafts where he was taken a year prior. This could set up a potentially huge comeback season at a much more affordable draft rate for anyone who decides to get back onto the Rendon bandwagon. Still only 25, Rendon has not all of a sudden forgotten how to hit. We would advise throwing out Rendon's 2015 season completely since he was never right physically. While the 17 stolen bases from 2014 may not be repeatable, the rest of Rendon's numbers could be reached with good health. Rendon was growing into his power prior to all the injuries and his hitting skills remain above-average. At the very least, you can project around 15-20 home runs with a .280 average and anything more would be a nice bonus. We side on the aisle that says Rendon will be back to performing like an upper-level player this season.

2016 PROJECTION: .286 17 HR 80 RBI 93 R 8 SB

7. Kyle Seager: A permanent member of our "All Favorite" fantasy baseball team includes Seattle Mariners veteran Kyle Seager holding down the third base spot. While Seager has not been embraced by all due to the West Coast bias and hesitancy of investing in hitter who play in Safeco Field, he has proceeded to post four straight seasons of very durable/productive results with the bat. One thing that instantly stands out is that during the 2015 season, Seager reached a career-high in home runs for the fourth straight year. Starting in 2012, Seager's home runs have read as the following: 20, 22, 25, and 26. While the lineup support has never been ideal prior to Nelson Cruz' arrival last season, Seager has also been a dependable runs and RBI man; finishing in the 75-90 range in both on a yearly basis. In addition, Seager also chips in around 7-10 stolen bases a season which helps adds yet more value to his name. Another crucial part of owning Seager that is often overlooked is the fact the guy is as durable as they get at a very physically demanding third base position. Seager has now logged at least 650 at-bats for four straight years which makes him a guy you can stick at third base and never have to worry about. While the batting average only hovers in the .265 range, the rest of the Seager profiles screams out "value play." While everyone else is fighting each other over Nolan Arenado, Manny Machado, and Josh Donaldson, you can just as easily stock up on other positions early and come back to Seager later. As safe a pick as one can make.

2016 PROJECTION: .265 25 HR 78 RBI 88 R 8 SB

8. Matt Carpenter: No longer carrying the more valuable second base eligibility heading into the 2015 fantasy baseball season, St. Louis Cardinals third baseman Matt Carpenter looked like a poor fit at his new spot due to his historically below-average power. With fantasy owners wanting home runs and RBI from their first and third baseman, Carpenter was largely ignored in drafts due to the fact he hit a grand total of 26 long balls from 2012 through the 2014 seasons. Well one of the bigger shocks of last season had to be Carpenter going out and slamming 28 home runs and driving in 101 batters as he showed a previously unknown ability to hit for power. Carpenter's home run output was as out-of-the-blue as you can get since he never hinted at that kind of production previously. More known for average and a high runs total due to batting at the top of the Cardinals lineup, the whole narrative has changed for Carpenter for the time being. What was interesting and maybe the reason for the severe uptick in power is that Carpenter changed his approach at the dish. Whether it was due to knowing he needed to hit for more power if he were to be the team's everyday third baseman, Carpenter was swinging for the fences like never before. The evidence of this was seen beyond the home run total as Carpenter's K rate went through the roof in 2015, with his 22.7 percent mark a full 7 points higher than his 15.7 number in

2014. Using a more grip-it-and-rip-it approach, it obviously worked for Carpenter in terms of the 28 home runs but his .272 average is well down from the .294 and .318 he batted from 2012-13. Of course .272 is not a terrible average by any means and we will gladly take that with the new power output. Having turned 30 in November, we now have to wonder if Carpenter can repeat his career-year numbers into 2016. We have our doubts as we always lean on overall averages when it comes to a player's career numbers than relying on one outlier season. Until Carpenter repeats his 2015 production, that will go into the outlier bin. Always be leery of investing in these type of surprising numbers and it is likely Carpenter will go above what we are comfortable paying since his draft price will rise to lofty territory after such a tremendous season.

2016 PROJECTION: .275 22 HR 95 RBI 88 R 4 SB

9. Adrian Beltre: There was a changing of the guard among third baseman in 2015 fantasy baseball, as new superstar arrivals like Josh Donaldson, Manny Machado, and Nolan Arenado helped push out the aging David Wright, Aramis Ramirez, and Adrian Beltre. As far as Beltre was concerned, his five season run as a borderline late first round pick came to a quick end starting in 2014 when his home run rate suddenly nosedived, going from 30 long balls the year prior to only 19. The 2015 season was no better as Beltre hit just 18 home runs in 577 at-bats. The dip in power is no shock since Beltre turns 37 in April and he has a ton of mileage on his aging frame. Despite the noticeable decline in the power numbers, Beltre is still hitting for a good average with .324 and .287 marks the last two seasons. With a tiny 10.5 percent K rate helping to stave off erosion in the average department, Beltre could possibly sneak out another decent season to warrant daily usage in 12-team mixed formats. However additional decline is likely since no player can escape the pull of age. Terrific overall career for sure but Beltre is another candidate who is starting the inevitable slide towards retirement.

2016 PROJECTION: .286 17 HR 77 RBI 75 R 1 SB

10. Evan Longoria: While aging third baseman like David Wright and Adrian Beltre have been pushed aside by the massive infusion of young power-hitting talent at the third base position, Tampa Bay Rays veteran and former first round favorite Evan Longoria is also becoming a forgotten player as well. Before the arrivals of Josh Donaldson, Nolan Arenado, and Todd Frazier, it was Longoria who was the exciting power-hitting third base upstart. That was fueled in large part to his amazing 2009 breakout (.281/33 HR/100 RBI/113 R/9 SB) that launched Longoria into first round territory in fantasy baseball for the next couple of years. Unfortunately 2009 will likely remain the high point in Longoria's still young career (he turned just 30 this past October) based on his changing statistical profile. For one thing, Longoria's ongoing propensity for striking out at a high rate have hurt him in the average department for a few years now. Over the last three seasons, Longoria has recorded shaky averages of .269, .253, and .270; with his K rate going over 19 percent in each of those campaigns. Longoria has also completely abandoned the stolen base game, having swiped just 11 total the last four years combined. Finally, Longoria's power has fallen off by more than a little as well. From 2009 through the 2012 seasons, Longoria hit the 30-home run mark in three of them. The last two years? Try only 22 and 21 respectively. This despite getting at least 670 at-bats in each season. The fact of the matter is that Longoria is a scaled-down version of his mid-20's self and that is obviously not a good thing. His draft price has plummeted as well which actually could make him somewhat of a good value considering he still is capable of 20 home runs and around 80 RBI. The shine has completely worn off here though which means Longoria should be in the conversation in the bottom percent of 12-team mixed league starting third baseman.

2016 PROJECTION: .272 22 HR 79 R 83 RBI 4 SB

11. Miguel Sano: While he was a bit late to the show last season, top Minnesota Twins third base prospect Miguel Sano added his name to the very potent bats that now permeate the position. A season-ending Tommy John elbow surgery set Sano a full year behind in his development in 2014 but the rebuilding Twins finally ushered in the youth movement of the team in the middle of last season. Joining outfielder Byron Buxton, Sano made his debut with the team in July and proceeded to instantly show the terrific power that made him a top prospect in the first place. In just 279 at-bats, Sano compiled 18 home runs, 52 RBI, and a .269 average. As an even more exciting bonus, Sano added shortstop eligibility in leagues that require only 5 starts late in the 2015 season. Turning just 23 in May, Sano has a very bright power-hitting future ahead of himself by the looks of things. We compare Sano very closely to the Pittsburgh Pirates' Pedro Alvarez who also came up to the majors with a slugging reputation. While both have the home runs down pat already, Sano also resembles Alvarez when it comes to their incredibly high K rate. Sano struck out in a horrid 35.5 percent of his at-bat as a rookie and only a ridiculously lucky and unsustainable .396 BABIP prevented him from batting under .230. While no one can doubt Sano's power potential, his average figures to be very ugly in 2016 which will take some of the shine off the home run totals. When you strike out as much as Sano does, you tend to make yourself one-dimensional as a hitter. With really just home runs, RBI, and runs to his name, Sano figures to be a bit overrated in 2016 drafts. While we are intrigued by anyone who can hit home runs at a high clip, things get a bit more gloomy when the average is such a liability.

2016 PROJECTION: .237 28 HR 75 RBI 73 R 5 SB

12. Maikel Franco: The Philadelphia Phillies finally welcomed in the Maikel Franco Era in 2015, plugging in the power-hitting third baseman at the hot corner for what they hope will be the next decade. After clearly showing he was not ready in his cup of coffee run with the team in late 2014 (.179/0 HR/58 at-bats), Franco looked much more comfortable at the dish last season (.277/13 HR/326 at-bats). Franco draws a decent amount of walks for a young power hitter and his 15.3 K rate last season was very solid for someone his age. Further improvement is expected in 2016, with Franco fully capable of swatting over 20 home runs with a useful average. The recent explosion of top-tier third baseman in 2015 has left Franco as a bit of a forgotten man entering the new season, which means he could be a nice steal as a middle round draft pick.

2016 PROJECTION: .281 21 HR 74 RBI 67 R 2 SB

13. Mike Moustakas: After seemingly waiting forever to make good on his status as the former number 2 pick overall in the 2007 draft and with the fantasy baseball community having long abandoned him, a sudden career-year was produced in 2015 by Kansas City Royals third baseman Mike Moustakas. Showing contact skills he never produced in his previous four years in the majors, Moustakas shocked everyone by hitting .297 in the first half of the season. This from the same guy who struggled to hit even .220 previously which was the primary reason nobody wanted to get involved with him for 2015. As nice as the average was, the flip side was the fact Moustakas hit only 7 home runs during that span which was a major drop off from his customary power rates. That leads one to conclude that Moustakas was finally making an effort to use the whole field and shorten his swing so that he could avoid another sub-.240 batting average. It was an interesting tradeoff in that most of Moustakas' value came with the home runs and RBI but at the same time it was nice to see the guy finally post even an average that wouldn't be a major liability. Perhaps most encouraging was the fact Moustakas blended the two as best he could in the second half, hitting 15 home runs and batting .269. We would gladly sign up tomorrow for the composite 22 home runs and .284 average Moustakas totaled last season but projecting him for 2016 is a bit difficult. The .284 average is in big outlier territory for Moustakas as he never came close to that number before. However there are signs that it was legitimate as Moustakas successfully lowered his K Rate to a very good 12.4 percent last season. Consider that in 2012 Moustakas' K rate was an ugly 20.2 percent and one can see how much improvement he has made there which correlates positively to the average gain. In addition, Moustakas' .294 BABIP a year ago was pretty much neutral, adding more legitimacy to his 2015 average. It is very possible Moustakas gives back a bit of the average but at the same time making a push toward 25 home runs. While we would never suggest paying anything more than a mid-round pick, it seems Moustakas is finally trending in the right direction.

2016 PROJECTION: .260 24 HR 84 RBI 75 R 1 SB

14. Matt Duffy: The San Francisco Giants uncovered a diamond in the rough in 2015 as former 2012 18th round draft pick Matt Duffy staked his claim as a future member of the infield at either first or third base for the team. With minor league numbers that showed good speed and batting average skills but little in the way of power, Duffy shocked many by hitting 12 home runs in 612 at-bats in his first extended look by the Giants last season. In addition, Duffy stole 12 bases and put up another good average at .295. It appears there is a nice blend of skills here, with the developing power taking Duffy's stock to another level. Keep in mind that in 2014 at Double-A, Duffy batted .332 and stole 20 bases which means the ability is clearly there in those categories. What also helps Duffy is a solid 15.7 K rate and the speed to get himself out of trouble. While the Giants are ready to give Duffy the inside track to the starting third base job for 2016, his draft price has not risen much at all from late round territory which adds to the buying appeal. Consider Duffy a moderate impact guy who could put up a 15/15/.300 campaign in 2016 as a late round upside pick.

2016 PROJECTION: .298 14 HR 79 RBI 86 R 15 SB

15. Justin Turner: When discussing some of the better pure hitters in Major League Baseball, no one would reflexively include Los Angeles Dodgers infielder Justin Turner. However that would be an oversight as Turner has hit .280, .340, and .290 over the last three seasons, fully unleashing himself as a classic late-bloomer who only turned into an everyday player at the age of 30. In fact getting back to how good a hitter Turner is, how about these batting averages for the months of May, June, and July? Try .318, .330, and .343. Turner did tail off during the second half of the season however, when a persistent knee issue had him in and out of the lineup. As we said earlier, Turner is already well into his prime at the age of 31 which means what you currently see numbers-wise is what you will continue to get. Still with eligibility all over the infield, Turner is a very valuable guy to draft for your bench as a super fill-in bat on light schedule days or when injuries strike your starters.

2016 PROJECTION: .305 12 HR 61 RBI 54 R 6 SB

16. Josh Harrison: Yet another guy we correctly labeled a bust candidate in last year's Draft Guide was Pittsburgh Pirates third baseman Josh Harrison. Serving as another example of not buying fully into career/outlier seasons, Harrison crashed back to earth in 2015 after his breakout campaign the year prior. Harrison put himself on the fantasy baseball map in 2014 when he finally latched onto a starting job and proceeded to hit 13 home runs, steal 18 bases, and bat .315. A utility guy the previous three years in the majors with the Pirates, Harrison showed little ability to handle the bat, having hit .250 or under both in 2012 and 2013. Injuries opened the door to more playing time a year later though and the career-best numbers followed. Of course we argued that Harrison's production that season was very fluky, since he never came close to those levels prior which was a stance that ultimately came true. Harrison went right to "work" making us look prophetic last season as he hit all of 4 long balls and scored a paltry 57 runs in 449 at-bats. Yes injuries hurt the counting stats and negatively impacted Harrison's swing but we were not impressed by anything we saw in 2015. While

Harrison could come back this season and split the difference between his statistics the previous two years, we are not paying much of anything to find out.

2016 PROJECTION: .280 8 HR 45 RBI 65 R 14 SB

17. Xander Bogaerts: Boston Red Sox infielder Xander Bogaerts did little to change his reputation as an empty batting average guy in 2015, hitting a pathetic 7 home runs and stealing just 7 bags in 645 at-bats. The Red Sox are committed to Bogaerts as their starting third baseman though, lauding his defense and maturity at the age of 23. That is all nice and well but in fantasy baseball where impact numbers are needed, the guy falls way short. Any Red Sox prospect always carries immense sleeper prices due to the high-visibility of the franchise and the swell ballpark but Bogaerts is to be ignored in anything but AL-only formats given the utter lack of impact numbers. While the 80-plus totals in runs and RBI are nice, even the .320 average Bogaerts put up last season was not believable due to a very lucky .372 BABIP that is not sustainable. Pass.

2016 PROJECTION: .293 9 HR 84 RBI 86 R 11 SB

18. Chase Headley: The New York Yankees were very foolish to give a four-year extension to third baseman Chase Headley at the end of 2014 and they surely are already regretting the move after seeing how terribly he played last season. Right at the top of the majors in errors at third base, Headley predictably did nothing much with the bat as he managed an inexcusable 11 home runs in 642 at-bats while playing half his games at Yankee Stadium. Headley engineered one of the biggest outlier seasons ever in 2012 with the San Diego Padres (31 HR/115 RBI/17 SB) and he can't even do half of that now in an offensive park. With a K rate over 20 percent and having not even swiped one base in 2015, Headley can be ignored in almost all formats.

2016 PROJECTION: .260 10 HR 78 R 67 RBI 1 SB

19. Martin Prado: Veteran infielder/outfielder Martin Prado kept going on in 2015, this time with the Miami Marlins after the New York Yankees sent him packing in a trade for Nathan Eovaldi the previous winter. The ballpark move was a big a change for the negative as a hitter could get and so it was no shock that Prado failed to move the impact meter much with the bat as he hit .288 but with just 9 home runs. Aging a bit at 32, Prado doesn't steal bases anymore and his power numbers are barely hanging on as well. He remains a high-contact hitter who is always a good average guy to hang around on your bench but Prado at this point has a very limited say in today's fantasy baseball.

2016 PROJECTION: .286 10 HR 55 RBI 67 R 1 SB

20. Trevor Plouffe: Minnesota Twins third baseman Trevor Plouffe is really kind of a "just there" guy in terms of being an annually boring/mediocre talent when it comes to fantasy baseball. While Plouffe has shown that he can get red hot for shorts spurts with his power, the overall results are underwhelming. It was standard operating procedure for Plouffe in 2015 as he batted an ugly .244 but still sent 22 baseballs out of the park with 86 RBI. A 19.6 percent K rate will continue to drag the average down and Plouffe has no speed to speak of which showcases his limitations. A solid AL-only third baseman, Plouffe is nothing but backup material in mixers.

2016 PROJECTION: .253 21 HR 83 RBI 73 R 2 SB

21. Joey Gallo: The Texas Rangers unveiled immensely powerful third base prospect Joey Gallo for his first major league foray in 2015 but needless to say the kid quickly proved he was not ready. As the 8th overall pick in the 2012 draft by the team, Gallo quickly began to earn a cult following at the team's minor league locales due to his light-tower home runs. The proverbial pure slugger, Gallo crushed the baseball with a ferocity few in the game could match but that is only when he is not piling up the strikeouts by the boatload. In one of the more staggering minor league statistics from 2015, Gallo struck out in an unbelievable 39.5 percent of his at-bats, while he also picked up 14 home runs. His 36-game stint with the Rangers was predictably ugly as Gallo pushed the K rate even higher to a ridiculous 46.3 percent which led to a .204 average. While the 6 home runs and 3 steals were nice, Gallo obviously needs more seasoning. Unfortunately, it is likely Gallo will pretty much stay the way he already is in terms of his hitting approach. That means even if he makes it onto the roster to start 2016, another demotion could always be possible due to the fact he likely won't hit over .230. That means Gallo better make a decent contribution in the power department in order to stay around. We always preach how guys with this kind of batting average issue are always a bad investment no matter how far they can slam a baseball and surely this is the case with Lamb as well . Stay as far away as you can.

2016 PROJECTION: .223 16 HR 48 RBI 45 R 5 SB

22. Pablo Sandoval: When you factor in both salary and the offensive potency of a player's home ballpark, you can argue that Boston Red Sox third baseman Pablo Sandoval was the worst every day hitter in the major leagues in 2015. After getting a crazy contract from the Red Sox as part of the their rebuilding plan leading into last season, Kung Fu Panda fell flat on his rotund face as he managed to hit a brutal .245 with 10 home runs and 47 RBI in 505 at-bats. That is unfathomable when you consider Sandoval was making as big a positive ballpark leap as a hitter can get in moving from San Francisco to Boston. Sandoval wound up with a career-high 14.5 K rate and he outdid his always low walk rate at 5.0 percent. There is never any reason for an opposing pitcher to throw Sandoval anything juicy to hit as he constantly gets himself out chasing pitches. Whereas Sandoval was once a well-sought after commodity early in his career, he is quickly becoming a guy you want to completely avoid.

2016 PROJECTION: .261 11 HR 55 RBI 52 R 0 SB

23. Luis Valbuena: The Houston Astros have cornered the market on ugly average/power hitting specialists in 2015 and that included third baseman Luis Valbuena who took that to a whole other level. In just 493 at-bats, Valbuena hit 25 home runs and collect 62 RBI for the playoff-bound Astros. However that power came with a price, mainly in the average department. Struggling to hit .200 for most of the season, Valbuena rallied a bit to finish with a still very ugly .224 average. While Valbuena does draw walks (10.1 percent), his 21.5 K rate is nasty. In Valbuena's defense though, his .235 BABIP was incredibly unlucky and in actuality he was more of a .250 hitter than .224. Either way, Valbuena is very limited and should really just be used in AL-only formats.

THE REST

24. David Freese: Other than one very fluky season (2012), veteran third baseman David Freese has had little to no fantasy baseball value since. Always injured and a guy who was already 29 when he finally broke through, Freese tried to rally his name brand in 2015 when he hit 14 home runs in 470 at-bats. That actually represented the second-highest total of Freese's career which speaks to how average a player he is. Annually having poor health and lacking sizable impact in any one category, Freese should not be drafted unless you take part in a very deep league.

25. Cody Asche: Acting simply as a mediocre placeholder until Maikel Franco was ready, Cody Asche has a very bleak immediate future with the Philadelphia Phillies. Asche would split the 2015 season with the Phillies and their Triple-A team, hitting just 12 home runs with a .245 average in 456 at-bats with the big league club. There is no value to be gained here unless Asche gets moved to another team where he has a chance to start but even under that scenario, his upside is very limited.

26. Jed Lowrie: With the Carlos Correa era fully underway with the Houston Astros, veteran infielder Jed Lowie moved over to be the team's full-time starting third baseman last season. Always a professional hitter who makes the most of his limited ability, Lowrie loses a tremendous chunk of his value by not being shortstop eligible any longer. At third base, Lowrie's numbers are simply subpar and we don't anticipate a sudden Matt Carpenter-like power uptick either. Lowrie batted just .222 in his 263 at-bats season, a campaign that was once again marred by injuries. On the back nine of his career as he turns 32 in April, Lowrie is nothing but a boring and very average player for fantasy baseball purposes.

27. Jake Lamb: The Arizona Diamondbacks have dabbled with young third base prospect Jake Lamb the last two seasons but were not likely impressed by what they saw. While Lamb has decent power, his 2015 campaign was nothing to write home about as he batted .263 with 6 home runs in 390 at-bats. The Diamondbacks will likely try to improve their lot at third base going forward and even if they give Lamb another extended look in 2016, this is just an AL-only play at best.

28. Chris Johnson: Once the Atlanta Braves accepted the fact that Chris Johnson's BABIP-fueled .321 batting average during the 2013 season was a complete fluke, they ultimately threw in the towel on the veteran when they gave him away to the Cleveland Indians to finish the 2015 season. Struggling to hit even 10 home runs and with the average now firmly under .260 where it belongs, Johnson should not be drafted.

29. Tyler Saladino: The Chicago White Sox decided to take a look at speedy third base prospect Tyler Saladino late in the 2015 season after the bottom completely fell out of their season. After swiping 25 bases at Triple-A, Saladino started running right away for the White Sox upon his promotion. While Saladino batted just .225, he wound up with 4 home runs and 8 steals in his 254 at-bats which at least is mildly interesting. Even at Triple-A last season though, Saladino was a shaky average guy as he batted just .255. That is usually a bad sign in terms of adjusting against major league pitching and as a result Saladino has just minimum AL-only value in the late rounds of your draft.

30. Conor Gillaspie: If you have Conor Gillaspie on your team this season for fantasy baseball, you really need to try something else. He has failed to do even anything remotely impressive in his six-year major league career and that won't change in 2016 either. Now let's go onto more important issues.

31. Juan Uribe: After a very productive and at times underrated career, Juan Uribe is now just a backup infielder at the major league level who can swat the occasional home run in a timeshare situation. Has nothing to offer at this stage of the game.

32. Will Middlebrooks: Even getting a much-needed trade out of the pressure-cooker in Boston did nothing to stop the runaway Will Middlebrooks train to irrelevance. After coming over in an offseason trade, the San Diego Padres could only stomach 270 at-bats where Middlebrooks hit a pathetic .212 with 9 home runs before optioning him to Triple-A El Paso in July. It was telling that the Padres didn't even call up Middlebrooks for September when rosters expanded, showing clearly that he is not a part of their future. While no one doubts Middlebrooks' power, the problem is that he simply can't make enough contact at the plate as evidenced by his career .231 average. Middlebrooks has struck out in about 25 percent of his at-bats in his four interrupted major league seasons and that simply won't work in terms of being a regular. Avoid altogether.

OUTFIELDERS

Draft Strategy: As we have already discussed, The Fantasy Sports Boss staff are of the mind that you should use your first or second round pick on a five-tool outfielder at the outset of your draft. When we say five-tool outfielder, we include the following names that are worthy of being selected in the first two rounds, as well as the slugging outfielders who made the top 24 grade:

Round 1: Mike Trout, Andrew McCutchen, Giancarlo Stanton, Bryce Harper

Round 2: Adam Jones. Ryan Braun, Charlie Blackmon, Carlos Gomez, A.J. Pollock (yes he is worth of such a grade now), Starling Marte, Nelson Cruz.

Any of these names can anchor your outfield, whether you start three or five. Those formats that use three should get their initial outfielder in the first two rounds, make an effort to grab a second before Round 8, and then round out the position in the middle rounds. With regards to five outfielder formats, make sure you have two by Round 7, following that up with two more by Round 14, and round things out with your fifth option in the latter rounds of the draft. Outfield runs the gamut in terms of all-around five-tool guys, .300-hitting sluggers, all the way to home run or stolen base one-trick ponies. There are more than enough options to go around here in the deepest position in the game outside of first base.

1. Mike Trout: Already the consensus number 1 player in all of fantasy baseball by a mile, Los Angeles Angels outfielder Mike Trout achieved yet another plateau of production in 2015 as he reached the 40-home mark for the first time with 41. It just added to the ridiculous set of numbers that Trout has produced on an annual basis, with no debate whatsoever about who should go number 1 in all drafts. What is truly amazing is that Trout begins the 2015 season still incredibly young at the age of 24 and that means he actually has a few seasons left of upside if you can believe it. There is nothing more to say here about what a dominant player Trout is and his five tool ability remains despite the fact his stolen bases sank to a career-low 11 in 2015. Clearly Trout is losing interest in steals now that he is hitting in the prime 3-4 spots in the order but that will also decrease any injury risk as well. Trout still strikes out a bit too much at 23.2 percent but he offsets that with a terrific 13.5 walk rate which helps him hover around the .300

mark in batting average. 45 home runs is the next benchmark and we have learned not to doubt Trout when it comes to any feat. If you don't land the top pick in your draft, you will be out of luck.

2016 PROJECTION: .288 42 HR 99 R 108 RBI 14 SB

2. Bryce Harper: So that is what a Bryce Harper breakout looks like. After a few years of disappointing production due mainly to injuries caused some to question if Harper would ever live up to the hype, the 2015 season turned out to be the full coming out party for the Washington Nationals outfielder. The numbers were straight out of a video game as Harper powered his way to 42 home runs, 118 RBI, and missed on the batting title by a single point with a .330 average. Simply put, Harper was the definition of ridiculous. Maturity was evident in Harper's approach as he lowered his K rate by more than 6 points from 2014 (26.3 to 20.0) which sent the average soaring. The 19.0 percent walk rate was phenomenal as well as Harper got the Barry Bonds treatment for most of the season. Just like with Mike Trout, Harper is still incredibly young as he turned just 23 in October. That means there are many more seasons of blockbuster numbers ahead of him and the only thing you can maybe nitpick about is the loss of stolen bases (only 6 in 654 at-bats last season). While Trout is still the number 1 guy to draft, Harper has now pushed himself firmly into the number 2 spot.

2016 PROJECTION: .318 40 HR 122 RBI 106 R 5 SB

3. Andrew McCutchen: While it was not a blockbuster season by any means, Pittsburgh Pirates perennial MVP candidate Andrew McCutchen made his usual contribution across all five standard ROTO categories in 2015. Dogged by some sort of leg/quad injury that was never officially confirmed by the team in the first half, McCutchen started out of the gates slowly for the second season in a row. April doesn't ever seem to agree with McCutchen as he batted just .197 with two home runs, and stole not even a single base. Things got going from there as usual though as McCutchen has always done his best hitting as the season goes along. The 23 home runs McCutchen hit were just two short of his 2014 tally and his 96 RBI was an improvement by 13 as well. On the negative side, McCutchen fell off dramatically in the stolen base department, with his total of 11 serving as a career-low by 7. In fact it is starting to look like McCutchen is ceding stolen bases as he pushes toward 30 since he has now declined in three straight seasons there.

Outside of the stolen bases, McCutchen was his usual top-notch self across the board with no noticeable declines anywhere else worth talking about. McCutchen remains a locked-in middle first round pick.

2016 PROJECTION: .304 24 HR 95 RBI 99 R 16 SB

4. Giancarlo Stanton: If there was ever such thing as a baseball magnet, the body of Miami Marlins outfield slugger Giancarlo Stanton surely would be it. How else to explain the fact that Stanton's last two seasons have been ruined by thrown baseballs that crashed into his face (2014) and hand (2015)? In between, Stanton has more than proven himself to be the best power hitter in the game but his losing battle with injuries is starting to cloud his overall outlook. As gruesome as the fractures and lacerations were that Stanton suffered after getting hit in the face by a Mike Fiers fastball two years ago, the one possible saving grace was that it occurred on Sept. 11th which robbed his owners of only three weeks of numbers, The fractured hamate bone that Stanton needed surgically removed last season however was even worse for his owners from a missed games standpoint since the slugger didn't play another game from June 26th onward. Leading up to the season-ending hand fracture, Stanton proved that there were no psychological effects from the facial HBP as he smashed a ridiculous 27 home runs and collected 67 RBI in only 279 at-bats. It looked like Stanton was on his way to the first 40-home run season of his young career until disaster struck with the hand. As a result of all the missed games, some are labeling Stanton as injury prone but that is a bit of an overreach. The fact of the matter is that both of the HBP's that Stanton suffered were freak incidents that could have happened to anyone. It is not like Stanton has suffered a series of leg or knee injuries like say a Jose Reyes that would call into question his durability. The best course of action is to chalk up Stanton as being a bit unlucky and buy right back in on his awesome power late in Round 1 of your draft. There is not a better per game home run hitter in baseball and his power numbers are even more impressive when you consider the spacious ballpark he plays in. Strikeouts remain a big problem (29.9 percent K rate in 2015) which accounts for the .270 lifetime average but power hitters like this at the still young age of 26 remain extremely valuable.

2015 PROJECTION: .267 39 HR 97 RBI 88 RBI 9 SB

5. Ryan Braun: Another season removed from the whole Biogenesis mess went a long way toward Ryan Braun getting the focus back onto what he does with a bat in his hand. While Braun will always carry around the PED stain and the fallout from it, there was no denying the fact that the Milwaukee Brewers outfielder put himself back into the outfielder 1 territory in 2015 with a very good set of numbers. Overall Braun hit .285 with 25 home runs, 84 RBI, and 24 stolen bases which was his best offensive production since before his PED bust. However there is also no denying the fact that while those numbers were impressive, they represent a clear drop in what Braun accomplished leading up to the Biogenesis fallout. Specifically speaking, being off the steroids has robbed Braun of his ability to hit .300-plus as he has been under that number each season since the suspension. In addition, Braun's days of hitting 30 home runs also appear to be gone for good as he has totaled 19 and 25 with 500-plus at-bats each of the last two seasons. Finally, Braun's three highest strikeout rates have come in the three seasons since the suspension, ranging between 18 and 22 percent. Basically what we are seeing now is the true version of Ryan Braun without the juice and that is still a very good player who makes the grade as a solid outfielder 1 but who also comes with baggage. In addition to the drop in numbers, another fall-out from the steroids can be seen in the breaking down of Braun's body. Anyone who has owned Braun over the last few years knows how he was constantly in a day-to-day situation with almost every part of his body hurt at one time or another. The biggest issue was quite serious when Braun couldn't finish his 2015 campaign due to a back injury that resulted in offseason surgery. A bad back is always troubling for any hitter but Braun was expected to be ready for spring training. Other than a slightly elevated .322 BABIP last season that will correct itself a bit with possibly a lower batting average in 2016, Braun should be able to repeat his number from last year as he continues on into his prime.

2016 PROJECTION: .281 24 HR 86 RBI 89 R 23 SB

6. A.J. Pollock: For a fleeting moment we thought about putting Arizona Diamondbacks All-Star outfielder A.J. Pollock on the cover of our 2016 draft guide after he went down as by far our most impactful sleeper recommendation for the 2015 fantasy baseball season. It was in these pages a year ago we told you all to reach a few rounds early for Pollock who we felt strongly was going to be a five-tool impact player in short order. Needless to say Pollock was utterly ridiculous last season as he turned himself into top tier outfielder status with dominant numbers across the board. There was not a single standard category that Pollock didn't reach a career-high in as he batted .315 with 20 home runs and a monstrous 39 stolen bases. In addition, Pollock scored 111 runs at or near the top of the D-Backs lineup and also collected 76 RBI. It was magical stuff from Pollock from the start of the season to the finish and at only 28, he looks here to stay for awhile as an outfield anchor. Many will debate whether Pollock can repeat such a terrific season but it says here he absolutely can. While the .338 BABIP was on the lucky side, guys with Pollock's speed can ward off the regression better than most. Also Pollock struck out in just 13.2 percent of his at-bats last season as he was constantly making contact. Be sure you don't hesitate for a second when it comes to making Pollock as high as a late second round pick this season.

2016 PROJECTION: .308 22 HR 75 RBI 108 R 35 SB

7. Adam Jones: Each and every season we speak out in glowing terms regarding the ultimate durability and consistency of Baltimore Orioles All-Star outfielder Adam Jones. A solid outfielder 1 in fantasy baseball circles for years, we feel Jones often gets overlooked when the discussion turns to the top players in the game at his position. The truth is that ever since Jones arrived in Baltimore via trade from the Seattle Mariners, you could pretty much write his yearly numbers in ink during spring training. For example, over the last five seasons Jones has hit the following total of home runs: 25, 32, 33, 29, and 27. He also has topped 80 RBI in each of those years as well. The batting average during that span? Try .280, .287, .285, .281, and .269. The .269 dip can be blamed on a back problem that plagued Jones during the second half of the season which impacted him at the dish to the tune of a .254 average. Otherwise it was vintage Jones as he continues to serve as one of the more underrated and less talked about top players in the game. We do have to understand however that Jones' back issues could be his body's way of telling him that he is now 30-years-old. While Jones is still in his prime, 30 is usually when physical aches start to crop up. Another indication that Jones is no longer a kid is that his past as a 15-stolen base guy seems finished for good. Over the last four years Jones' stolen bases totals have slid every season, coming in with the following totals: 16, 14, 7, and 3. Overall there is some slight leakage of numbers but Jones has another few seasons of top play remaining.

2015 PROJECTION: .280 28 HR 88 RBI 86 R 5 SB

8. Jose Bautista: Despite turning 36 in October, Toronto Blue Jays outfielder Jose Bautista continues to remain as one of the best home run hitters in baseball in coming off a 2015 season when he sent 40 baseballs over the fence. Some have been predicting Bautista's demise for the last few seasons but the guy refuses to go along with that narrative since his last two years have seen more home runs than his 2012-13 stretch. What also makes Bautista much more than a home run specialist is the fact his counting statistics in both RBI and runs routinely go past the 100 mark due to a high walk rate (16.5 percent in 2015) and a solid K rate (15.9 percent) for a slugger. The average is noticeably slipping though, as Bautista's last four seasons have come in at the following sketchy numbers: .241, .259, .288, and last season's .256. We have started to believe that Bautista will ultimately go the way of David Ortiz in terms of continually putting up 30-40 home run seasons as he reaches the age of 40. The evidence so far backs this up. While you have to always be leery in using an early round pick on a player over the age of 35, Bautista is so far showing he should be considered an exception.

2016 PROJECTION: .253 35 HR 100 RBI 93 R 5 SB

9. Nelson Cruz: Even Safeco Field couldn't hold the extreme power of Nelson Cruz as evidenced by the mammoth 44 home runs he hit last season which somehow bettered the 40 he slammed the year prior but in a much better ballpark in Baltimore. What was even more shocking perhaps was the fact Cruz batted a career-high .303, again while calling one of the worst ballparks in the game his home. Cruz continues to surprise us as he reaches his mid-30's and right now we have to stop knocking the guy as he is in a major run right now. Power hitters always age better and hold onto their statistics longer than speed guys and that means Cruz can still be counted as a low-end outfielder 1. While the .303 average was terrific, throw that number out into the outlier bin as Cruz was helped big-time with a very lucky .330 BABIP). Other than that, Cruz looks to be on his way to another 30-plus home runs.

2016 PROJECTION: .273 35 HR 97 RBI 88 R 4 SB

10. Starling Marte: After hinting at outfielder 1 value since coming into the majors in 2012, Pittsburgh Pirates outfielder Starling Marte joined teammate Andrew McCutchen into that coveted tier during the 2015 season. Marte was simply fantastic as he reached career-highs in home runs (19), runs (84), and RBI (81); while also swiping 30 bases and posting a solid .287 average. Yes Marte now has all five ROTO categories covered and at 27 he could improve slightly more in 2016. Marte showed his maturity as a hitter last season by lowering his K rate to 19.4 percent, down from the 24.0 mark he put up in 2014. While we want to see Marte walk more, his ability to both hit for power and steal bases is a very impressive set of skills. A third round pick is what it deservedly will take now to get him onto your roster.

2016 PROJECTION: .286 22 HR 84 RBI 86 R 28 SB

11. Mookie Betts: Sometimes a guy seems destined to become a top-end player and one clearly could have made that argument for Boston Red Sox outfielder Mookie Betts heading into the 2015 season. After Betts absolutely tore up both Double-A (.355/6 HR/22 SB) AND Triple-A (.335/5 HR/11 SB) during the early portion of 2014, the Red Sox had no choice but to call him up for a trial run. Despite being only 21, Betts didn't embarrass himself as he batted .291 with 5 home runs and 7 stolen bases in 52 games with the Red Sox. It was more than enough for Betts to shoot right to the top of the "must have sleeper" list for the fantasy baseball community as the Red Sox committed to him being the team's everyday outfielder for the start of the 2015 season. With a draft price that was extremely pricey for someone so young and inexperienced at the major league level, the early returns were not overly impressive as Betts batted just .230 in April and .259 in May. Clearly there was some sort of an adjustment period for Betts as major league pitchers had a whole offseason to formulate an attack in terms of how to pitch to him. Like a seasoned veteran though, Betts figured things out and responded by hitting .300 or better in three of the last four months of the season, including a ridiculous .389 September. The end result was a tremendous five-category campaign where Betts batted .291 with 18 home runs and 21 stolen bases at the age of 22. Needless to say, Betts is here to stay as an immensely talented outfielder who is already knocking on the door to top tier status. Betts has uncanny contact ability for such a young player, with a tiny 12.5 percent K rate in 2015 that will always keep him secure as a batting average asset. In addition, Betts has the top-end speed down to swipe 20-plus bases the next few seasons as well, while also showing power that will only improve as he moves toward his prime seasons. There is simply nothing negative to say about Betts in looking ahead to 2016 and as a result he should be well-worth a pick in the Round 3-4 range.

2016 PROJECTION: .308 22 HR 98 R 84 RBI 25 SB

12. Yoenis Cespedes: The award for the "Greatest Impact Acquisition" at last season's trading deadline no doubt went to the New York Mets when they completed a last minute deal with the Detroit Tigers for outfielder Yoenis Cespedes. Already in the midst of personal bests in every category but steals, Cespedes blew the top off his numbers by slamming a crazy 17 home runs, collecting 44 RBI, and hitting .287 in just 230 at-bats for the Mets. If there were any way a guy who played only two months in one league could be an MVP, Cespedes would have been it for the NL given how incredible his performance was. His run with the Mets put the finishing touches on a monster career-year where Cespedes hit 35 home runs, drove in 105, scored 101, and batted .291. That set Cespedes up perfectly for free agency where he remains as of this writing. The fact Cespedes was able to do all that power damage while operating in two of the best pitching parks in baseball in Comerica and Citi Field speaks volumes of how good he was last season. A clear outfielder 1 whose main asset is power, Cespedes will be a tremendous early round pick no matter where he ends up this winter. Cespedes still strikes out too much (20.9 percent in 2015) which makes repeating his .291 average unlikely but everything else is repeatable. Bank on another 30 home runs and 100 RBI for this durable slugger.

2016 PROJECTION: .284 33 HR 104 RBI 95 R 5 SB

13. Charlie Blackmon: We admit we were part of the chorus that said the very good 2014 breakout season engineered by Colorado Rockies outfielder Charlie Blackmon was not likely to be repeated. The reason we felt that way was due to the fact after his scorching April was in the books, Blackmon was just decent the remaining five months. However Blackmon clearly got the last laugh on us in 2015 as he went ballistic in putting up an outfielder 1 campaign, highlighted by his 17 home runs and 43 stolen bases. Our rule has always been that if a player can put back-to-back seasons of very productive numbers together, the legitimate stamp gets put on them. Blackmon has solidified himself as a 15-20 home run guy, with an average in the .280-.290 range, and high-end steal totals that go towards the 40 mark. That is tremendous overall production as Blackmon can safely be added to the rare five tool player tier in today's fantasy baseball.

2016 PROJECTION: .288 17 HR 67 RBI 90 R 37 SB

14. Justin Upton: Whether it is Arizona, Atlanta, or San Diego, the theme remains the same as far as outfielder Justin Upton constantly leaving his owners wanting more. Having never come close to living up to his number 1 draft pick status, Upton moving to San Diego and spacious Petco Park prior to 2015 was not a recipe for finally unleashing what many once said was can't miss ability. Once again Upton did some good things (26 home runs and 85 RBI), mixed in with some bad (a career-low .251 average). Petco Park proved not to be an issue though as Upton hit 15 of his home runs at home. In addition, Upton was much more aggressive on the base paths last season, with his 19 stolen bases being his highest tally there since 2011. Now that Upton is 28-years-old though, what you see is what you get in terms of numbers. The K rate remains a big problem for Upton, as he struck out in 25.6 percent of his at-bats last season. That will continue to drag down the batting average and thus take some value away from the positives Upton brings in the home run column. Also the 19 steals may not be repeatable as Upton swiped a total of just 16 the two years prior to that. A free agent as of this writing, we could fall for Upton one more time if he ends up in a prime hitting environment like Toronto, Colorado, or Philadelphia but until that time comes, it is best to put him in the high outfielder 2 tier.

2016 PROJECTION: .259 27 HR 86 R 84 RBI 14 SB

15. George Springer: While Springer lost a big chunk of the 2015 season to injury, the ultra-talented outfielder made some very positive strides in his game. Springer pretty much improved in every category across the board, with the most positive development being the reduction in his K Rate from an insane 33.0 mark as a rookie to last season's 24.2 percent. As a result, Springer saw a drastic improvement in batting average, going from .231 in 2014 to a .276 mark a year ago. In addition, Springer found his stolen base legs after being very hesitant as a rookie. With tremendous natural power, Springer posted a 16/16 line last season that has much more room for growth. We have a strong belief that Springer is set for a monster breakout season, one that could have him in the 25/25 range if he can stay healthy. It is imperative that Springer continue working on his K rate because his value will explode if he can get to be even just a .280 hitter. Be aggressive here as the payoff could be monstrous.

2016 PROJECTION: .266 24 HR 79 R 77 RBI 23 SB

16. Lorenzo Cain: A new member of the upper tier five-category club was Kansas City Royals outfielder Lorenzo Cain in 2015. After more than a few flashes during his first few seasons in the majors of such ability, Cain never stayed healthy enough to full unleash his potential. Things started to come together during the second half of the 2014 season, as Cain helped the Royals make the postseason for the first time in decades. Proving his mini-breakout was no fluke, Cain cemented his status as one of the best outfielders in baseball by hitting 16 home runs, stealing 28 bases, and batting 307 last season. Throw in an excellent 102 runs scored and 72 RBI and one can see the precious five-tool ability that we all are willing to pay so much for at the draft table. Turning 30 in April, Cain's 2015 season is likely as good as it will get in terms of numbers but that is still a terrific statistical place to be. The .347 BABIP was clearly in the lucky zone but Cain was at .380 in 2014 as his speed continues to beat the curve there. With only a 16.2 percent K rate, there is no reason Cain should not be in the ballpark of his 2014 numbers this season.

2016 PROJECTION: .304 17 HR 70 RBI 98 R 29 SB

17. Hanley Ramirez: The era of Hanley Ramirez as a shortstop-eligible superstar hitter have officially come to an end after he spent all of the 2015 season manning leftfield for the Boston Red Sox. As scary as that proposition was defensively, Ramirez took full advantage of his first ever season hitting in an offensive park after spending his entire previous career with the Marlins and Dodgers. Ramirez predictably came out of the gates on fire with the bat, slamming 10 home runs and driving in 22 with a .293 batting average in April. It surely looked like Ramirez was ready to put up another dominant offensive campaign after he dealt with rampant injuries that derailed his previous two seasons. Alas the good times ended there as Ramirez once again came down with a variety of ailments that would have made for a good episode of Grey's Anatomy. He would go on to hit .235 or lower in three of his last four months of the season as an active player, missing all of September as the Red Sox finally shut Ramirez down with a persistent shoulder problem. All those years of manning the physically intense shortstop spot tend to wear down players quicker than let's say an outfielder or a first baseman and that seems to be what is taking place with Ramirez now as he enters into his age-32 season. Digging into the numbers, the 19 home runs in 430 at-bats were excellent but that is about the only good thing Ramirez did in 2015. For one thing, Ramirez' days of being a stolen base asset are almost completely finished as he swiped only 6 bags last season. In addition, the 4.9 percent walk rate Ramirez put up a year ago was a career-low by a wide margin which shows you how much of a hacker he has become. Surely the allure of swinging for the Green Monster is a part of the decline but that free-swinging approach has had a disastrous impact on Ramirez' batting average, which came in at another career-low of .249. An unlucky .257 BABIP was partly to blame but it is obvious that Ramirez has turned into a shell of his former first round fantasy baseball self. Losing shortstop eligibility is a tremendous blow to Ramirez' value, as he would still be a top 1-3 guy there in 2016 if the eligibility was intact. Instead as an outfield-eligible guy only to start the season, Ramirez is really nothing more than a low-end OF 2 given the numbers and declining health. The physical problems will only get more pronounced as Ramirez gets older and at this point he really only looks like a home run/RBI asset and not much more. Fading.

2016 PROJECTION: .262 17 HR 65 RBI 74 R 5 SB

18. Carlos Gonzalez: Classifying the season of Colorado Rockies outfielder Carlos Gonzalez would prove to be a futile venture, so crazy were the swings in production. It looked early on in 2015 that Gonzalez was a major shell of his former outfielder 1 self as he crashed to the tune of just a .259 average and 13 home runs during the first half of the year. What happened next almost defied belief as Gonzalez went on a power run that would make Adam Dunn envious. In just 260 at-bats during the second half of the season, Gonzalez hit an insane 27 home runs and drove in 62. Finishing the year with a career-high 40 homers and 97 RBI, Gonzalez put himself squarely back into outfielder 1 territory. The path Gonzalez took there was a much different one from his earlier days however, with the increase in power overcoming the almost complete loss of stolen bases. Gone forever are the days where Gonzalez went 20/20 as he swiped just 2 bags all of last season. No doubt years of leg injuries and the fact he is now 30 means Gonzalez' days of taking bases are finished. Still we can more than overlook that development if Gonzalez can continue staying healthy and hitting home runs at his 2015 rate. Gonzalez has actually become a better overall hitter, posting a 21.9 percent K rate that was lower than both his 2013 and 2014 marks. He also pushed up his walk rate to 7.6 last season, bettering the mid-6.0 range he was at the two years prior. The injury threat has not all of a sudden gone away here as Gonzalez cemented his reputation as a health mess a long time ago. You still need to proceed very cautiously here and at least for now his 2015 home run production should be considered an outlier. We are still very leery of Gonzalez given his history and now even more so due to the fact his big 2015 figures to push his value quite a bit higher than we are willing to pay.

2016 PROJECTION: .274 27 HR 94 RBI 84 R 4 SB

19. J.D. Martinez: Boy did the Houston Astros miss the mark when it came to their development of outfielder J.D. Martinez. After Martinez showed some promise coming up the team's farm system, the Astros seemed to run out of patience after the 2013 season when the traded him away to the Detroit Tigers. While not an ideal landing spot for a burgeoning power hitter due to the vast dimensions of Comerica Park, Martinez put together a nice 2014 by clubbing 23 home runs and collecting 76 RBI with a .315 average. While any fantasy baseball owner of Martinez going into 2015 would have been fine with a repeat of those numbers, the youngster instead decided to go bonkers in the power department by clubbing 38 home runs and collecting 102 RBI. No doubt Martinez benefitted greatly from hitting in front of or behind Miguel Cabrera in the order, pretty much the most cushy spot in the game in terms of getting good fastballs to slam. Martinez will be right back in that precious spot for 2016 as well so the home runs will likely continue to fly out. The one knock on Martinez last season was the fact his K Rate got a bit out of whack at 27.1 percent, perhaps a sign that he was swinging for the fences more than ever. Still Martinez was able to bat a solid .282, helped along by a lucky .339 BABIP. While you may automatically think Martinez will slide back in the average department in 2016, keep in mind he is one of those guys who seems to beat the BABIP curve every season with three straight years in the plus-.300 area code. Asking for a repeat of 38 home runs could be a bit too much but 30-plus seems like a very good likelihood.

2016 PROJECTION: .280 34 HR 97 RBI 91 R 4 SB

20. Carlos Gomez: It was a beyond frustrating season for Houston Astros outfielder Carlos Gomez and those who owned shares in him during 2015 fantasy baseball. Never right physically at any point in the season as he battled oblique/hamstring/ankle injuries, Gomez had his worst offensive campaign since 2011 as he hit just 12 home runs and stole a depressed 17 bases. Needless to say Gomez failed to come anywhere close to his late first round ADP but at a still young 30, we think a bit of a mulligan should be placed on his 2015 numbers. With full health, Gomez should be fully capable of going right back past the 20-steal mark with ease and the power could creep right back near the 20 mark as well. While Gomez still is an undisciplined hitter even through his big seasons from 2012-14, his athleticism remains very impressive. The draft price should drop into the Round 3 or 4 range and at that spot investing in a bounce back from Gomez is a solid ploy.

2016 PROJECTION: .278 17 HR 73 RBI 84 R 26 SB

21. Corey Dickerson: A popular target in 2015 fantasy baseball drafts due to his ballpark and burgeoning power numbers, it looked like Colorado Rockies outfielder Corey Dickerson was headed for a monster season in 2015 when he broke out of the gates to swat 5 home runs and batted .329 in his first 21 April games. Just as the excitement really began to build for his owners though, disaster struck in the form of the dreaded plantar fasciitis in his foot. A debilitating injury that can only be remedied through surgery, Dickerson was determined to play through the pain. After a DL stint that went from late April into mid-May, Dickerson returned a much different player and for the worse. Not being able to generate power in his swing due to the pain in his foot, Dickerson failed to hit a home run in 10 games before he went right back onto the DL. With frustration at peak levels, Dickerson returned in September to hit 5 home runs in his last 22 games. Clearly that production fell under the "too little/too late" heading but at the very least Dickerson will be 100 percent healthy for 2016 spring training after getting the foot taken care of over the winter. Turning just 27 in May, Dickerson seems primed to pick up right where he left off last April in pushing toward a 30-home run season with a good batting average for the Rockies. Like most Rockies hitters, Dickerson benefits tremendously from his ballpark and is a much scaled-down version of his hitting self on the road. For his career, Dickerson is a dominant .355 hitter at home with 24 home runs. On the road those totals drop to .249 and 15. So obviously there is a split to be aware of when Dickerson is on the road. However the bottom line is that Dickerson should be at the doorstep of 30 home runs if his body cooperates and that should keep him right in the ballpark of being an early round pick.

2016 PROJECTION: .309 28 HR 89 RBI 93 R 7 SB

22. Hunter Pence: Age spares no one when it comes to being a professional athlete and the aftereffects begin to crop up once a player passes the age of 30 in terms of increased risk of injury and a drop in numbers. Even arguably the most dependable outfielder in fantasy baseball in the form of the perennially underrated Hunter Pence could not hold off this unyielding trend. Counted on once again as a low-end OF 1 or a high-end OF 2 coming into 2015, Pence was set to continue posting his quietly effective five-tool numbers in anchoring the San Francisco Giants lineup. The first bad omen for Pence came at the start of spring training games when he suffered a fractured left forearm that kept him out until mid-May due to an HBP. Upon his return, Pence quickly got back to supplying his five category contributions, hitting 9 home runs, stealing 4 bases, and driving in 40 batters in only 223 at-bats. Alas there was no at-bat number 224 as Pence came down with a dreaded oblique strain on August 17th that wound up costing him the rest of the season. It was the icing on the cake of a frustrating year both for Pence and his fantasy baseball owners. Truth be told however, it was really just the first disappointing campaign from Pence in his entire career which began in 2007. That speaks volumes about how dependable and durable Pence had been previously and one can understand the thought of giving Pence a full mulligan for 2015, especially when you consider the HBP was a freak accident. The fact Pence kept hitting close to his career levels when he was on the field also is a nice sign that he could squeeze out another 1-2 years of standard production before the decline phase sets in. There are some signs of statistical leakage though in the form of a K rate that came in at a career-high 21.5 percent in 2015. Hitting .280-plus could be a challenge if Pence stays on that trend. In addition, Pence's days of being a stolen base asset could be fading as he has gone from 22 to 13 to 4 over the last four years. Again we could be nitpicking here given that the injuries could have caused the numbers decline but at 33 in April, we have to factor in age as something that could impact Pence's production. If you can draft Pence as a mid-level outfielder 2, you did well.

2016 PROJECTION: .277 19 HR 79 RBI 75 R 8 SB

23. Jason Heyward: The ongoing drama that comes with owning outfielder Jason Heyward continued on into the 2015 season, as he mixed awful and brilliant play over the six-months of play. With the Atlanta Braves having run out of patience with his underwhelming play since debuting with the team in 2010, a winter trade to the St. Louis Cardinals offered Heyward a fresh start going into 2015. It looked early on that the Cardinals made a rare error with the swap, what with Miller pitching like an ace for the Braves and Heyward logging a listless .217 average in April. However Heyward stayed true to his tendency of hitting better as the season moves along, actually ending up on some back-end MVP ballots by the end of the year. Heyward would ultimately finish the season with 13 home runs, 23 stolen bases, and a career-best .293 average. While the home run totals have been somewhat of a disappointment over the last three years (14, 11, and 13), Heyward made nice strides with his approach at the dish last season which allowed for the average boost. Primarily speaking, Heyward's 14.8 K rate was the best of his career and he walked at a high 9.2 percent clip as well. While it does seem as though Heyward's stronger skills were in the speed and stolen base department (three of the last four years at 20-plus) as opposed to the power, this is something we are willing to overlook if he can continue hitting above .280. Maybe Heyward has not fulfilled the once lofty expectations we all had for him a few years ago but the fact of the matter is that he is developing into a very good outfielder 2.

2016 PROJECTION: .284 15 HR 63 RBI 83 R 22 SB

24. Jacoby Ellsbury: The flip side to the hitter who is aging nicely like Jose Bautista is the case of rapid decline like we are seeing out of New York Yankees outfielder Jacoby Ellsbury. Already the Yanks likely are having major regret just two seasons into the crazy 7-year contract they gave Ellsbury prior to the start of 2014. Ellsbury is serving as the latest example of how players whose biggest strength is speed tend to decline much more quickly than sluggers and this trend can start as soon as they pass the age of 30. While Ellsbury started the 2015 season well enough (.318/14 SB/32 R in April/May), a knee injury soon shelved him until mid-July. Always a slow healer and having one of the more pronounced tendencies for getting injured, Ellsbury was a joke when he finally returned. From

July through the end of the season, Ellsbury batted a listless .220 and stole only 7 bases. The end result was a pathetic .257 average, 66 runs, and 21 stolen bases. Now an old 32, Ellsbury already looks like a shell of his former early round/outfielder 1 self. Even moving past the fact Ellsbury remains a major injury headache (an issue that will just get worse as he continues to get older), his speed seems to be eroding as well since the 21 steals were his worst performance by far in a season when he has over 500 at-bats. Also, hitting just 7 home runs while playing half your games at Yankee Stadium is truly awful. In addition, Ellsbury's K rate is jogging steadily northward, going from 14.6 percent in 2014 to 17.2 percent last season. We have constantly shared with you our hesitancy in using an early round pick on Ellsbury due to his fragile nature but that line of thinking is even urgent so now that his numbers are falling apart. No longer qualifying as an outfielder 1, Ellsbury seems like he is ready to plummet fast in his somewhat disappointing career.

2016 PROJECTION: .275 6 HR 44 RBI 77 R 23 SB

25. Kole Calhoun: Los Angeles Angels outfielder Kole Calhoun had been a player who was universally embraced by the fantasy baseball community going into the 2015 season for a number of reasons. The first is that Calhoun annoyed some by not being a stolen base guy despite the fact the Angels planted him in the leadoff spot often during the 2014 season. In addition, Calhoun battled injuries which kept the cap on his statistical capabilities. Well 2015 brought a full Calhoun breakout as he surprised many by cracking 26 home runs and collecting 83 RBI while playing a full season with 630 at-bats. Clearly Calhoun had more power than most anticipated and the Angels finally found a spot for him in the middle of the lineup given his lack of speed. However Calhoun is still a bit rough around the edges in that his average dropped to a shaky .256 mark and only 4 stolen bases show he continually won't be a help there. What you see is what you get now out of Calhoun who is in his prime at the age of 28. The K rate jumped last season to 23.9 percent which caused the average to drop and that is the one variable that can change the outlook on Calhoun a bit in 2016. If he cuts the K's a bit, Calhoun could bat .275 which makes him gain a bit more value to go with the home runs.

2016 PROJECTION: .266 24 HR 82 RBI 80 R 3 SB

26. Gregory Polanco: Already possessing two five-tool outfielders in Andrew McCutchen and Starling Marte, it looks like the Pittsburgh Pirates might be adding a third there in the form of the speedy Gregory Polanco. Polanco is no sudden star either as he put himself toward the top of prospect lists in 2014 when he hit 7 home runs, stole 16 bases, and batted .328 at Triple-A. He didn't embarrass himself when called up that year either, putting up a 7/14 line but with a shaky .235 average. With a full offseason to work on his skills, Polanco got off to a nice start to the 2015 season before fading a bit late. Holding the leadoff spot that Marte was ill-suited for, Polanco was a stolen base weapon as he swiped 27 bags and combined that nice haul with 83 runs scored. Polanco was also not a zero in the home run category as he hit 9 long balls in 652 at-bats. In fact Polanco reminds us of Marte whose best attribute was the stolen base when he first debuted, with the power showing up a few years later. Polanco seems like he is on the same path and more growth in power is likely. Also, Polanco's positive minor league batting averages have failed to make the jump to the majors as he hit just .256 last season but the advanced numbers point to more there as well. An 18.6 K rate is not terrible for someone so young and an 8.4 walk rate is also a nice number. Already a low-end outfielder 2, it would not shock us in the least if Polanco made it to outfielder 1 status in 2016.

2016 PROJECTION: .265 14 HR 63 RBI 88 R 29 SB

27. Christian Yelich: While the knee-jerk feeling would be that Miami Marlins outfielder Christian Yelich was a disappointment in 2015, the truth is that the youngster made some nice strides in his development into what many think will be upper-level production. The former 2010 first round pick (23rd overall), Yelich fought through an early DL stint to post a .300 average, 7 home runs, and 16 stolen bases in 126 games. Surely the numbers don't jump off the page and when you take into account the high expectations going into the season, there is some understanding of why Yelich was a bit of a letdown to some. However Yelich turns just 24 in December and he still has the natural tools to be at least an outfielder 2 soon enough. Strikeouts were a problem for Yelich when he broke in as a rookie in 2013 as he posted a very high 24.2 percent K rate. However Yelich got that number down to 19.2 percent last season which alone shows improvement. The .300 average was fueled some by the very lucky .370 BABIP Yelich posted but guys with his type of high-end speed usually go above .300 by a decent margin anyways. What we really need to determine is how much of a gain Yelich will make with his power to go along with the speed. We envision Yelich as a 15/25/.290 guy as soon as this season and a line like that would put him into the outfielder 2 realm we anticipated all along. With the draft price more affordable this time around, Yelich is absolutely worth a long look again.

2016 PROJECTION: .284 11 HR 53 RBI 84 R 24 SB

28. Brett Gardner: The nice mid-career elevation of New York Yankees outfielder Brett Gardner continues on during the 2015 season, as the speedster was named an All-Star for the first time in his career at the age of 32. While Gardner came into the majors as a 40-stolen base dynamo, he has changed his statistical profile over the last few years for an overall better impact in fantasy baseball. Gardner is no longer the stolen base weapon he was earlier in his career (four straight years of under 25 in that category) but on the flip side he has become more of a home run hitter. After having never reached double digits in home runs during his first six years in baseball, Gardner has now hit 17 and 16 the last two seasons respectively. Toss in a run total that has gone over 80 five years running and Gardner is a good asset in three standard league categories. We all know leadoff guys like Gardner don't put up a ton of RBI but his batting average has been quite ugly in his career. This has been especially true lately as Gardner's plus-20 percent K rate has not allowed him to bat over .260 the last two years. The fact that coincides with Gardner's recent power boost is not just a coincidence either. The last issue to be aware of is the fact Gardner has struggles badly during the second half of the last two seasons, with his all-out approach causing the aches and pains that are the likely cause of the swoons. So keep this in mind during the summer if you are a Gardner owner since it would be a good idea to sell high at that point in the season.

2016 PROJECTION: .257 16 HR 65 RBI 88 R 19 SB

29. Jay Bruce: It was another typical season from Cincinnati Reds outfielder Jay Bruce in 2015, as he once again hit for good power (26 home runs) but struggled badly with the batting average (.226). Now a full veteran in his prime at the age of 29 in April, Bruce has actually gotten worse in the average department compared to his initial few seasons in the league when he was between .252 and .281 from 2010-13. However over the last two years that number has dropped to

.217 and .226 which is a big problem. On the plus side, Bruce's very good power remains impressive as he pretty much is a lock for 25 home runs and 80 RBI. Those are really the only two categories that Bruce is a help in fantasy baseball though and we have been correctly pointing out that he has been overrated for years. The fact of the matter is that Bruce has not lived up to the initial hype when he first came up and things won't change now that he is close to the age of 30. Not our cup of tea as Bruce is quite limited considering where he annually gets picked in drafts.

2016 PROJECTION: .244 25 HR 86 RBI 70 R 8 SB

30. Adam Eaton: It took a little longer than expected but Chicago White Sox outfielder Adam Eaton finally started showing what all the fuss was about when he was considered a top prospect coming up the Arizona Diamondbacks system. A pure leadoff hitter who had a string of .300-plus averages and who stole as many as 38 bags in a season on the farm, Eaton went bust both in his initial 2013 and 2014 forays into the majors. The proverbial light bulb flashed on in 2015 however as Easton finally managed to stay healthy after more than a few injury woes his first two years and the result was a 14/18 campaign in the power/speed categories that hint at maybe more to come. In addition, Eaton batted .287 and scored a tremendous 98 runs as he became a terrific value play since his draft value had sunk more than a little going into the season. Turning just 27 in December, Eaton has quickly graduated near the border between OF 2 and OF 3 status, with a tiny bit of ceiling left for some more numbers. A .345 BABIP was clearly in the lucky range but guys with Eaton's speed can ward off regression better than most other players. We are fully back on board this train.

2016 PROJECTION: .290 15 HR 59 RBI 100 R 20 SB

31. Michael Conforto: The New York Mets have been lauded all over baseball for having the most dominant and impressive arsenal of young pitching the game and no doubt Jacob DeGrom, Matt Harvey, Noah Syndegaard, and Steven Matz have more than legitimized the accolades. The Mets farm system was not all about pitching though as prized outfield prospect Michael Conforto completed a rapid ascent up the minor league ladder to debut straight from Double-A in 2015. Conforto was the 10th overall pick in the 2014 draft but his off-the-charts hitting approach enabled him to take the express train to the Mets where he hit .270

with 16 home runs in 468 at-bats. The maturity and poise here is tremendous and Conforto has the rare type of natural power that screams out future 30 home run star. Perhaps even more impressive, Conforto is not a hacking slugger either since he struck out at a decent 20.1 percent for a rookie. In addition, Conforto was hitting a terrific .321 at Double-A. Incredibly young at the age of only 23 this March, Conforto is right there at the top in terms of the being the best young power prospect in all of baseball. Well worth acting on a round or two early in order to secure this future star.

2016 PROJECTION: .278 24 HR 74 RBI 65 R 7 SB

32. Stephen Piscotty: One of the prime reasons the St. Louis Cardinals are known as arguably the most successful organization in baseball is due to their uncanny ability to develop high-end hitting and pitching prospects. With Carlos Martinez covering the pitching side of that trend in 2015, outfielder Stephen Piscotty filled the hitting quotient. A classic smooth and compact swinger with good patience, Piscotty looked like a seasoned veteran as a rookie by hitting .310 with 7 home runs and 39 RBI in only 252 at-bats. A very scary outfield collision with Peter Bourjos was the only hiccup but overall Piscotty came through that all right considering how ugly it looked. Still quite young at 25, Piscotty is growing into his power and looks like a classic 20-HR/.300-hitting outfielder for the next decade. Prior to his promotion last season, Piscotty hit 11 home runs and batted .272 while showing a knack for walks (12.4 percent) and a solid K rate (167) on the farm. The reason for Piscotty hitting better average-wise with the Cards was due to his extremely lucky .379 BABIP; a number that can't possibly come close to being repeated. As a result we need to downgrade Piscotty in the average department for 2016 but at the same time he should make gains everywhere else. There is not much speed here so don't think you are snagging a five-tool outfielder but Piscotty looks like a guy who is primed for another solid step up in production this season. The Cardinals' prospect history says as much.

2016 PROJECTION: .284 16 HR 74 RBI 71 R 8 SB

33. Gerardo Parra: As much as we talk about how the Arizona Diamondbacks have collected a very impressive batch of young outfielders, one guy they let slip away was leadoff speedster Gerardo Parra. A good but not overly hyped prospect coming up the D-Backs' system, Parra was a useful player in his four-plus years with the team. What made Parra so interesting was that he flashed five-category ability, having hit 10 home runs in a season and also stealing as many as 15 bags. Alas Arizona played the matchups when it came to Parra and their other outfielders and that hurt the his counting numbers season after season. Things all came together for Parra in 2015 however as a season split between the Milwaukee Brewers and Baltimore Orioles resulted in a career-year. Parra would go on to hit .291 with 14 home runs and 14 stolen bases, while also scoring 83 runs. Still quite young as he turns 29 in May, Parra has now graduated into an everyday leadoff man who can post a .300/15-HR/20-SB/90-R/60-RBI line if all breaks right. The hype has grown a bit after Parra's big year, especially in a high-attention locale like Baltimore but few guys are better outfielder 3 candidates.

2016 PROJECTION: .298 15 HR 57 RBI 95 R 17 SB

34. Yasiel Puig: The riddle that is Los Angeles Dodgers outfielder Yasiel Puig continued in 2015, with no clear answers as to how good the Cuban import really is. While Puig's off-the-field troubles and diva attitude have drawn more than a few rebukes since arriving in the States, his propensity for missing games is also becoming a major part of the disappointing narrative. This was never more true than last season when Puig netted just 306 at-bats due to a slew of oblique and hamstring injuries. Even in those 306 at-bats however, Puig failed to impress much outside of his 11 home runs. For one thing, Puig struck out in 21.2 percent of his at-bats, resulting in a very shaky .256 batting average. The average was a major drop from the .296 Puig hit in 2014 and the .319 mark he put up as a rookie. What was real key there was the fact that Puig had ridiculously lucky BABIP's in both 2013 (.383) and 2014 (.356) which were bound to be corrected to the mean. That is what happened last season as Puig's .297 BABIP was right there in the neutral region which resulted in the batting average drop. If Puig's does not get more BABIP luck in 2016, he will be a liability in average again due to his 20-plus percent K rate that he has been producing since making his debut. Moving away from the average, Puig's slugging percentage has dropped each of his first three years in the majors, which accounted for the dip in his home run rate in 2015. While Puig does have good speed, his high in stolen bases is a modest 11, which is dimming any thoughts of him ever being a 20/20 player. With all of the negatives we just went over with Puig, one can really start to wonder just how good of a player he really is. The evidence is suggesting Puig is not much more than an outfielder 3, despite all the hype that arrived when he was a rookie a few seasons ago. The petulance and immaturity is also a big problem that further threatens what Puig could turn out to be. The fact of the matter is that Puig was one of the biggest headaches for anyone to own last season in fantasy baseball and that makes investing in him for 2016 a very shaky proposition.

2016 PROJECTION: .273 17 HR 59 RBI 70 R 8 SB

35. Billy Hamilton: The ultimate one-trick pony, Cincinnati Reds outfielder Billy Hamilton's second MLB season went pretty much the same as the first. That meant a whole bunch of stolen bases (57), an ugly batting average (.226), and not much of anything else to speak of. The Reds tried Hamilton out of the leadoff spot initially to begin 2015 but his utter lack of walks (6.2 %) and high K rate (16.5 %) made him a terrible fit there. Moved to the bottom of the order, Hamilton did his stolen base thing with little else happening. It all ended badly as well, with Hamilton needing season-ending shoulder surgery. Now 26-years-old, Hamilton is already close to his prime which means he is pretty much what will be going forward with his numbers. Batting at the bottom of the Reds order in 2016 will be rough for his bottom line value as Hamilton won't get many good pitches to hit and as a result we could see a slight drop in steals and runs as well. We have spoken many times about how overrated a player Hamilton is, with many being seduced by his ridiculous minor league stolen base totals. That was never going to be repeated at the major league level as we have seen and in actuality, there are also many more valuable stolen base assets who can help in batting average and runs. Leave Hamilton to someone else.

2016 PROJECTION: .243 5 HR 35 RBI 59 R 54 SB

36. Alex Gordon: The career of veteran outfielder Alex Gordon has been somewhat a frustrating one for his fantasy baseball owners each season. When owning Gordon, you always feel disappointed in his aggregate numbers, wanting more from a guy who came up as the number 2 overall pick in his draft class. Still the Royals continually stated that Gordon was their MVP and that makes sense when you consider how good a defensive player he is, in addition to his contributions as a hitter. Still we don't count defense in fantasy baseball and the numbers are where things become a bit of a letdown. Case in point was the 2015 season as Gordon once again was solid but far from spectacular as he batted .271 with 13 home runs and 48 RBI in 422 at-bats. Gordon battled injuries which no doubt hurt his counting statistics but as he turns 32 in February, age is starting to change his number landscape some. For one, Gordon's days of helping in the steals category could be quickly coming to an end, as he took just two bags last season. Gordon also is a bit of a shaky average guy due to struggles against righties and a K Rate that still straddles around the 20.0 mark. The best you can ask for now with Gordon is a 20/15 season to go with a .275 average and that makes him nothing more than an outfielder 3 in fantasy baseball.

2016 PROJECTION: .273 17 HR 86 R 78 RBI 8 SB

37. Joc Pederson: There were a ton of sky-high expectations for Los Angeles Dodgers top outfield prospect Joc Pederson heading into the 2015 season, with this publication being firmly planted on that bandwagon. It was an understandable way of thinking after we saw Pederson hit 33 home runs and steal 30 bases in 2014 at Triple-A which gave him the look of the next great power/speed outfield dynamo. Well Pederson seemed primed to fulfill that expectation early on during the season, as he began hitting light-tower home runs that had him sitting on 20 long balls at the All-Star Break. Having been selected an All-Star, it was easy to overlook the red flag that was Pederson's .230 batting average, with many chalking that up to him being raw. Well the All-Star Game became the last highlight for Pederson in 2015 as his second half was epically bad. With a strikeout rate that was off-the-charts, Pederson batted just .178 while hitting only 6 home runs in 180 at-bats in that span. Pederson was so bad that he was taken out of the precious leadoff spot and shoved way down in the order. By the end of the year Pederson was an automatic out and his insane 29.1 percent K rate showed that he still needs more than a little work with the bat. On the positive side, 26 home runs from any rookie is very impressive but Pederson also failed to come through in the stolen base department as he took just 4 bags. Pederson couldn't seem to get his timing down with the steals, much in the same way George Springer struggled there as a rookie in 2014. Springer started figuring things out in 2015 however and the hope is that Pederson can start running so that he can offset the damage his ugly batting average will bring. Simply put, a whole bunch of shine has come off on Pederson as the home runs he hits get offset by the hurt he puts on your team batting average. While we still like

Pederson's long-term potential, his shortcomings threaten to undermine his overall impact.

2016 PROJECTION: .235 28 HR 63 RBI 74 R 9 SB

38. Shin-Soo Choo: Just when the fantasy baseball community was prepared to cast outfielder Shin-Soo Choo aside forever, the veteran came back yet again in 2015 to show he is not finished just yet. While Choo no doubt has changed as a player, he took advantage of the friendly confines of his ballpark in Texas to match a previous career-high in home runs with 22. Always a high on-base guy to begin with, Choo also put up very good totals in the areas of runs (94) and RBI (82). Alas Choo is far removed from his early 20/20 days with the Cleveland Indians and his last gasp performance there with the Cincinnati Reds in 2013 when he hit 21 home runs and stole 20 bases. The fact of the matter is that Choo's speed looks gone for good as he has stolen a grand total of just 7 bases over the last two years. Outside of that though, Choo remains productive as he managed to hit a respectable .276 last season which made him a contributor in four out of the five standard categories. The best part is that no one seems to want to own Choo anymore as he gets knocked a bit too unfairly for losing his speed. This is one of the trends we always see in fantasy baseball in terms of a guy losing almost all of his past appeal due to eroding numbers in one category. This is what is taking place with Choo who, while he is in fact aging as he turns 34, remains a solid impact player. Take advantage of the dirt cheap draft price and add Choo for one more run as your third outfielder.

2016 PROJECTION: .267 20 HR 84 RBI 93 R 3 SB

39. Dexter Fowler: The Chicago Cubs became the latest team to attempt to unlock the once much-hyped ability of outfielder Dexter Fowler heading into the 2015 season and in going along with their recent trend of rolling 7's on player investments, they were rewarded with his best major league campaign yet. Batting in the leadoff spot for most of the year, Fowler reached career-highs in runs (102), homers (17), and stolen bases (20) to supply some terrific outfielder 3 value. Considering the fact Fowler was largely ignored in drafts due to the string of disappointing seasons earlier in his career with the Colorado Rockies and Houston Astros, his 17/20 line in the power/speed categories was very helpful for his owners. We can knock Fowler for his ugly .250 batting average but his .308

BABIP, while being a neutral number, was quite low for someone with his speed. We think Fowler can move back up to the .260 range which will change the outlook here for the better and his power/speed numbers are looking very repeatable as well. The draft price might creep up a bit again but as an outfielder 3 Fowler looks like one of the more effective players in that tier.

2016 PROJECTION: .263 16 HR 48 RBI 95 R 22 SB

40. Michael Brantley: After several years performing as a solid but unspectacular outfielder for the Cleveland Indians, 2014 brought an unexpected career year from Michael Brantley in the form of a .327 average, 20 home runs, and 23 stolen bases. In addition, Brantley scored 94 runs and drove in 97 as he suddenly turned into a five-tool outfielder right before our eyes. However there was a stark divide after that terrific season was in the books and this primarily centered on believers who argued Brantley tapped into his prime at the age of 27, while the other side screamed "outlier." Count us among the latter crowd as we were very skeptical about Brantley for a number of reasons. First off, Brantley's .333 BABIP was a career-high and quite a bit into the "lucky" territory which added skepticism to the .327 average. In addition, Brantley's home run rate was in fluke territory when compared to his career norms. As a result, we advised caution when it came to investing in Brantley for 2015, predicting in last year's draft guide that the power would scale back. That is exactly what it did as Brantley hit just 15 home runs as his long ball rate went back to his previous levels. In addition, Brantley swiped just 15 bases and saw his average drop to .310 as his BABIP normalized to a more neutral .318. Now 29, Brantley is firmly into his prime years and so he should be graded on the levels he had established in 6 of his previous 7 seasons. We respect the fact Brantley helps in all five categories but he doesn't excel in any one. That works fine as a solid outfielder 2 but not as the outfielder 1 many incorrectly thought they were getting last season. Finally and most concerning, Brantley underwent shoulder surgery in November which will keep him out until May at the earliest.

2016 PROJECTION: .307 16 HR 86 RBI 77 R 17 SB

41. Matt Holliday: The bottom is starting to fall out completely on the career of St. Louis Cardinals outfielder Matt Holliday, as the veteran was able to get into only 229 games last season due to a myriad of injuries. One of the best pure hitters of his generation, Holliday is on the fast track toward oblivion by the looks of things as he turns 36 in January. Overall Holliday hit just 4 home runs, drove in 35, and batted .279 for the Cardinals in 2015 and one has to wonder how much longer both he and the team can go on together. Having hit over .290 every season of his 10-year career leading into 2014, Holliday has been under .280 the last two seasons which is a clear sign of decline. In addition, Holliday's home run rate is slipping noticeably, as his season totals since 2012 have read 27, 22, 20, and 4. While Holliday still walks a ton (14.1 percent) which should keep the average steady enough, the rest of the statistical package is looking quite shoddy. Another guy where you salute the career and bid him a goodbye.

2016 PROJECTION: .275 14 HR 65 RBI 67 R 1 SB

42. Curtis Granderson: Eyebrows were raised when the New York Mets signed free agent outfielder Curtis Granderson to a four-year deal prior to the 2014 season and the critics began to howl when the veteran went out and batted just .227 with 20 home runs in his first year with the team. However the Mets began to look very smart for making that deal when Granderson became the top leader on a young team that reached the World Series, sacrificing some of his numbers in accepting a move to the leadoff spot when no other candidate in the clubhouse was adequate enough for the job. The results were a quietly very good year from Granderson that was highlighted by the veteran hitting 26 long balls and scoring 98 runs, while pushing his average back up a bit to .257. Clearly Granderson is far from the 40-home run guy he was with the New York Yankees due to the extreme ballpark downgrade but he has done a nice job shortening his swing with the Mets in lowering his K rate to the 21-22 range after being as high as 28.5 percent across town. With the ability to still collect some steals (11 in 2015), Granderson should supply outfielder 3 numbers once again this season.

2016 PROJECTION: .255 25 HR 73 RBI 93 R 10 SB

43. Matt Kemp: For the second season in a row, the fantasy baseball community was ready to give last rites to San Diego Padres outfielder Matt Kemp, only to see him rally with a very good second half that helped keep his bat relevant for another year. This trend all started after the 2013 season which was a complete disaster for Kemp as he hit just 6 home runs and batted .270 in 73 games as his body began to completely fall apart physically. As a result there were very low expectations for Kemp as 2014 dawned and that seemed to be right on target as he proceeded to hit just .260 during the first half of the season with 8 home runs in 305 at-bats. However Kemp more than saved his year by getting locked-in at the dish during the second half to the tune of 17 home runs and a .305 average. Still the positive vibes didn't get to last long once the season was through as the Los Angeles Dodgers traded him to the San Diego Padres during the winter. With Kemp having lost a ton of speed, most of his fantasy baseball value was tied into home runs which would now be a challenge in calling Petco Park home. Alas just like in Los Angeles, Kemp did almost a perfect carbon copy of his first half (.250/8 HR) and second half (.286/15 HR) split. Considering the ballpark, Kemp's final tally of 23 home runs and 100 RBI was a very impressive feat, while at the same time upholding his outfielder 2 status for fantasy baseball. Now 31-years-old, Kemp is a much different player than he was just a few years ago with the Dodgers. The most obvious change is the loss of stolen bases as Kemp seems to have lost a good deal of his speed. Having swiped as many as 40 bases in his monstrous 2012, Kemp posted underwhelming totals in that category of 9, 9, 8, and 12. Another issue is the batting average as Kemp's days of hitting .300 are also looking to be gone for good. Kemp has settled into the .265-.280 range over the last three seasons which is not terrible but also not terrific either. On the positive side, the power is still there and Kemp also had his best K rate since 2007 which is a positive. Injuries are perhaps the biggest story though as Kemp has had a ton of them ranging from back and shoulder surgery, to a torn tendon in his finger that also needed to be fixed. Lack of health is always the biggest problem when it comes to players who pass the age of 30 as it often is related to a drop in production. Kemp still has the goods to help again as a middle-tier outfielder 2 but this is a guy who has seen better days.

2016 PROJECTION: .275 22 HR 89 RBI 86 R 11 SB

44. Kevin Pillar: The 2015 Toronto Blue Jays stormed to the AL East division title on the literal strength of their veteran power-packed lineup. However they also got an unexpected boost from former 2011 32nd round pick Kevin Pillar who was able to solidify a starting outfield spot over Dalton Pompey at the start of the season. Known for his speed, Pillar didn't disappoint as he stole 25 bases and scored 76 runs. However Pillar surprised by hitting 12 home runs which changed the whole scope of his impact. Pillar is showing quite an advanced approach to hitting already as he struck out in just 13.5 percent of his at-bats in 2015. If he can add to his low 4.5 percent walk rate, Pillar can string together a bunch of .300 hitting campaigns. The 12 home runs may not be repeatable as Pillar didn't show much in the way of power coming up the team's farm system but playing half your games in Rogers Center will give him a good chance to do so. This one is turning out better than anyone thought was possible.

2016 PROJECTION: .286 11 HR 80 R 59 RBI 27 SB

45. Rusney Castillo: Anyone who invested into the hype of top Boston Red Sox Cuban outfielder Rusney Castillo prior to the 2015 season had to be pulling their hair out of their heads. After a spring training oblique injury kept Castillo from making the Opening Day roster, the Red Sox didn't start giving the kid consistent work until the second half of the year. While Castillo flashed the big-time speed and developing power that made so many clamor for him in the first place, the overall result last season was a shoddy 5 home runs, 4 stolen bases, and a .253 average in 80 games. With the Red Sox in rebuilding mode after a horrid season, Castillo will join Mookie Betts and Jackie Bradley Jr. to give the team arguably the best young outfield in the game. Getting back to the numbers, Castillo was not dominant at Triple-A last season either as he batted .282 with 3 home runs and 10 steals in 40 games. Believe it or not Castillo turns 29 in July so he is older than you think and that should somewhat cap your views on how good he can be. There is no denying the power/speed ability that is lurking under the surface but Castillo has to start quickly in 2016 or else we will start wondering if he was more hype than anything.

2016 PROJECTION: .278 12 HR 67 R 63 RBI 16 SB

46. Jorge Soler: There were immense expectations attached to top Chicago Cubs outfielder prospect Jorge Soler, with the consensus being that he would become the latest in the recent run of instant impact Cuban stars arriving into Major League Baseball. It was an understandable way of thinking as Soler has natural power that screamed out "future 25 home run slugger." Of course projections are mostly just conjecture and Soler failed to come through in 2015 as he battled serious oblique issues that limited him to just 101 games played. When in the lineup, Soler batted a listless .262 as he struck out in a crazy high 30.0 percent of his at-bats. The power was not there either, as Soler hit just 10 home runs and drove in 47. No matter how you look at his season, Soler went bust. We have seen countless cases of post-hype sleepers who figured things out eventually and we have the sneaking suspicion Soler will start realizing his vast potential in 2016. The very high K rate cools the jets just a bit on the ceiling but his power is too good to keep down for much longer.

2016 PROJECTION: .276 19 HR 74 RBI 65 R 7 SB

47. Ender Inciarte: The Arizona Diamondbacks are the envy of baseball in terms of young and impactful hitters, a group that includes the speedy Ender Inciarte. A natural leadoff man, Inciarte used his very high contact rate to hit .303 with 6 home runs and 21 stolen bases in 2015. This came on the heels of a 19-steal 2014 debut that hinted at more to come across the board. While the home runs are not going to be much of a factor here, Inciarte is already a three-category help in runs, steals, and average. Very rarely do you see a young hitter like Inciarte (turned only 25 in October) put up a 10.3 percent K rate like he did last season. That means Inciarte can hit for a good average year after year to go with potential 25-30 steal speed. The D-Backs need to clear the glut a bit in the outfield as Yasmani Tomas and David Peralta will also vie for time but Inciarte looks like a very good late round investment who can pay off nicely if he can continue to develop.

2016 PROJECTION: .310 7 HR 84 R 48 RBI 24 SB

48. Billy Burns: One theme we always harp on each fantasy baseball season is to never draft pure speed guys until the very late rounds, as new names reveal themselves each and every year. Case in point was the job Oakland A's leadoff man Billy Burns performed in his 2015 rookie season, as he grabbed hold of a daily spot in the lineup early on and proceeded to showcase classic skills from the top of the order. Burns would go on to hit .294 with 70 runs scored and 26 stolen bases for the A's, a development that squarely had him in the outfielder 3 tier. With a tiny 14.6 percent K rate, Burns works the count and gets good pitches to hit to help prop up the average. Once on base, Burns shows the aggressiveness to steal bases and 30 is very much in play for 2016. Another young player who is on the rise, Burns can be a terrific plug-and-play guy you never have to stress over.

2016 PROJECTION: .300 6 HR 53 RBI 79 R 29 SB

49. Wil Myers: In the span of just three short years, Wil Myers has gone from one of the most highly regarded power prospects in the minor leagues to someone who now just elicits a shrug in the fantasy baseball community when his name is mentioned. After a nice rookie campaign in 2013 when Myers hit 13 home runs in 373 at-bats for the Tampa Bay Rays, his 2014 season was set to be a major breakout. A serious wrist injury derailed those hopes however as Myers got into just 87 games that netted a horrid .222 average and 6 home runs. The Rays thought nothing of it to deal Myers to the San Diego Padres prior to 2015, with the latter believing they were still getting a top-end talent at a buy low rate. Much like the year before though, Myers was dogged both by more injuries and with shaky offensive numbers. Myers suffered an oblique strain that landed him on the DL and then more wrist problems undermined his second half as well. The result was a second straight dud of a season as Myers hit just .253 with 8 home runs in 253 at-bats. It appears as though Myers' swing is having an adverse effect on his wrist and that is something which has to be weighed heavily if you are thinking of making a buy low investment. Myers was used as the Padres' leadoff man last season but that is not an ideal spot for him either in terms of the power game. With that said, the home runs have not exactly flashed for Myers and the holes in his swing (21.7 percent K rate) have continued to undermine him. If it sounds like we are saying nothing but negative things about Myers, it is because he has simply been terrible over the last two seasons. We went on record last year saying Myers was overrated and that rings especially true now.

2016 PROJECTION: .259 14 HR 53 RBI 63 R 7 SB

50. Odubel Herrera: The Philadelphia Phillies opened up an outfield slot for speedy prospect Odubel Herrera last season and he kid proved to be part of the future of the team by hitting a very impressive .297 with 8 home runs and 16 stolen bases in 537 at-bats. Herrera was well off the radar both in the minors and in 2015 due to awful state of the Phillies but he is absolutely worth checking out for your outfield 3 spot due to his underrated power/speed ability. While Herrera's power potential is not nearly on par with his stolen base prowess, this is a player on the upswing who will have a guaranteed spot to continue his development in the Phillies' outfield this season. Other than the guarantee of Herrera's average dropping a bit due to an extremely high .387 BABIP, we like the direction this is going.

2016 PROJECTION: .284 10 HR 74 R 47 RBI 20 SB

51. David Peralta: The Arizona Diamondbacks have a good problem on their hands in terms of having an abundance of young and/or promising outfielders on their hands, highlighted by All-Star A.J. Pollock and supplemented by Ender Inciarte, Yasmani Tomas, and David Peralta. The late-blooming Peralta (he already turns 29 in August), started making a name for himself during an intriguing rookie campaign in 2014 when he hit 8 home runs and stole 6 bases in 348 at-bats for the team. While still not playing on an everyday basis, Peralta did even better last season when he cracked 17 home runs, stole 9 bases, and batted .312. That is a very nice set of numbers for a guy who plays half of his games in a power ballpark and the Diamondbacks will likely make it their business to get Peralta some more consistent work in 2016. While Peralta does strike out a bit (20.7 percent), he offsets that with a good 8.5 walk rate. He has also beaten the BABIP curve in both of his MLB seasons, coming in with lucky rates of .328 and .368 which means another good batting average is likely. Throw in a bit of speed and there is quite a bit to work with here. The ceiling may already be close at hand given Peralta's age but it won't cost you that much to find out since he remains off the radar.

2016 PROJECTION: .289 19 HR 83 RBI 66 R 10 SB

52. Marcell Ozuna: The Miami Marlins and young outfielder Marcell Ozuna were a strange storyline for a large chunk of the 2015 season, much to chagrin of his fantasy baseball owners. Coming off a terrific breakout 2014 campaign when Ozuna showed off his power by hitting 23 home runs and knocking in 85 runs, he proceeded to suffer from almost a complete outage in that category during the first half of the 2015 season. Things got only worse when the Marlins sent Ozuna back down to the minor leagues in July amid reports he was having some run-ins with teammates and the managerial staff. After just a 4 HR/.249 first half, Ozuna responded in the second half when he was brought back up after some humble pie in August by hitting .278 with 6 long balls. Still the bottom line numbers were shaky with a composite .259 average and just 10 home runs in 494 at-bats. Since Ozuna has zero speed, he has to hit at least 20 home runs to warrant usage in daily leagues. While his K rate improved last season, it was still on the high side at 22.3 percent and the .259 average should have even been lower due to a lucky

.320 BABIP. What made Ozuna so interesting in the first place was the upward trajectory he was showing as a power hitter but now he is pretty much back to the drawing board in terms of value.

2016 PROJECTION: .263 19 HR 74 RBI 77 R 2 SB

53. Ben Revere: Cheap speed, cheap speed, cheap speed. We have been fans of outfielder Ben Revere for a few years now as the guy always supplies some decent value despite the fact he is annually ignored at the draft table. Revere gets pigeonholed as a guy who is just a stolen base specialist but that is not the case here as he is a career .295 hitter and has gone for 71 and 84 runs scored the last two seasons. The steals are the big catch though as Revere has gone over 40 swipes twice in the last four years and he should be a given for at least another 30 in 2016. While you literally get zero power, Revere is the type of outfielder 3 who can really boost your steals category while helping in two other columns for a bargain-basement price.

2016 PROJECTION: .280 1 HR 34 RBI 83 R 33 SB

54. Avisail Garcia: The Chicago White Sox were enthusiastic about outfield prospect Avisail Garcia heading into the 2015 season, so much so that they opened up a spot for him in the everyday lineup. While still a work in progress, Garcia showed enough to have us intrigued again for the 2016 season as he hit 13 home runs and stole 7 bases in 601 at-bats. Garcia has to make inroads on his high K rate (23.5 percent) in order to improve his mediocre .257 average but the power/speed ability is very interesting in a good hitting ballpark. Not turning 25 until June, Garcia has another ceiling to tap into while carrying a decent draft price.

2016 PROJECTION: .266 15 HR 66 RBI 73 R 9 SB

55. Denard Span: Nothing went right for Denard Span in 2015, as the Washington Nats outfielder and leadoff man underwent back surgery before the season even began and then was shut down in August due to needing a hip procedure. In between Span once again showed some quietly impactful five-category skills in hitting 5 home runs, stealing 11 bases, and batting .301 in 275 plate appearances. Now 32 and facing an uncertain immediate future after the hip surgery (one of the more tougher procedures for a hitter to come back from),

Span has a lot to prove in 2016 in terms of staying healthy and showing he can still be an everyday leadoff hitter.

2016 PROJECTION: .296 7 HR 85 R 34 RBI 23 SB

56. Steven Souza: Young Tampa Bay Rays outfield prospect Steven Souza was a moderate sleeper heading into the 2015 season after an 18-home run/26-stolen base Triple-A campaign in the Washington Nationals farm system put him on the map. While we were on board, there was the not so small issue of Souza's high strikeout totals that even included the minors leagues. Well Souza lived up to his billing completely in his first full major league season, posting a 16/12 line in the home run/steals categories, while also hitting a woeful .225. Souza was downright hideous with the strikeouts, whiffing at an inexcusable 33.8 percent clip. That simply won't work as you can't take that kind of average hit no matter what Souza does in the power/speed categories. Also Souza is older than you think as he turns 27 in April so his upside is not as vast as one would imagine and we may already have seen his best.

2016 PROJECTION: .233 19 HR 56 RBI 67 R 14 SB

57. Yasmani Tomas: Sort of along the same lines of Jorge Soler with the Chicago Cubs, Cuban import Yasmani Tomas failed to come anywhere near the hype attached to his name once the Arizona Diamondbacks opened up the vault to sign him last offseason. The D-Backs foolishly tried to have Tomas work as their starting third baseman in spring training but his awful defense necessitated a move to the outfield in order to try and better hide his glove. All the defensive struggles seemed to negatively impact Tomas' work at the dish which was supposed to be his strength. As a result Arizona was forced to send Tomas to the minor leagues at the start of the season but he was brought back quickly enough in mid-April. What was really interesting is that when Tomas did return, he failed to hit for the power that was advertised. However, on the flip side Tomas also surprised by hitting .313. With a well-earned reputation for striking out, it was expected Tomas would be an initial average liability but that his power would compensate. Well nothing went according to plan for Tomas and his owners and the second half of the season was rough as well since the average sank down to a composite .273, while the power failed to materialize. Only 9 home runs in 426 at-bats while playing half your games at Chase Field is a big letdown for sure and the .273 average should have been lower due to Tomas' lucky .354 BABIP. Despite all the negatives, Tomas just turned 25 this past November which is still very young. We are willing to give him another try in 2016 now that the hype has ebbed a bit but we are not sure how legitimate the power really is.

2016 PROJECTION: .265 16 HR 59 RBI 55 R 6 SB

58. Khris Davis: Sometimes the boring veteran guy rotting on the waiver wire can help you win a league title and such a case was seen in the powerful second half of the season engineered by Milwaukee Brewers outfielder Khris Davis a year ago. Having already proven himself to be a 20-plus home run guy in 2014, Davis was largely ignored for 2015 fantasy baseball due to batting average struggles and a limited overall game based almost all on power. That became even more pronounced when Davis hit just six first half home runs last season with an ugly .245 average. Well Davis was only getting warmed up with his power stroke as he went on a big tear from July onward by hitting 21 home runs in just 233 at-bats. No doubt Davis literally provided big bang for the waiver wire bucks but that will likely be forgotten when 2016 drafts come around. Again Davis is pretty much a one-category home run guy all the way, as he has not even reached the 70-RBI mark as a pro. Also consider the fact Davis has batted just .244 and .247 the last two seasons and there is really no reason to invest in the guy again as anything but a bench power bat. Ride him when the home runs start sailing out but otherwise Davis is not going to be very useful.

2016 PROJECTION: .244 22 HR 65 RBI 57 R 5 SB

59. Carlos Beltran: It was a classic last hurrah season for New York Yankees outfielder Carlos Beltran in 2015, as the veteran proved to be arguably the team's most effective hitter during the second half of the year on his way to a 19-home run/.276 campaign for the team. This after a horrid 2014 that led many to think Beltran was finished as an everyday player. While Beltran's speed is long gone and he is taped up like a mummy, his power is holding on as he approaches 40. Now in the last year of his deal with the Yankees, Beltran has motivation to squeeze out one more deal before he goes off into retirement. Of course investing in someone at Beltran's advanced age is never a smart idea and he should really just be looked at in AL-only formats or as the fifth outfielder in mixed leagues which go that deep.

2016 PROJECTION: .266 17 HR 53 RBI 46 R 0 SB

60. Randal Grichuk: The St. Louis Cardinals are at a crossroads in their outfield as veteran Matt Holliday is looking completely washed up, while youngster Randal Grichuk is doing everything he can to warrant more playing time in 2016. A former 2009 first round pick (24th overall by the Los Angeles Angels), Grichuk did very well in his first extended major league look in 2015 by hitting 17 home runs and batting .276 in just 350 at-bats. Grichuk even ran a bit with 4 stolen bases as well. Power is where Grichuk hangs his hat though and he looks like a sure bet to reach the 20-home run mark this season with 400-plus at-bats. A 31.4 percent K rate shows that Grichuk is far from a finished product but the tools are obvious here. Bank on the St. Louis pedigree and keep a late round pick handy for the kid.

2016 PROJECTION: .266 22 HR 66 RBI 65 R 6 SB

61. Josh Reddick: Pretty much waiver wire garbage since his big but fluky 2012 breakout with the Oakland A's (32-HR/11-SB/85-RBI), Josh Reddick did a nice job salvaging his fledgling career in 2015 by hitting 20 home runs and stealing 10 bags in 582 at-bats. Perhaps most encouraging, Reddick managed to hit .272 which was a career-best number in that category. It is apparent that Reddick changed his hitting approach, knowing full well how things were starting to spiral out of control during his ugly 2013 and 2014 seasons. Pushing his K rate down to a career-best 11.2 mark allowed Reddick to make such inroads with his average in 2015 and at the same time add some home runs as well. Reddick has always had underrated speed that is capable of netting around 10 stolen bases and with the improved average, that helps place him near outfielder 3 status once again. Still just 29 in February, Reddick is an especially smart late-round investment in five outfielder formats.

2016 PROJECTION: .266 22 HR 79 RBI 65 R 9 SB

62. Cameron Maybin: Talk about better late than never. After bottoming out both in the San Diego Padres and Miami Marlins organizations, leave it to the completely rebuilding Atlanta Braves to finally unlock some of the potential in outfielder Cameron Maybin last season. Some horrific strikeout rates and complete inability to work counts doomed Maybin year after year and eventually it got to the point he was almost out of chances. The Braves gave him one last shot however and Maybin clearly took it seriously as he batted .267 with 10 home runs and 23 stolen bases. The .267 average was the highest of Maybin's career, as well as the 10 home runs. Always one who had good speed, the 23 stolen bases were about the only thing that wasn't surprising about Maybin last season. While it seems like he has been around forever, Maybin is still just going to turn 29 in April. There have been scores of post-hype sleepers such as this in the past and the value that comes with them is always a recipe for fantasy baseball success. We won't go too crazy here as Maybin has to prove 2015 was no fluke but at least he is back in the conversation as an outfielder 3. However the Braves apparently didn't believe in the emergence of Maybin since the dealt him early in the winter to the Detroit Tigers. Very telling.

2016 PROJECTION: .265 9 HR 55 RBI 63 R 20 SB

63. Jayson Werth: We have now reached the time where the Washington Nationals are going to really regret giving that ridiculous 7-year contract to Jayson Werth prior to 2011. Werth was a complete health mess in 2015, logging just 88 games with the team, his numbers tumbling everywhere. Turning 37 in May, Werth is looking totally shot, as he batted just .221 last season with 12 home runs in 378 at-bats. In addition, Werth has completely lost his speed as he stole ZERO bases; a development not surprising in the least given his age. The Nats almost have to play Werth given how much they are paying him but you don't have to do the same. Simply put, there is nothing left to give here.

2016 PROJECTION: .254 14 HR 63 R 56 RBI 1 SB

64. Marlon Byrd: The very late-career power run of Marlon Byrd continued on in 2015, despite his numbers slipping pretty much everywhere else. In a year split between the Philadelphia Phillies and San Francisco Giants, Byrd hit 23 home runs and collected 83 RBI to keep his name relevant in fantasy baseball for maybe one more season. The K Rate is starting to get a bit out of hand now as Byrd has been at 29.0 and 26.7 percent the last two years as he swings for the fences more than ever. Never one to take many walks, Byrd is really just one-dimensional in the home run category, which means he is barely making it into OF 3 territory in mixed setups. Turning 39 in August, Byrd is likely on his last legs.

2016 PROJECTION: .237 19 HR 65 RBI 55 R 1 SB

65. Melky Cabrera: We hate to put it this way but unless on the juice, Melky Cabrera is pretty much a non-entity in fantasy baseball. The latest evidence came in 2015 during his first season with the Chicago White Sox after signing on as a free agent. Cabrera was a disappointment as he hit just .273 with 12 home runs and 3 stolen bases despite being in a big offensive park. The almost complete lack of steals has now cemented the fact Cabrera can't run anymore, with just 11 total swipes over the last three years. That development also pretty much takes away any value Cabrera once had as stolen bases was one of his primary strengths during his Kansas City Royal and San Francisco Giant days. 12 home runs is decent enough but when you play half your games in that ballpark, it really is not that impressive. Turning 32 in August and with a K rate that jumped two full points last season, Cabrera is nothing but a boring bench guy at this point in his career.

2016 PROJECTION: .272 11 HR 73 RBI 65 R 4 SB

66. Anthony Gose: After stalling while trying to make his way to the majors in the Toronto Blue Jays organization, speedy outfielder Anthony Gose got a prime opportunity with the Detroit Tigers for 2015 after coming over via trade. The Tigers proceeded to throw Gose right into the leadoff spot and for awhile the kid did a terrific job scoring runs and swiping bases like a top of the order weapon should do. The long grinding season eventually took a toll but Gose did enough in hitting .254 with 73 runs scored and 23 stolen bases that he should be the favorite to serve as the team's leadoff batter again for 2016. Gose has some work to do though, particularly in the strikeout department as he whiffed at a 27.1 percent clip which no doubt will hurt the average. Another example of cheap speed, Gose can work as your outfielder 3 with some upside left to his name.

2016 PROJECTION: .265 6 HR 34 RBI 77 R 26 SB

67. Alex Guerrero: It has not been the best transition to Major League Baseball for Los Angeles Dodgers Cuban import Alex Guerrero through his first two seasons in the States. After being beaten out by Dee Gordon for the starting second base job and then sent to the minors in to begin the 2014 season, Guerrero failed to carve out a spot in the team's crowded outfield despite a torrid April at the dish when he hit 5 home runs and batted a scorching .423. With no DH at his disposal, manager Don Mattingly rotated Guerrero with fellow outfielders Yasiel Puig, Carl Crawford, Joc Pederson, and Andre Ethier. When all was said and done, the year was a big waste for Guerrero who received just 219 at-bats total. While Guerrero's home run rate was very good with 11 in such a limited amount of time at the dish, his .233 average was not so hot. Of course Guerrero deserves a bit of a break there due to the very inconsistent playing time which is extremely tough on a raw international player. With Mattingly now out of the picture, Guerrero should get his chance in 2016 under a new regime. With Crawford looking finished and Ethier on the trade block again, Guerrero should get a prime crack at a starting spot for the upcoming season. What Guerrero needs to do to help maximize that chance is cut into his high 24.8 K rate which takes a major toll on his batting average. What is not up for debate is the power, with Guerrero being very capable of hitting 25 home runs if he can scratch out a decent amount of at-bats. Perhaps most attractive of all, nobody will want Guerrero this time around after he failed to meet expectations last season. This will depress Guerrero's draft price to the point he could end up being a terrific steal. Don't forget about him.

2016 PROJECTION: .257 19 HR 65 RBI 55 R 4 SB

68. Jackie Bradley Jr.: The Boston Red Sox are clearly in rebuild mode after a very ugly 2015 last-place season but their outfield shows tremendous promise since each of the three spots is manned by a young hitter that has some solid ceiling left to their names. While Mookie Betts and to a lesser extent Rusney Castillo got most of the pub, Jackie Bradley Jr. became a bit of a forgotten man after he proved completely unready to be a major league player in 2014 amid some solid expectations. Striking out in a crazy 28.6 percent of his at-bats that led to a .198 average and just 1 home run, Bradley Jr. was sent back to Triple-A for more seasoning. He would fail to latch on for the start of 2015 as well, forced to wait his turn on the farm for another opportunity that was not guaranteed to come any time soon. Well once the Red Sox realized they were toast in terms of the division, Bradley Jr. got another chance. While the results were not mind-blowing, Bradley Jr. hit 10 home runs in just 255 at-bats but again the average was an issue at .249. Bradley Jr. still strikes out a ton as evidenced by his 27.1 percent K rate and he has not shown big aptitude in the steals department either despite some very good speed. For the power progress alone, Bradley Jr. is back on the fantasy baseball radar but we still think he is too rough around the edges to be anything but a very late round grab.

2016 PROJECTION: .255 15 HR 57 RBI 59 R 5 SB

69. Aaron Hicks: The Minnesota Twins started to finally get a return on the 2008 first round pick (14th overall) they used on speedy leadoff hitter Aaron Hicks. After toiling in the team's minor league system since 2008, Hicks began to take the shuttle back and forth between Triple-A and the big league team from 2013-14. During that time with the Twins, Hicks simply did not hit and pretty much was an afterthought when 2015 began. Some nice early work at Triple-A where he batted .342 was enough to get Hicks one last chance to show what he can do and this time he made the most of it. While the average remained a struggle at .256, Hicks was able to muscle out 7 home runs and use his speed to steal 13 bags in 390 at-bats. Alas the Twins dealt Hicks to the New York Yankees during the first installment of the Winter Meetings, placing him in a blockbuster of an offensive park. That means Hicks should get around a 2-3 home run and 7-10 RBI boost since he will be playing half his games at Yankee Stadium. Ultimately what helped Hicks last season was getting his K rate somewhat under control at 16.9 percent. Since he does draw a decent amount of walks (8.7 percent), a decent improvement in average is also very possible this season. That is especially true when you look at his unlucky .285 BABIP. Either way, Hicks should be in play as a late round stab given the improvement we saw last season and he can be boosted even higher in the rankings if the Yankees deal Brett Gardner and thus open up a starting spot for him.

2016 PROJECTION: .265 10 HR 53 RBI 63 R 19 SB

70. Jarrod Dyson: The Kansas City Royals have done nothing but praise the work of speed specialist Jarrod Dyson who has cemented his spot as a part-time player and late-inning runner for the team. When injuries strike down a starting outfield, Dyson becomes an overnight value play due to his big stolen base ability. Consider that despite not getting more than 250 at-bats each of the last three years, Dyson has stolen more than 30 bags in each. Again Dyson is a specialist all the way as he struggles in the average department in hovering around the .260 mark and he has not an ounce of power as well. Ultimately though, the stolen base ability makes him a great guy to stash on your bench when you need help in that area.

2016 PROJECTION: .257 2 HR 23 RBI 45 R 34 SB

71. Colby Rasmus: On and on the very boring and ultimately disappointing career of Colby Rasmus went in 2015. Having failed to make it as a first round pick of the St. Louis Cardinals of all teams, Rasmus has begun an odyssey that has taken him from the Toronto Blue Jays to the Houston Astros over the last few years. Always a good power hitter no matter the locale, Rasmus never figured out the strike zone or closed the massive holes in his swing as he gained more experience. While the 25 home runs he hit last season were impressive and also a career-high, they came with another ugly average of .238. Rasmus' already very high K rate has only gotten worse, topping 30 percent each of the last two years which speaks to the severe limitations here. With his once moderate speed now gone as well, Rasmus is truly just a one category home run specialist.

2016 PROJECTION: .235 22 HR 63 RBI 60 R 3 SB

72. Byron Buxton: The Minnesota Twins finally unveiled the ballyhooed prospect duo of Miguel Sano and Byron Buxton last season but the results for both were the polar opposite. While Sano excelled right out of the major league gate in showcasing his tremendous power, Buxton failed to come anywhere close to living up to his hype as arguably the top outfield prospect in all of baseball. A good deal of the blame could fall on health as Buxton has not even gotten a total of 600 at-bats the last two years combined between the minors and majors. As a result, we can give Buxton a mulligan on the ugly .209 average and 2 home runs he hit in 138 at-bats with the Twins last season. Keep in mind Buxton is only going to be 22 in December which is incredibly young for any player. While Buxton has not hit for much power since being drafted, he already is a big speed guy who is destined for 30-plus steals with the Twins before too long. A 31.9 percent K rate has to be addressed obviously and there is at least some concern that Buxton is more athlete than major league hitter. 2016 will go a long way in determining where this goes but Buxton is way too young for anyone to be concerned just yet.

2016 PROJECTION: .255 7 HR 55 RBI 73 R 23 SB

73. Michael Cuddyer: One of the first free agents to sign onto the dotted line last offseason was the New York Mets inking Michael Cuddyer to a two-year deal to help both in the outfield and at first base. Coming off a tremendous two-year run with the Colorado Rockies (which included a batting title), it was easy to see why we chose Cuddyer to be on our BUST list in last season's draft guide. What stood out the most was Cuddyer making as big a ballpark change for the worse in going from Coors Field to Citi Field. The average was obviously going to plummet, with Cuddyer also losing home runs from his already decreasing total. Well Cuddyer was even worse than what we anticipated, as he was nothing but a part-time player by the end of the 2015 season. Hitting just .259 with 10 home runs in 408 at-bats, Cuddyer also battled his usual assortment of injuries. Now a very old 37 in March, Cuddyer could have a tough time amassing even 400 at-bats this season on a Mets team that wants to get Michael Conforto into the outfield on an everyday basis in 2016.

2016 PROJECTION: .253 11 HR 53 RBI 56 R 2 SB

74. Rajai Davis: Speed-driven outfielder Rajai Davis has made a nice career for himself in the major leagues, mostly through the stolen base. Almost every year of Davis' 10-year career had him going in as a platoon or bench guy but more often than not he found his way to 400-plus at-bats. As a result Davis put up some very impressive stolen base seasons, four times going for more than 40. Unfortunately for Davis, the ride looks like it will be closing soon as he stole just 18 bags in a 2015 season where he only played in 112 games due to injury. Now 35-years-old, Davis also saw his K rate rise sharply last season, going from 2014's rate of 15.2 percent to 2015's 20.5. Will likely have to settle for another platoon situation but with eroding speed, Davis doesn't offer much help anymore.

2016 PROJECTION: .257 7 HR 44 RBI 53 R 16 SB

75. Domonic Brown: We had Brown pegged perfectly when we called out his 2013 "breakout" season for the absolute fluke it was. While Brown impressively hit 27 home runs that put himself on the fantasy baseball map, we were not believers for a number of reasons. The first was that Brown's terrible walk rates and high strikeout totals were an awful match in terms of future production. Once major league pitchers realized that Brown had virtually no patience and swung at everything, they began pitching to him much more freely. Soon the outs piled up as Brown made us look clairvoyant when he hit .235 with only 10 home runs. Just an off year after his breakout the season? Not a chance as Brown was even worse in 2015 with 5 home runs and a .228 average as he played in only 63 games. First it was a persistent Achilles tendon injury that had Brown on the DL in

April and kept him there until June 14th. Next it was a concussion suffered on September 2nd that wound up keeping Brown out for the remainder of the season. In between Brown continued to show horrific plate discipline and major holes in his swing that makes him nothing but a bench option at best in terms of fantasy baseball.

2016 PROJECTION: .239 14 HR 52 RBI 47 R 4 SB

76. Desmond Jennings: Unmet expectations are the name of the game here as Desmond Jennings simply has not developed like many in the fantasy baseball community and the Tampa Bay Rays for that matter envisioned. Compared to the Rays version of Carl Crawford in terms of possessing leadoff skills that could yield a bunch of runs and stolen bases when he first came up, Jennings instead has struggled badly in the average department and now his body is beginning to betray him. Now five full seasons into his career, Jennings has a mediocre career average of .249 and he has failed to score more than 82 runs or steal more than 20 bases since 2013. The biggest problem for Jennings is a brutal K rate which is never a good match for a leadoff hitter. With the exception of last season, Jennings's K rate has been 19 percent or higher going back to 2011 and his stolen base numbers have dropped for three straight years despite still only being 29. Jennings amassed just 97 at-bats in 2015 as a chronic knee injury plagued him most of the season and then a tooth infection finished him for good in September. Right now Jennings barely qualifies as an outfielder 3 and ideally he is more a bench option than anything.

2016 PROJECTION: .257 11 HR 52 RBI 74 R 17 SB

<u>**THE REST**</u>

77. Andre Ethier: Injuries to Yasiel Puig and Carl Crawford forced the Los Angeles Dodgers to dust off Andre Ethier to help fill the void in the team's outfield. Having been stuck with Ethier due to the foolish contract extension the Dodgers signed him to a few years ago, the veteran had his best season since 2012 as he batted .294 with 14 home runs in 445 at-bats. While he still struggles against lefties, Ethier's 16.9 percent K Rate in 2015 was his lowest since 2009 and he can still hit the baseball a long way but not as often as earlier in his career. The Dodgers will likely try to move him again during the offseason but at 34 in April, they are not likely going to have any luck moving forward. A bench bat all the way.

78. Jarrett Parker: Deep sleeper alert. The San Francisco Giants got a real talent on their hands in the form of outfielder Jarrett Parker. The team's second round pick in 2010, Parker tore up Triple-A to the tune of 20 home runs and 23 stolen bases in 504 at-bats before getting a late cup of coffee run with the Giants to close out last season. Even though Parker received just 54 at-bats with the team, he managed to hit 6 home runs and post a .347 average in that span which helped open more than a few eyes. The kid has good patience at the dish, with a walk rate habitually being in the low teens in the minors. In addition, Parker has very good speed and developing power that makes him your classic home run/stolen base asset. The big red flag comes in the strikeout department as Parker struck out at a 32.5 percent clip last season at Triple-A despite all those glowing power/speed statistics and that number climbed to 38.9 with the Giants. A very good comparison is Joc Pederson with a bit less power. That is a comparison worth checking out this drafting season but keep in mind the average is a potential problem.

79. Chris Coghlan: The Chicago Cubs got very solid part-time work from Chris Coghlan in 2015, coming just one year after the team rescued the former 2009 Rookie of the Year from premature retirement after a string of terrible seasons. While Coghlan struggled hitting for average at just .250, he was able to crack 16 home runs and steal 11 bases in just 503 at-bats. Coghlan got unlucky with a .284 BABIP though, which meant the average should have been higher as well. Despite the feeling that Coghlan has been around forever, he turns just 31 in June which means he has another few solid seasons left in the tank. Look for Coghlan to be in the ballpark of his 2015 numbers but nothing more as he is still not going to play every day for the team.

80. Kevin Kiermaier: Over the last two years, Kevin Kiermaier has hit 10 home runs and batted .263 in each of those campaigns as mediocre consistency seems to be his thing. Where Kiermaier did make improvements was in the stolen base column as he reached double digits last season with 18. Not much has been said about Kiermaier since he goes quite a bit under the radar in Tampa Bay but there are some workable tools here. The fact of the matter is that Kiermaier has shown he is an everyday player for the Rays and he has proved himself as a very good AL-only outfielder as well. In mixed leagues Kiermaier still needs to improve another level before we try him on as anything more than a stream guy on light schedule days but at least he has some ability worth checking out.

81. Delino DeShields: Proving to be a chip off the old block, Delino DeShields showed he could be every bit the stolen base weapon his father was in his first extended major league look with the Texas Rangers in 2015. Despite some ugly batting averages in the minor leagues, DeShields put himself on the fantasy baseball map when he stole 54 bags in 2014 at Double-A and it is that skill only that has him relevant going forward. DeShields batted just .261 for the Rangers last season but his 25 stolen bases and 83 runs scored in just 492 at-bats look just fine. There is some Dee Gordon (before he figured out how to hit .300-plus) value here in terms of where DeShields currently is in his development but that just puts him barely into the third outfielder realm for 2016 fantasy baseball. With no power to speak of and a batting average that could get worse instead of getting better given the 20.5 percent K rate, DeShields is just a support player at best.

82. Nori Aoki: The San Francisco Giants got more than they expected out of leadoff veteran outfielder Nori Aoki in 2015. After a rough 2014 season that called into question whether Aoki could hold down an everyday gig in the majors any longer, the Giants gave him a chance to full their ongoing leadoff void. While injuries only allowed Aoki to play in 93 games, he responded with a very solid season in hitting .287 with 5 home runs and 14 stolen bases. Of course Aoki is still chasing his 2012 rookie year that has been his best performance in Major League Baseball thus far but the guy still has something to offer those who take part in five outfielder formats and especially in NL-only setups. Aoki is no spring chicken as he turns 34 in January and the speed is declining as it should given his advancing age. However Aoki is one of the toughest guys to strike out in all of baseball (6.4 percent K rate) and that means a good average with a decent run total is almost a given.

83. Alex Rios: While the Kansas City Royals have a knack for getting something out of washed up veterans, they struck out in the case of outfielder Alex Rios last season. Looking like he is on his last legs after a solid but somewhat up-and-down career, Rios managed to bat just .255 with 4 home runs and 9 stolen bases in 411 at-bats. With his health declining as well, Rios has now hit just 8 total home runs over the last two years and his stolen bases are falling off a cliff as well. While you always wanted a bit more out of Rios, now is not the time to revisit the guy at the age of 35 and with numbers that are barely worth using in any format.

84. Coco Crisp: Long another favorite of ours due to always carrying good draft value combined with effective power/speed numbers, it looks like the end is near for veteran outfielder Coco Crisp. Now 36, Crisp may not even be an everyday starter anymore after injuries kept him out for all but 44 games last season. When on the field, Crisp was a non-factor as he batted just .175 and stole all of 2 bases. With the speed now looking shot, Crisp really has nothing left to offer any of his owners, even in AL-only formats.

85. Austin Jackson: For the second season in a row, Austin Jackson played for two different teams as he enters into the journeyman portion of his career. That is not a place where you go looking for fantasy baseball help and truth be told Jackson is the definition of a mediocre player. He never turned out anywhere near as good as some pegged him to be when Jackson first came up in the Detroit Tigers system and the big issue is the utter lack of impact numbers both in the home run and stolen base categories. Now Jackson did go 9/17 in 2015 which is nothing to scoff at but a 23.9 percent K rate and 5.5 percent walk rate show a completely unrefined hitter who won't be changing much now that he is a veteran who turns 30 in February. We'll pass.

86. Carl Crawford: The narrative has remained the same over the last four years for Los Angeles Dodgers outfielder Carl Crawford. The former first round five category dynamo is now nothing but a part-time player who is constantly injured. In addition, Crawford barely even steals bases anymore, with just 10 last season. Crawford can't hit much anymore either, with his K rate going over the 20 mark for the first time in his career in 2015 at 21.2 percent. A complete waste of roster space if you do foolishly draft the fading veteran.

87. Dalton Pompey: The Toronto Blue Jays seem to be determined to trade speedy outfield prospect Dalton Pompey, going fully in on fellow youngster Kevin Pillar instead. A speed/stolen base weapon who has a bit of pop in the Rajai Davis mold, Pillar is only interesting in five outfielder formats if he finds a starting spot somewhere.

88. Nick Markakis: We are still scratching our heads regarding the foolish free agent contract the Atlanta Braves handed Nick Markakis prior to the 2015 season for more than a few reasons. The first was that when the ink was not even dry on the deal, Markakis underwent a neck procedure. In addition, the guy is as pronounced an empty average as you can get as he hit all of 3 home runs and stole just 2 bases in his 686 at-bats last season. Unless you are Nick Markakis' mom, there is absolutely no reason at all you should go near this washed-up veteran.

89. Drew Stubbs: We are well past the curiosity stage of Drew Stubbs' career, as he has now failed to make it in two of the best offensive ballparks in the majors with the Cincinnati Reds and Colorado Rockies. Things have gotten so bad now that Stubbs spent time back at Triple-A in 2015 and then proceeded to hit a woeful .195 with the Rockies in 140 at-bats. You are simply not trying if he is on your roster.

90. Angel Pagan: Yet another aging, speed-oriented player who is facing the end of his career, the numbers are falling off the map for San Francisco Giants outfielder Angel Pagan. Always battling injuries, Pagan hit just .262 in 2015 while stealing only 12 bases in 551 at-bats. With steals being the main draw in owning Pagan in the past, the fact he is drying up in that category while also seeing his average sink due to a rising K rate (16.9 percent last season) means there is nothing left to go on here.

91. Alejandro De Aza: Talk about entering into the journeyman phase of one's career. That is the present situation for outfielder Alejandro De Aza who spent stints with three different teams in 2015, not the best sign for a guy who is going to turn just 32 in April. Despite all the movement, De Aza is still useful enough as he posted a 7/7 line in the home run/stolen base columns, while also adding a decent enough .262 average. On the flip side, De Aza has seen his K rate spike over the 20 percent mark each of the last two years and again there is no given that he has a starting spot locked up somewhere for this season. Only interesting if playing time develops but don't hold your breath there.

92. Chris Young: A former mid-level draft pick during his Arizona Diamondback days, Chris Young is now just a part-time player who is in the lineup mostly when a lefty is on the mound. Young just can't hit righties anymore and truth be told he was never so great there even in his prime. 14 home runs in just 356 at-bats for the New York Yankees last season show that Young can still drive the baseball but he has pretty much no value to you anymore.

93. Jake Marsinick: Sometimes a fluke is easy to spot such as the early first half performance of Jake Marsinick for the Houston Astros last season. Nothing but a mediocre player even in the minor leagues, Marsinick took advantage of early playing time due to George Springer going out injured to hit .379 in April with 2 home runs and 8 stolen bases. Alas Marsinick stopped catching major league pitchers off guard as the year went on and by August he was nothing but a backup for the Astros. Now 9 home runs and 24 steals in just 372 at-bats is certainly noteworthy but a .236 average and horrible 28.2 K rate reveal the fluky nature of those numbers. The Astros will be fully stocked in their outfield for 2016 and Marsinick won't be a factor until injuries strike again. Don't wait around for that to occur.

94. Juan Lagares: An early elbow injury and the eventual arrival of Yoenis Cespedes and Michael Conforto relegated Juan Lagares to a spot on the bench for the New York Mets as the 2015 season moved along. Blessed with tremendous speed and off-the-charts defensive ability, Lagares' tools have not shown themselves in the hitting numbers. The power has simply not developed yet and Lagares stealing only 7 bases in 465 at-bats last season is inexcusable considering how good he runs. Already turning 27 in March, it could very well be that this is who Lagares is and no further improvement will be made. Under that scenario, Lagares has pretty much no value even with Cespedes likely moving on in free agency.

95. David Murphy: If there were only lefties circulating major league pitching staffs, David Murphy would be a very solid fantasy baseball outfielder. Since lefties only make up a small minority of pitchers though, Murphy is just a non-story in our fake game. A part-time guy no matter where he has been, Murphy can be ignored completely.

96. Seth Smith: Sort of along the same lines of David Murphy, Seth Smith is another guy who destroys lefty pitching but is greatly exposed against a righty. If you fail to make it as an everyday guy with the Colorado Rockies like Smith was unable to do, you deserve to sit on the waiver wire for the entire season.

97. Brandon Guyer: It has taken Brandon Guyer a very long time to settle in as a major league player as he already turns 30 in January but the guy did a pretty solid job when given a chance to play in 2015. Filling in due to a slew of injuries that impacted the Tampa Bay lineup, Guyer hit .265 with 8 home runs and 10 stolen bases for the team in just 385 at-bats. Still the Rays plan on Guyer being a bench bat at best for 2016 and if you take as long as he did to make it to the majors, it reveals how there really is nothing to get overly excited about here.

98. Will Venable: The 2013 season turned out to be a very fleeting one when it came to the fantasy baseball value of Will Venable. He earned props by hitting 22 home runs and stealing 22 bases that season but the haul proved to be a gross outlier as Venable was downright brutal over the last two years. The San Diego Padres had no use for Venable from the start of the 2015 season and that didn't change much during the year as he got just 390 at-bats. Venable still can run as he stole 16 bases his 135 games but his 24.1 percent K rate and an ugly .244 batting average reveal some major shortcomings. These are shortcomings you can do without.

99. Michael Bourn: One of the more proven trends in fantasy baseball centers around guys whose games are build on speed tending to fade away much more quickly than those whose main skill is power. Michael Bourn has taken that early fade despite turning just 32 in December. The fact of the matter is that Bourn can hardly run anymore as a series of leg injuries in his late 20's stole his speed and pretty much his entire game. With no power or average ability to speak of, Bourn has been completely negated in fantasy baseball circles.

100. Franklin Gutierrez: One of the better stories in all of baseball last season was the terrific comeback made by Seattle Mariners outfielder Franklin Gutierrez. After Gutierrez was almost into retirement due to a serious illness, he proceeded to fight his way back to the Mariners during the middle of the 2015 season. What happened next was nothing short of amazing as Gutierrez hit 15 home runs in just 189 at-bats while also batting .292. Consider that during his entire previous career, Gutierrez hit more than 15 home runs only once. Gutierrez will be 33 in February and you have to wonder how much adrenaline was at work with his nice comeback last season. Ultimately in terms of fantasy baseball, Gutierrez is just a very late round grab or a waiver guy for when injuries strike.

101. Jeff Francoeur: Another out of the blue comeback story emerged in Philadelphia last season when Jeff Francoeur returned to the majors with the Phillies. One of the more popular players during his early years with the Atlanta Braves due to an extreme "swing at everything" approach, Francoeur was back at it in 2015 when he hit 13 home runs and walked in just 3.8 percent of his at-bats. Francoeur will turn only 32 in January which his amazing considering he debuted back in 2005. A fun story for sure but nothing worth talking about when we look toward 2016 fantasy baseball.

102. Melvin Upton: Even the arrival of brother Justin did nothing to shake Melvin Upton out of his insane hitting struggles in 2015 with the San Diego Padres. Now just strictly a part-time player, Upton's .259 batting average last season was actually his highest since 2008 which shows you terribly he has played. While he can still steal some bags, Upton is about as radioactive a name as one can get.

103. Ichiro Suzuki: The march toward 3,000 hits continues for first ballot Hall of Fame candidate Ichiro Suzuki. Having turned 42 in October, Ichiro is just a part-time bat on the Miami Marlins who brought him back on a one-year deal. It was shocking to see Ichiro hit just .229 last season and his steals are almost completely shot as well since he had just 11. It is not going to be a very pretty ending here.

104. Grady Sizemore: Yet another aging veteran holding on by his finger nails is former first round star Grady Sizemore. With his speed long gone due to some serious injuries over the years, Sizemore did next to nothing between two teams in 2015 when he hit six home runs and batted .253 in 296 at-bats. It is debatable regarding whether Sizemore gets another chance with a major league team.

105. Preston Tucker: Lost in the well-deserved hype of George Springer and Carlos Correa ever since 2014, the Houston Astros also got their first look at 2012 7th round pick Preston Tucker last season. After smacking 11 home runs in just 143 at-bats at Triple-A, Tucker was promoted by the Astros where he hit another 13 long balls in 98 games. A .243 average showed some limitations and truth be told Tucker never hit above .300 from Double-A on up. Still an unlucky .274 BABIP was at least partially to blame and Tucker has natural power that could get him near the 20 mark which is valuable in any format. Youth and some more upside combine to make Tucker a good late round grab.

106. Aaron Altherr: Another kid who the Philadelphia Phillies tried out late in the 2015 season was the speedy Aaron Altherr, with the team seeing enough to give the kid a chance to stake a claim to a starting outfield spot for 2016. Altherr didn't embarrass himself during his 161 at-bat trial run with the Phillies, hitting 5 home runs and stealing 6 bases with a .241 average. Yeah the average was ugly as Altherr struck out in 25.5 percent of his at-bats but the power/speed numbers were somewhat interesting. Altherr had a collective 14/16 line between Double and Triple-A last season so he has some tools to work with. The batting average won't be pretty due to all the whiffs but Altherr could be worth monitoring early on if he can land a spot on the team.

107. Shane Victorino: Say goodnight. It is time to wave goodbye as Shane Victorino goes off into the fantasy baseball sunset. A very solid and underrated player in his career, Victorino is one big health mess whose numbers are a disaster everywhere. Stop living in the past.

108. Matt Joyce: Yeah Matt Joyce is still kicking around but he received just 284 at-bats last season with the Los Angeles Angels. Known for his April and May hot streaks and then for the complete falling off that comes over the last four months of a season, Joyce is barely even a major league player at this stage of the game.

109. Josh Hamilton: It almost feels silly talking about Josh Hamilton's hitting numbers as that issue takes a back seat to his more pressing off-the-field problems. Of course we are referring to the drug relapse Hamilton prior to the start of 2015 that threatened his standing as a major league baseball player. Commissioner Rob Manfred had sympathy for Hamilton however and allowed him to serve the drug suspension concurrently while he was out with an injury. The Los Angeles Angels threw in the towel on Hamilton by trading him back to the Texas Rangers where looked like Mickey Mantle for a brief portion of his troubled career but even returning "home" didn't ignite his sliding bat. Hamilton would hit just .257 with 6 home runs and 21 RBI in 144 at-bats, going on the shelf again at the start of September due to a torn meniscus in his knee that required surgery. While it was at least a bit intriguing with Hamilton going back to Texas, he is now nothing but an aging slugger whose very high K rate indicates the holes in his swing are growing. It was a fun story a few years ago when Hamilton was hitting those tape-measure home runs with the Rangers but now the narrative has changed to a bit of a tragedy.

110. Michael Saunders: Mildly intriguing going into the 2015 season after ending up with the Toronto Blue Jays and operating in offensive haven Rogers Center, Saunders was a complete health disaster as he accrued just 9 games of useless numbers before checking out for good in August with persistent knee trouble. The 19-HR/21-SB season in 2012 is becoming more and more of a distant memory.

111. Leonys Martin: It was another season of unmet expectations from speedy outfielder Leonys Martin in 2015. After being given a golden opportunity to serve as the Texas Rangers' leadoff batter entering into the season, Martin immediately struggled with the bat to the point that he eventually was benched outright by the team. While no one ever questions Martin's speed and ability to swipe some bases, his struggles to get on base have made those skills moot. Strikeouts were the biggest issue as Martin posted an ugly 22.0 K rate, a tremendous negative for a potential leadoff hitter. In addition, Martin has next-to-no patience (posting a pathetic 5.2 BB/9 in 2015) which again makes him ill-suited for the leadoff spot. The end result was a terrible .220 batting average and only 14 stolen bases in 309 at-bats before Martin underwent surgery to remove the hamate bone in his hand which finished his season early. An offseason trade to the Seattle Mariners gives Martin a fresh start but don't hold your breath here.

112. Oswaldo Arcia: It appears as though the Minnesota Twins don't view power-hitting outfielder Oswaldo Arcia as part of their present and future plans considering they gave him only 58 at-bats with the team in 2015 despite being in the heat of a pennant race. While no one can debate the raw power Arcia has, the massive holes in his swing make him a strikeout machine that shows up in a string of ugly batting averages. Through three partial seasons with the team, Arcia is just a .243 hitter and some have questioned his work ethic as well. The cost conscious Twins could give Arcia another look in 2016 and his power could result in a very cheap 20 home runs under that scenario. We land on the side of seeing Arcia as nothing more than a waiver add when he proves he can stick with the club.

113. Brandon Barnes: About the only good thing we can say about Brandon Barnes is that he plays for the Colorado Rockies. Despite being in the offensive haven that is Coors Field, Barnes hit all of 2 home runs and batted a terrible .251 in 281 at-bats. Just a backup guy on his own team, Barnes should not be touched in fantasy baseball leagues.

UTIL/DH

1. Alex Rodriguez: Talk about being a pariah. There was not a more radioactive name both in real-life and in fantasy baseball heading into the 2015 season than New York Yankees third baseman Alex Rodriguez. Of course by now it is old news that Rodriguez was suspended for the entire 2014 season for getting caught up in and lying about his involvement with Biogenesis. With two surgical procedures on his hips already in the books and Rodriguez turning 40 during his return season in 2015, there was pretty much no reason whatsoever to invest in the guy for in terms of fantasy baseball. A crucial thing happened during the initial days of spring training however when Yankees manager Joe Girardi announced Rodriguez would be the team's everyday DH in order to preserve his body and have him focus on just hitting. While this sounded nice, Rodriguez still had to show he could hit off such a long layoff and more surgeries. Well needless to say Girardi made the right call as Rodriguez was shockingly very good in 2015, as he cracked 33 home runs and drove in 86 batters in 620 at-bats. Rodriguez was especially good during the first half of the season when he hit .278 with 18 of his home runs, with some debating whether he deserved an All-Star nod. Predictably though, the long grind of a major league season on a 40-year-old body took its toll as Rodriguez was terrible in the second half when he batted just .218 (but with a still very solid 15 home runs). Clearly fatigue was a major issue for Rodriguez as the summer moved along and that is a trend that will likely continue on into 2016 as he turns another year older. Rodriguez showed that his power swing is still in fine working order and serving as the primary DH kept him almost completely healthy as he sail past the 600 at-bat mark. No longer eligible anywhere but UTIL or DH, Rodriguez is tough to own on that limited usage alone. If you do take a very late round stab, try and cash out in July. Good luck with that though as the dye has been cast here for the fantasy baseball community to digest.

2016 PROJECTION: .248 27 HR 84 RBI 80 R 2 SB

2. Evan Gattis: One of the more talked about trades of the 2015 Hot Stove Season was the Atlanta Braves dealing away catcher/outfielder Evan Gattis to the Houston Astros, with the latter planning on operating their new acquisition as the team's everyday DH. Retaining the precious catcher eligibility for one more season at least, Gattis was all of a sudden looking like a tremendous fantasy baseball option at that always shallow position. What with playing every day at DH (which would keep his always fragile body fresh and eliminate rest off days), Gattis seemed primed for a run at 30 home runs. Well like many knee-jerk predictions, Gattis didn't go along with the plan at first. In a comically bad April debut with the Astros, Gattis picked up just 12 hits while batting .164. As a result Gattis unbelievably found his name on more than a few waiver wires. We told you all to stay with him though, understanding that there is always a bit of a learning curve for any hitter switching leagues. Well Gattis justified that faith as he then went out and cracked 9 home runs with a .276 average in May. All was well. While Gattis stayed true to his hot and cold spells, he finished with a career-high 27 home runs and 88 RBI. Manning DH also kept Gattis healthy which had been a big challenge previously. Now a veteran at the age of 29, Gattis will once again be the Astros' primary DH in 2016 which should have him in play for similar numbers to last season. No longer carrying catching eligibility is a big knock to his value however, so impressive was Gattis' power totals there. UTIL or DH-only in most setups, Gattis is not a guy you want to spend a high draft price on due to his overall limitations. While the home runs and RBI are very good, the .246 average Gattis put up last season was ugly. With a 19.7 percent K rate, Gattis is a pure slugger who will continue being a liability in average. Target more heavily in AL-only leagues but use only as a late round target in everywhere else.

2016 PROJECTION: .253 28 HR 89 RBI 65 R 2 SB

STARTING PITCHING

Draft Strategy: Despite some of the impressive breakthroughs among the hitting fraternity last season, we head into 2016 fantasy baseball firmly planted into the era of pitching dominance with no end in sight. As a result, starting pitching goes incredibly deep once again this season, to the point where you can get a solid fantasy baseball ace-level arm as late as the sixth round. Such ace starters who fell on average to the fifth round or later a year ago included Cole Hamels, Corey Kluber, Matt Harvey, Jacob DeGrom, Gerrit Cole, Jake Arrieta, Jon Lester, Jordan Zimmerman, and Sonny Gray. In addition, there annually is a batch of hurlers who are middle-to-late-round picks that make the jump to sudden ace level like 2015 cases Chris Archer, Danny Salazar, Hector Santiago, Dallas Keuchel, Jason Hammel, Shelby Miller, Noah Syndegaard, and Carlos Martinez. As a result, it would be foolish to draft a pitcher before Round 5 and ideally you can wait as late as Round 6 and still get an ace and also be able to build a potent staff. The numbers don't lie.

1. Clayton Kershaw: As if there were any doubt that Clayton Kershaw was not far and away the best starting pitcher by a mile, he went out in 2015 and added to his litany of eye-opening numbers by becoming the first hurler since Randy Johnson to strike out 300 batters (301 to be exact) in his 232.2 innings. Having already won multiple Cy Young Awards prior to turning 28, Kershaw is already opening up talk regarding being of the very best pitchers of all-time. The numbers certainly back the argument that he is as Kershaw's career ERA through 8 MLB seasons is an unbelievable 2.43 and his WHIP comes in at a puny 1.03. Even better, over the last three years Kershaw's highest ERA was the 2.13 he had in 2015. Want more? Kershaw must have been bored the first two months of last season as his April/May ERA's were 3.73 and 3.97. Including a 0.27 July mark, Kershaw's second half ERA was 1.31 with 141 K's in 109.2 innings. There is simply nothing more to say that hasn't already been talked about in terms of the pure domination of Kershaw and while we don't advise using a first round pick on a pitcher, he is the one obvious exception to the rule.

2016 PROJECTION: 19-4 2.01 ERA 0.95 WHIP 279 K

2. Max Scherzer: Having already won a Cy Young Award and established himself as a top candidate for the mantle of being the best pitcher in baseball not named

Clayton Kershaw during his stint with the Detroit Tigers, one could only shudder at the thought of how dominant Max Scherzer could be after landing in the easier National League with the Washington Nationals as a free agent for 2015. Well we got our answer in spades as Scherzer became only the fifth pitcher in Major League Baseball history to throw TWO no-hitters in one season (the second a 17-strikeout assault on the New York Mets to finish the season where he struck out 11 straight batters at one point). It really was no shock that an already excellent Scherzer recorded a career-best in ERA (2.79), WHIP (0.92), and strikeouts (276) in 228 innings. Long past early issues with elbow trouble and control issues, Scherzer is just about the toughest pitches to get a hit off of in the game. Combine that with his insane 10.86 K/9 and another career-best in control (1.34/9) and Scherzer should once again be the second pitcher off the board this season.

2016 PROJECTION: 19-9 2.84 ERA 0.99 WHIP 259 K

3. Madison Bumgarner: So much for Madison Bumgarner having a tired arm. Long a booster of Bumgarner going back to his rookie debut with the San Francisco Giants, we finally showed some hesitation when it came to his outlook for the 2015 season. The reason of course was due to the much-discussed heavy workload for Bumgarner during the Giants' Word Series Championship season in 2014. Including the playoffs, Bumgarner logged over 270 innings which brought forth legitimate concern about him feeling the effects going forward. While eventually Bumgarner will have to pay the piper for all those massive inning totals early in his career, last season was not that time as the lefty posted a sub-3.00 ERA for the third year in a row at 2.98, while also winning 18 games. In addition, Bumgarner struck out a career-high 234 batters as his K/9 IP rose to another personal best of 9.65. As hard as it may be to believe, Bumgarner is still getting better as his K rate has improved every season the last four years, while his control also came in at a career-best 1.16 in 2015. We are running out of positive adjectives to describe how dominant a pitcher Bumgarner is and the fact he is still just 26 makes it a good bet he will remain at that level for quite awhile longer. As durable an arm as there is in the game, Bumgarner's dependability at the always volatile pitching fraternity makes him arguably the best pitching buy in fantasy baseball.

2016 PROJECTION: 19-7 2.88 ERA 0.99 WHIP 239 K

4. Zack Greinke: When you are a member of a Los Angeles Dodgers pitching staff that includes the best arm on the planet in Clayton Kershaw, it can be difficult to stand out. That certainly wasn't the case though for the 2015 National League ERA leader Zack Greinke, whose 1.66 mark brought back memories of another Dodgers great Sandy Koufax. With a crazy 45.2 scoreless inning streak included in the domination, Greinke had his best season ever which includes the Cy Young award he won with the Kansas City Royals. In addition to leading the majors in ERA, Greinke also had the best hit rate in the game, with only 148 surrendered in his 222.2 innings. While Greinke's velocity has been on a two-season decline, he is racking up the K's with incredible movement on his pitches to go along with a top-notch 1.62 BB/9 rate. Having logged two straight 200-plus strikeout seasons in a row with ERA's of 2.71 and 1.66 with the Dodgers, there is no reason to think Greinke won't be a top five pitcher again in 2016. This despite the fact that at press time Greinke was a free agent after opting out of his contract. We have championed Greinke's cause more than any other publication going back a decade and we surely won't stop now.

2016 PROJECTION: 17-7 2.27 ERA 0.95 WHIP 210 K

5. David Price: It was another Cy Young-caliber season for David Price in 2015, a season that was split between the Detroit Tigers and the playoff-bound Toronto Blue Jays. Despite pitching for almost all his career in the brutal AL East, Price has been a top ten fantasy baseball ace going back to the 2010 season. We did correctly call out the 271 strikeouts Price recorded in 2014 as a clear outlier and that was proven correct last season as he punched out a still very impressive 225 in 220.1 innings. Still Price's composite 2.45 ERA was a full run better than his 3.59 mark the year prior and his 0.69 HR/9 rate was especially impressive when you consider he spent two months pitching in Rogers Center. A free agent as of press time, Price is a locked-in ace no matter where he ends up signing. If he ends up in the National League though, we could be looking at truly remarkable numbers.

2016 PROJECTION: 19-7 2.77 ERA 1.07 WHIP 205 K

6. Jake Arrieta: There is dominance and then there is what Chicago Cubs ace SP Jake Arrieta achieved in a 2015 season for the ages. Already coming off a major breakthrough campaign in 2014 when he pitched to a 2.53 ERA, 0.99 WHIP, and striking out 167 batters in 156.2 innings, Arrieta took things up another notch in 2015 as he won the NL Cy Young Award. In numbers that were Clayton Kershaw-like, Arrieta posted a 1.77 ERA, 0.86 WHIP, and struck out a staggering 236 batters in 229 innings. No matter where you looked in his statistical profile, Arrieta was off the charts. A classic late bloomer who bombed out with the Baltimore Orioles, Arrieta has taken off to dramatic heights almost from the moment he arrived with the Cubs. In what has to be considered the most awesome statistic of the 2015 season, Arrieta compiled a 0.75 ERA, 0.73 WHIP, and struck out 113 batters in his 107.2 second half innings in the heat of a pennant race. Also there was the 0.29 HR/9 rate and 9.28 K/9 to marvel at. While there may have been some slight apprehension in totally embracing Arrieta prior to 2015 coming off an unexpected breakout season, there is no doubt now that he belongs as one of the very best ace starters in fantasy baseball. Still in his prime at the age of 30, Arrieta looks here to stay as a rotation anchor for your team.

2016 PROJECTION: 17-8 2.34 ERA 1.05 WHIP 209 K

7. Gerrit Cole: Some guys are just destined for greatness, so high is the natural ability a certain player like this possesses in terms of their pitching and hitting skills. This grouping included flame-throwing Pittsburgh Pirates ace Gerrit Cole, who used the 2015 season to show just how overpowering his repertoire can be. Putting himself squarely into the Cy Young discussion, Cole posted a 19-8 record with a 2.60 ERA, 1.09 WHIP, and 202 strikeouts in 208 innings. The first pick in the 2011 draft, Cole needed the 2013 and 2014 seasons to gain control of his stuff and become more of a "pitcher" and not a "thrower." Blessed with a 100-mph fastball, Cole immediately brought forth comparisons to a young Justin Verlander. Like with Verlander early in his career, Cole fought through some shaky control issues and the tendency to throw as hard as he could on every pitch. Fast forward to 2015 and Cole spoke in spring training about how he was ready to pitch more to contact and rear back a bit on the 100-mph lasers. The results were spectacular to say the least and as a result Cole has firmly established himself as a rock solid top ten fantasy baseball ace. Digging into the numbers a bit more, Cole stayed true to his word to dial back the fastball a bit, as his K/9 IP went from 2014's mark of 9.00 to 2015's tally of 8.74. In addition, easing up on the fastball allowed Cole to control his stuff better, posting a career-best 1.90 BB/9 IP. Having posted a .304 BABIP, there is nothing fluky at all regarding Cole's 2015 campaign and he should safely be drafted as the anchor of your rotation this season.

2016 PROJECTION: 20-8 2.54 ERA 1.07 WHIP 207 K

8. Chris Sale: Ladies and gentleman we present to you the most awesome strikeout machine in fantasy baseball, Mr. Chris Sale. It was another eye-opening season for the Chicago White Sox ace in 2015, as he redefined his power pitching reputation in striking out a purely insane 274 batters in just 208.2 innings. That 11.82 K/9 is top closer territory and not something you see out of a starting pitcher across that many innings. When it comes to the art of striking guys out, there is not a better starter in the game outside of maybe Clayton Kershaw. In addition to the strikeouts, Sale is just about as tough a pitcher to get a hit off of which is why he has a career ERA of 2.91 and WHIP of 1.07. If Sale wasn't always worrying us about injuries, he would be fully deserving of being the second starter off the fantasy baseball pitching board. Injuries do have to be weighed heavily though as Sale's noted jerky delivery puts undue stress on his elbow and shoulder. Sale has had more than a few scares over the years with both joints, having spent time on the DL each year he has been a starter going back to 2011. In his defense though, Sale has been able to reach the 200-inning mark in two of the last three seasons which is a positive. There really is nothing to talk about here that we don't already know. You have to swallow a bit harder in drafting Sale than some other aces around his tier but the numbers will blow you away when he is active.

2016 PROJECTION: 14-10 2.88 ERA 1.05 WHIP 271 K

9. Corey Kluber: One of the all-time great "value" seasons in recent memory came in 2014 when a hot start to the season ended up in a Cy Young-winning campaign for the Cleveland Indians' Corey Kluber. In an incredible performance from start to finish, Kluber recorded a 2.44 ERA, 1.09 WHIP, and a monstrous 269 strikeouts in 235.2 innings. We all marveled about how Kluber seemingly came out of nowhere but the truth was that there were signs along the way in terms of his ability. For one thing, Kluber was putting up some very good K rates at the minor league level before making his way to the majors. Secondly, Kluber actually started to introduce himself to the masses in 2013 when he threw to a 3.85 ERA in 147.1 innings. It took Kluber some time to make his way to Cleveland but he is now here to stay as a top ten fantasy baseball ace. While Kluber saw his ERA jump a full run to 3.49 last season, the rest of his numbers remained dominant such as his 1.05 WHIP and 245 K's. Outside of Clayton Kershaw, Max Scherzer, and Chris Sale, there may not be a better strikeout artist in the game. Finally, the 3.49 ERA put up by Kluber in 2015 was hurt by some bad BABIP luck (.315 resulting in a FIP of 2.97) which means he was pretty much as good as he was in 2014. Clearly Kluber can be trusted as a dominant ace and he would make for a great anchor for any rotation.

2016 PROJECTION: 15-9 3.17 ERA 1.05 WHIP 240 K

10. Felix Hernandez: Houston we have a problem. Or better yet, Seattle we have a problem. Without sounding overly dramatic, the 2015 season was quite concerning from this peanut stand when it came to longtime Mariners ace Felix Hernandez. Ever since Hernandez first broke in with the Mariners as a 19-year-old in 2005, he has served as a dominant top five fantasy baseball ace for over a decade. Hernandez was your classic power pitcher from the start, showcasing a blazing 98-plus mph fastball to go with knee-buckling secondary stuff. It had appeared as though Hernandez was even getting better when he registered a career-low 2.14 ERA and a career-high 248 strikeouts in 2014. Outside of the always stellar numbers, an often overlooked aspect of Hernandez has been his extreme durability which is no small thing among the fragile pitching fraternity. As clear evidence of this, beginning in 2008 Hernandez reeled off 8 straight seasons of 200-plus innings pitched, making him as dependable a pitcher as one can get. Alas the 2015 season brought forth a whole new narrative when it came to Hernandez and a lot of it was not good. In a bit of foreshadowing on our part, we mentioned in last season's draft guide that all those years of very high inning totals would eventually have to be answered for and not in a good way like we have seen in recent examples of aces gone bad such as Matt Cain and Tim Lincecum. While both Cain and Lincecum are still quite young, both pitchers began piling up very high inning totals starting at a young age for the San Francisco Giants. As both reached closer to their 30's, injuries began to crop up and their numbers plummeted. Of course Hernandez has not undergone that dramatic a decline like his two West Coast counterparts but the signs were starting to show up last season for sure. In fact the numbers were almost all going in the wrong direction for Hernandez in 2015, starting with his 3.53 ERA that was his highest by a wide margin since 2007. Digging under the statistical hood, Hernandez' 8.52 K/9 IP was a full run lower than 2014 and his lowest since 2010. Hernandez has been leaking fastball velocity for four years and counting but up until last season it was not hurting his numbers. Unfortunately we could now be reaching that stage as opposing pitchers were able to catch up to his stuff like never before. Want more evidence? How about a 1.03 HR/9 IP, which was only the second time in Hernandez' entire career that this number has been above 1.00. The last time that occurred? Try way back in 2006. Finally, Hernandez is starting to lose control of his stuff as his 2.59 BB/9 last season was almost a full run higher from the 1.75 mark he posted in 2014. Just when you thought things couldn't be more disturbing when it came to Hernandez, he came down with a sore elbow in September that forced Seattle to shut him down early. No structural issues were found but this is a reminder of the rampant talk around baseball regarding Hernandez' jerky delivery putting stress on the joint. So as we look ahead to 2016, there is more concern then every before when it comes to investing in Hernandez. No longer do we feel 100 percent secure in thinking we will be getting ace numbers from Hernandez and again all those massive inning totals starting at a young age have brought down scores of fellow starters before. With starting pitching as deep as ever, there is no need to test fate here when it comes to using a high pick on Hernandez. Again you just can't live in the statistical past when it comes to players, no matter how big the name is. We find it hard to believe we are saying this but your best bet is to avoid Hernandez for the first time ever this season.

2016 PROJECTION: 14-10 3.22 ERA 1.11 WHIP 188 K

11. Jacob DeGrom: While there was no doubt that Matt Harvey, Noah Syndegaard, and Steven Matz were all considered top-of-the-line power pitching prospects, the same was not said about fellow New York Mets farmhand Jacob DeGrom. Originally just a ninth round pick of the team in 2009, DeGrom was underwhelming with his early minor league numbers. After missing all of the 2011 A-Ball season due to having undergone Tommy John elbow surgery, DeGrom struggled badly at Double-A (4.80 ERA) AND Triple-A (4.52 ERA) during the 2013 season. Those ugly performances included unimpressive K rates that had DeGrom on nobody's prospect radar. A funny thing happened in 2014 however, as a good start to DeGrom's season at Triple-A earned him an early promotion to serve as an extra bullpen arm in none other than the Subway Series versus the New York Yankees. In an amazing twist of fate, DeGrom instead wound up becoming an emergency starter against the Yankees that night and proceeded to pitch very well in a no-decision. The wheels were then fully put in motion with regards to DeGrom engineering one of the best out-of-nowhere debuts in recent MLB history. Pitching like an ace starter almost throughout 2014, DeGrom won the NL Rookie of the Year Award by posting a 2.69 ERA, 1.14 WHIP, and having struck out 144 batters in just 140.1 innings. Considering that DeGrom had never had a K/9 even higher than the mid-7.00 range in the minors prior to 2014, the kid was almost like a brand new pitcher once he reached the majors. Eventually it was found that DeGrom had GAINED 2-3 mph on his fastball since the surgery, helping to explain some of the boost in the K's. In addition, DeGrom refined his off-speed stuff so well that it made his fastball that much more effective. The result was a season that many, while no doubt impressed, were skeptical of as 2015 came around. While we too were a bit leery buying in fully on a shockingly good story like DeGrom had, his .297 BABIP from 2014 showed there was no luck involved. DeGrom would show that he was in fact legit and in an even more powerful way last season, improving his numbers across the board as he cemented his status as a top ten fantasy baseball starter after only two seasons. With a 2.54 ERA and 0.98 WHIP, DeGrom was unhittable at times when on the mound. In addition, he crossed the 200-K mark in 2015, striking out 205 hitters in his 195 innings. On a staff with Harvey, Syndegaard, and Matz, DeGrom was considered the best starter on the NL East-winning Mets last season. When you look at what DeGrom has done from an advanced statistics angle, his K/9 continues to improve from 2014's 9.24 to last season's 9.66. In addition, DeGrom has terrific control with a 1.79 BB/9 and he keeps the ball in park with a 0.75 HR/9. Other than some BABIP luck last season (.271=2.70 FIP), DeGrom is ready to continue on as a top fantasy baseball ace for quite awhile. Buy in completely this season.

2016 PROJECTION: 15-7 2.57 ERA 1.04 WHIP 204 K

12. Stephen Strasburg: While it ended well enough, it was a beyond rough beginning to the 2015 season for Washington Nationals ace pitcher Stephen

Strasburg. Drafted as high as the second round, Strasburg was expected to put up another monster strikeout season for his owners. Instead Strasburg was right at the top of the biggest bust lists during the first half of the season, as he went into the All-Star Break with a horrid 5.16 ERA and 1.49 WHIP. Making matters even worse, Strasburg was placed on the DL with a back/neck issue to further inflame his owners. While Strasburg was pitching badly, he also was dealing with some terrible luck with the batted ball and with his strand rate. Thus it stood to reason that when he returned to the mound, Strasburg had a good chance to return to being a top ace. That is exactly what happened as Strasburg was truly dominant from late July onward, finishing the second half with a tiny 1.90 ERA and 0.75 WHIP with a insane 92 K's in 66.2 innings. In other words, all is forgiven. With a healthy body and his BABIP moving to the norm, Strasburg was back to his old ace self starting in the summer. He also had his highest K/9 rate (10.96) since 2012 and his walk rate has been under 2.00 the last two seasons as well. While his rough delivery still makes Strasburg a big injury risk and with some velocity leaking away, Strasburg seems just as potent as ever.

2016 PROJECTION: 15-10 3.17 ERA 1.10 WHIP 202 K

13. Matt Harvey: It was full of drama but Matt Harvey came back as strong as ever from the Tommy John surgery that wiped out his entire 2014 season. The New York Mets made it a point in not allowing Harvey to come back and pitch at the end of 2014 with the idea of giving him some extra recovery months, which in turn would lessen the after-effects from the surgery. As a result when Harvey toed the rubber for the start of the 2015 season, he was right back to his pre-surgery ace form. Racking up the strikeouts in bunches with his overpowering fastball and wicked curveball, Harvey rocked a 2.71 ERA and 1.02 WHIP, striking out 188 batters in 189.1 innings. Of course this being Matt Harvey, there was a soap opera theme to his season, such as having agent Scott Boras bring up his desire for Harvey to be capped at 180 innings due to the previous Tommy John. Harvey also missed the first postseason workout as the Mets prepared for their series against the Los Angeles Dodgers which raised more than a few eyebrows. Be that as it may, all you needed to be concerned with is what Harvey does on the mound and on that front, few pitchers are better. He has yet to have an ERA over 3.00 in three MLB seasons and Harvey's K/9 has been 8.94 or better during that span as well. Ignore the off-the-field stuff and tab Harvey as your staff ace. Just be aware of the fact that the 211 innings Harvey tossed last season were the most ever for someone coming back from Tommy John. While we are not saying this means Harvey is guaranteed to get hurt, it is something to weight when thinking about making an investment with the guy.

2015 PROJECTION: 15-6 2.78 ERA 1.00 WHIP 204 K

14. Jon Lester: If the Major League Baseball Season was only five months long and did not include April, Jon Lester would be right there as one of the most dominant pitchers of his era. The jewel of the Chicago Cubs offseason overhaul, Lester continued his career-long pattern of struggling out of the gates as he posted a hideous 6.23 ERA and 1.57 WHIP last April as talk already began to percolate that he was a gigantic bust both in free agency and in fantasy baseball. We knew better however and suggested on our website almost on a daily basis in April to try and buy low on Lester given his stark career trends. With another horrific April in the bag, Lester now has a career ERA of 4.02 in that month, to go with a 1.34 WHIP in 257.2 innings. In no other month for his career does Lester come near those numbers as he gets stronger as the season goes on. That was the result yet again in 2015 as Lester's 3.59 first half ERA was dwarfed by his 3.04 mark in the second half. With it being firmly established that Lester is a monster second-half starter and somewhat of a slow starter, let's look at the numbers more closely from last season. The first thing that needs to be discussed is Lester's strikeouts. On the eve of free agency in 2014, Lester put up 220 strikeouts which were his most since 2010. We hedged a bit on buying in on that number, given the recent history and the coincidence that burst came with dollars at stake. In the end though Lester validated that 2014 mark as he put up 207 strikeouts last season. The dip Lester took in that category from 2011 through 2013 can likely be blamed on some fatigue as Lester's innings began to really pile up after starting at a very young age with the Boston Red Sox. Unlike many pitchers who begin to hemorrhage strikeouts when their arm gets worn due to heavy usage, Lester was able to rediscover those lost K's based on his last two season totals. So we can now safely predict Lester to stay at or near that range again for 2016. In addition, Lester has become so much more efficient at this stage of his career, posting personal bests in WHIP at 1.12 each of the last two seasons. Always having some control issues during his heyday with the Sox, Lester is now almost a 2.00 BB/9 IP guy which was a range he never approached just a few seasons ago. Finally, Lester remains one of the toughest pitchers to get a hit off of in all of baseball, with no letup there in 2015. So as we look to the new season, Lester can be written in ink as a fantasy baseball ace who will supply his usual haul of numbers.

2016 PROJECTION: 17-7 3.29 ERA 1.14 WHIP 201 K

15. Dallas Keuchel: While Dallas Keuchel showed himself to be a very good starting pitcher in his breakout 2014 campaign (2.93 ERA/1.18 WHIP/146 K in 200 IP), no one could have foreseen the dramatic elevation he undertook last season that earned him the American League Cy Young award. The lefty continued showcasing upper-level control (1.98 K/BB) but his new trick was a launched K rate that climbed almost two strikeouts per nine from 2014 (6.57 to last season's 8.38). With Keuchel's rubber arm piling up 232 innings as the ace of the Astros staff, the result was a monstrous 216 strikeouts that thrust him into the fantasy baseball ace class. There was no letup at all for Keuchel throughout 2015, as he dominated the New York Yankees in the Astros' wild card victory as well. Now fully into his prime at the age of 28, we have to gauge whether or not there was a bit of an outlier effect to Keuchel's 2015 season. In digging into the numbers a bit, Keuchel did have some help with the batted ball, as his .269 BABIP was on the lucky side. Both Keuchel's FIP (2.91) and XFIP (2.75) were both under 3.00 though which is a positive going forward. In addition, it is tough to bank on such a rapid K/9 increase like we saw from Keuchel last season, so it is a good idea to keep expectations in check there as well. Finally we don't ever advise jumping in heavily on career years from guys who were not considered top prospects previously. Keuchel got hit pretty hard while coming up the minor league ladder and he was just a 7th round pick in his 2009 draft class. While we have all the respect in the world for what Keuchel accomplished in 2015, we prefer placing him in the SP 2 class and not as an ace.

2016 PROJECTION: 16-8 3.10 ERA 1.06 WHIP 190 K

16. Jose Fernandez: Outside of only Clayton Kershaw, we think there is not a better pitcher in all of baseball than the Miami Marlins' Jose Fernandez. With a fastball that nearly reaches triple-digits, to off-speed stuff that defies the laws of science with its movement, Fernandez has it all. What the Cuban import did as a rookie in 2013 was one of the all-time great debuts by a starting pitcher given the fact he was only 21 (2.19 ERA/0.98 WHIP/187 K in 172.2 IP). Fernandez was unbelievably off to a better start in 2014, registering an insane 12.19 K/9 in his first 51.2 innings until disaster struck in the form of Tommy John elbow surgery. Even the biggest Miami haters had to be disappointed in seeing such a talent like Fernandez go under the knife so early in his career but the kid fought back diligently in his rehab to return for the start of July. While there were some stumbles, Fernandez quickly re-established his ace form by pitching to a 2.92 ERA in his 64.2 innings. More encouraging was the fact that Fernandez actually improved his BB/9 to a career-best 1.95 in showing none of the typical fallout from the surgery. With the K rate once again in double-digits at 10.99, Fernandez is set to be a top 5-10 starter in 2016. The sky remains the limit.

2016 PROJECTION: 12-6 2.89 ERA 1.07 WHIP 181 K

17. Chris Archer: As if we didn't already know that the Tampa Bay Rays are among the best organizations in baseball when it comes to developing power pitching prospects, the incredible career-year posted by Chris Archer in 2015 stamped that reputation firmly. From start to finish, Archer was absolutely dominant as he improved on previous weaknesses and rapidly pushed up his K/9 rate. The result was a 3.23 ERA, 1.14 WHIP, and unfathomable 252 strikeouts in just 212 innings. The strikeouts clearly stand out here as Archer's previous high was a modest 173 but there were a few factors at work that helped him make the jump well past the 200 mark. The biggest was the fact Archer improved his control from a 2014 BB/9 of 3.33 to last season's 2.80. With Archer throwing much more in the way of strikes, opposing pitchers could no longer sit back and wait for walks. In addition, Archer's batting average against went from .243 the previous season to only .220 last year. Combine the two together and you get a ridiculous 10.70 K/9, which is doubly impressive in the American League. Other than some very slight BABIP luck (.295), Archer was as potent as any pitcher in baseball. Repeating such a monster career season is foolish as 2015 was a bit in outlier territory for Archer (especially when it comes to the strikeouts) but the track record of the Rays and young pitchers make it likely he will turn in another set of numbers which mirror those of an ace.

2016 PROJECTION: 14-10 3.29 ERA 1.16 WHIP 219 K

18. Noah Syndegaard: The man New York Mets fan affectionately call "Thor" for his immense size and flowing locks, Noah Syndegaard became the latest power pitching gem to come out of the team's system. Joining Jacob DeGrom and Matt Harvey as instant high-impact starters, the 6-6 Syndegaard wound up spending most of the 2015 season in the top five in all of baseball when it came to average fastball velocity at 98.5 percent. The big return for the Mets in the R.A. Dickey deal, Syndegaard already looks like a sure-fire ace starter who will pile up an immense amount of strikeouts. Overall Syndegaard finished with a 3.24 ERA and 1.05 WHIP as he punched out 166 batters in his 150 innings, then took it a step further by excelling in the postseason. A few noticeable things stand out with Syndegaard, not the least of which is his 9.96 K/9. Perhaps even more shocking was the 1.86 BB/9 that Syndegaard achieved last season, notable because the big knock on him prior to 2015 was his control issues. There were no such problems during his rookie season with the Mets and the sky is the limit here. Syndegaard could very well turn out to be the best among the Harvey-DeGrom triumvirate and he will be more unleashed in 2016 as he moves in on 200 strikeouts. Reach as high as you can for this right-handed Randy Johnson clone.

2016 PROJECTION: 14-7 3.17 ERA 1.04 WHIP 194 K

19. Johnny Cueto: Entering into the 2015 season, few probably realized the extent of how dominant Johnny Cueto had annually been going all the way back to 2011. A universally acclaimed top pitching prospect when coming up the Cincinnati Reds system, Cueto struggled badly through his first two years in the big leagues before he began harnessing his stuff in 2010. With a fastball that reached the upper 90's, Cueto only had to learn to cut down both his walks and home runs surrendered. Well Cueto made those improvements, which as a result launched him to the stratosphere of the starting pitching fraternity. Beginning in that 2011 season, Cueto reeled off four straight years with an ERA under the 3.00 mark. We are talking Clayton Kershaw territory here in terms of that statistic, as Cueto had no extended struggles at any point during that four season range. In addition to the drastically lowered ratios, Cueto also bumped up his K rate as he struck out as many as 242 batters in 2014. This all set the stage for an interesting 2015 season since Cueto was entering into his walk year amid strong rumors he would be getting dealt. As the trade chatter emanated, Cueto was once again doing his sub-3.00 ERA thing (2.62 with the Reds) and racking up the K's (120 in

130.2 innings) before he was finally moved to the Kansas City Royals right before the July 31 deadline. While Cueto was surely improving his chances to make the postseason with the first place Royals, at the same time he was moving into the much tougher American League and their stronger lineups. In serving as a clear piece of evidence of how ratios get negatively impacted by making such a jump, Cueto struggled badly at times with the Royals as he finished the season with a very ugly 4.76 ERA and 1.45 WHIP in his two months with the team. The difference was startling when it came to Cueto's performance in the NL and the AL and that has to enter into his mind as he ponders free agency. Clearly Cueto's stuff is explosive in the National League given the excellent numbers he continually achieved with the Reds in a tough park compared to his awful stint with the Royals in the DH-league. If Cueto ends up back in the NL, continue projecting him as a low-end fantasy baseball ace. If he stays put in the AL, knock him down to SP 2 status.

2016 PROJECTION: 15-9 3.18 ERA 1.04 WHIP 185 K

20. Sonny Gray: As if there were any doubts before, Oakland A's pitcher Sonny Gray firmly established himself as one of the best ace starters in the game in 2015. Still only 26, Gray won 14 games on a terrible A's team with a 2.73 ERA and 1.08 WHIP. Now with 491 major league innings under his belt, Gray's composite ERA is 2.88 which speaks to how tremendous a pitcher he is. There are a few things to note though, starting with the fact Gray's 2013 debut K rate of 9.42 has not been approached in the two years since and in fact has dropped each season of that span (7.52 in 2014, 7.31 in 2015). We are not talking about a 200-K number 1 starter like a Gerrit Cole or a Jacob DeGrom. What Gray does do exceptionally well is yield as low a hit rate as there is in baseball. Last season alone Gray surrendered just 166 hits in his 208 innings which is pretty much as good as you can get from a starter. Alas Gray was not able to add to those 208 innings as he was shut down early with a hip injury that does not figure to be a factor in 2016. Outside of a .255 BABIP that was quite lucky, nothing about Gray's 2015 should be seen as anything but exemplary.

2016 PROJECTION: 15-7 2.97 ERA 1.10 WHIP 176 K

21. Carlos Carrasco: When you want to talk about the definition of an "electric" pitching arm, look no further than new Cleveland Indians ace Carlos Carrasco. We say new because Carrasco first burst onto the scene during the second half of the 2014 season in a classic 'light bulb going on' performance after years of underachievement. Looking nothing like a pitching bust while fighting constant injuries and posting ERA's of 4.62 and 6.75 in 2012 and 2013, the Indians didn't even know what to do with Carrasco anymore. They eventually had him begin 2014 in the bullpen, hoping there was some way to unleash his 98-mph fastball to better effect. Injuries to other members of the Cleveland rotation however forced the reinsertion of Carrasco as a starting pitcher. The rest as they say is history as Carrasco suddenly became Pedro Martinez almost overnight. In a performance that won many of his owners a league championship, Carrasco proceeded to register a ridiculous 1.72 ERA, 0.90 WHIP, and struck out 86 batters in his 78.2 second-half innings. The hype machine went right into overdrive as the offseason began and it continued on into 2015 drafts where Carrasco was a guy we all fought over to get onto our rosters. At least early on though, it looked like Carrasco was back to driving us all crazy and failing to find any sort of consistency as he posted ERA's north of 4.00 in each of the first three months of the season. While his big second half run showed Carrasco finally gaining control of his past problems with walks and the home run ball, those issues resurfaced somewhat to begin 2015 which was mainly why the ERA spiked. With three months of the same type of results, it again seemed like Carrasco was nothing but a tease. However in an almost carbon copy performance in the second half, Carrasco once again turned back into Pedro Martinez as he registered a glowing 2.99 ERA, .090 WHIP, and struck out an insane 94 batters in 75.1 innings. All was forgiven. For the season as a whole, Carrasco did a nice Chris Sale impersonation by striking out 216 batters in his 183.2 innings, which was good for a dominant 10.58 K/9 IP which bettered his 9.40 mark from 2014. What really has launched Carrasco was his vast control improvement, as his BB/9 IP has come in at a splendid 1.95 and 2.11 mark the last two seasons. Prior to that, Carrasco was a mess who went as high as 3.47. In addition, Carrasco gives up virtually no home runs at this stage, which was a struggle for him in the past. The 0.47 HR/9 from last season is as good as it can get in the AL and again points to the massive development taking place here. So with Carrasco not beating himself any longer with walks and home runs, his strikeout stuff has been that much more potent. Place Carrasco squarely into the ace tier for 2016.

2016 PROJECTION: 14-10 33.41 ERA 1.05 WHIP 226 K

22. Lance McCullers: A major reason for the Houston Astros' amazing resurgence in 2015 was the strength of the team's starting rotation. Led by AL Cy Young winner Dallas Keuchel, the back-end was solidified by top minor league pitching prospect Lance McCullers. The hard-throwing McCullers was an instant hit for the Astros after being promoted in late May, going into the All-Star Break with a 2.52 ERA, 1.10 WHIP, and 71 strikeouts in 64.1 innings. With an explosive fastball that reached near 100-mph, McCullers is all power as evidenced by the 13.50 K/9 he had in the 32 Double-A innings he pitched prior to his promotion. While McCullers ran into some trouble during the second half as fatigue became a factor when the innings piled up, he still finished the season with a terrific 3.22 ERA, 1.19 WHIP, and 129 K in 125.2 innings. While McCullers's control is not ideal yet (3.22 BB/9), his combination of heavy strikeouts and knack for keeping the ball in the park makes him a very good bet to serve as a front-of-the-rotation arm for quite awhile. The kid has future ace written all over him.

2016 PROJECTION: 15-8 3.18 ERA 1.17 WHIP 178 K

23. Yu Darvish: The first major injury of the 2015 fantasy baseball season came just days into spring training when it was revealed that Texas Rangers ace Yu Darvish would need to undergo Tommy John surgery. Darvish of course missed the entire season and now is pointing to an early 2016 return. A truly dominant strikeout machine prior to the surgery (three straight 10.00-plus K/9 seasons to begin his major league career), Darvish should be able to rediscover most of his past dominance like we have seen from Jose Fernandez and Matt Harvey in their returns. We add the caveat that Darvish brings some extra risk due to the heavy usage he endured during his tenure pitching in Japan. Keep in mind that Japanese pitchers often break down and see their numbers erode within just a few years after arriving in the States. Remember how quickly Hideo Nomo lost his stuff after his incredible debut season with the Los Angeles Dodgers? While we're not saying Darvish will follow such a path, it is something to weigh during this year's draft. Still just 29, Darvish will get help at the top of the Rangers rotation in Cole Hamels which should lessen the pressure on him to be the ace. There will be a sizable discount this time around as well, which could make Darvish a swell bargain if he returns to his old form.

2016 PROJECTION: 14-8 3.27 ERA 1.21 WHIP 188 K

24. Adam Wainwright: One guy who was prominent on our 2015 Bust list as seen in last year' guide, was St. Louis Cardinals ace starting pitcher Adam Wainwright. Alarms were blaring at the end of 2014 when Wainwright began complaining about soreness in his pitching elbow, especially when you considered his past as a Tommy John surgery victim. With Wainwright having thrown a very high amount of innings since coming back from the procedure and with his 2014 K rate dropping sharply, we advised staying clear of him going into last season for good reason. It turns out it was a torn Achilles tendon and not anything to do with the elbow that knocked Wainwright out for almost the entire 2015 season. He made his last start on April 25th and in his short time in the rotation, was very good with a 1.44 ERA and 1.01 WHIP. Despite only throwing 28 innings, Wainwright's K rate dropped again to a very mediocre 6.43. That continued the decline trend from the 7.10 in 2014, 8.16 in 2013, and 8.32 in 2012. This is a big problem as Wainwright is older than you might think at 34 and with a ton of mileage on his arm already. Those strikeouts are not coming back to past levels given his age and this will in turn make Wainwright more hittable than ever before. Throw in the injury concerns and what you have here is a clearly declining ace that is getting by now more on name value than his actual body of work.

2016 PROJECTION: 14-8 3.29 ERA 1.08 WHIP 167 K

25. Carlos Martinez: More than a curiosity going into the 2015 fantasy baseball season based on his 180-plus ADP in drafts, St. Louis Cardinals fireballer Carlos Martinez became one of the best values in the game as he put up ace-like numbers to the tune of a 3.01 ERA and 1.29 WHIP, while also striking out 184 batters in 179.2 innings. Part of the trepidation when it came to investing in Martinez prior to last season was the fact he was making the transition from being a 2014 bullpen arm to a full-time member of the Cardinals' rotation. In addition, Martinez also had some pronounced control problems, posting a very high 3.63 BB/9 a year ago. In the end though, talent won out as Martinez' power repertoire brought forth a ton of swings and misses as evidenced by his splendid 9.22 K/9 IP. Martinez is a classic ace-like pitcher already due to the strength of his near 100-mph fastball and we all know the Cardinals are one of the most accomplished teams in baseball when it comes to developing top-end prospects.

Walks were still a bit of an issue for Martinez last season as the BB/9 was still north of 3.00 at 3.16. However when you give up only 168 hits in those 179.2 innings and strike out as many guys as Martinez does, the ratios will remain attractive. The only thing that is concerning (and not mildly we might add) is the fact Martinez was shut down in late September with a strained right pitching shoulder. Martinez is already included in our "Tommy John Watch" list given his classic surgery traits of being young and a very hard-thrower and the fact his shoulder came up lame is an issue not to be ignored. He should still be more than ready to go for the start of spring training but Martinez could also be slightly overpriced given the 2015 numbers combined with the injury concerns. Be a bit wary on how much you are willing to invest.

2016 PROJECTION: 14-5 3.15 ERA 1.27 WHIP 195 K

26. Cole Hamels: Another one of our annual favorites, veteran ace lefty Cole Hamels has made good on whatever you paid for him at the draft table for almost a decade. With his annual April issues aside, Hamels has now recorded 7 straight seasons with an ERA under 4.00 (twice under 3.00) and also has posted 200-plus strikeouts four times in that span. For his career, Hamels checks in with an ERA of 3.31 to go with a 1.15 WHIP; ace numbers no matter how you slice it. The 2015 season was another good one for Hamels but a new wrinkle was added to the statistical equation. We of course are referring to Hamels being dealt to the Texas Rangers and into the dreaded American League at the July 31 trade deadline. While Citizens Bank Park was never a picnic, Hamels was still operating in the much easier National League and feasted on the weaker lineups. The move to Texas changed all that and the results from August to the end of the regular seasons reflected the move. While the ERA's were almost identical (3.64 with Philly/3.66 with Texas), Hamels' K rate dropped by a decent enough margin in moving from the NL to the AL. With no more pitchers to pad the K's, Hamels will take a hit in the overall strikeout department this season. His days of 200-plus K's could be done for now as a result of the move and the WHIP should inch up a bit as well. On the flip side, the composite 3.65 ERA Hamels put up a year ago was his worst since 2013 and prior to that 2009. That means Hamels should actually see a lower ERA this season, albeit more in the 3.40 range and no longer in the 3.20 area code now that he is no longer in the National League. With a tendency to give up home runs a decent concern in Texas, Hamels has to be downgraded a bit from his past norms. While he is still a fantasy baseball ace until proven otherwise, you want to push Hamels down around the low-end SP 1 range.

2016 PROJECTION: 15-10 3.39 ERA 1.19 WHIP 195 K

27. Jordan Zimmerman: For years in these pages, we have continually spoken about how vastly underrated Washington Nationals veteran pitcher Jordan Zimmerman has been. Overshadowed at times in his own rotation by the more heralded Stephen Strasburg, Zimmerman instead has been the more accomplished pitcher of the two over the last five years. While Zimmerman doesn't have the K rate that some other top starters have, his ratios prove he deserves mention as a number 1 starter. Coming into the 2015 season, Zimmerman had logged four straight seasons with an ERA between 3.25 and 2.66, showcasing darting movement on all his pitches that resulted in one of the lower hit rates in the game. Combined with improved control every step of the way, Zimmerman always provided major value for your draft dollars. We expected nothing but another dominant season out of Zimmerman as the 2015 season dawned, as free agency and a giant payday awaited. Unfortunately things didn't go exactly as planned. The first issue was the fact Zimmerman's velocity was down 2-3 mph during spring training. While Zimmerman brushed it off as no concern, he opened April with a 4.89 ERA as he gave up 32 hits in 27.2 innings. He soon worked through that bump in the road to post a very good May (1.91) and June (3.00) but the wheels came off again in the second half of the year (4.20). The result is that Zimmerman finished the year with his highest ever ERA (3.66), WHIP (1.20), and having lost 18 strikeouts from the season prior despite tossing 2 more innings. With free agency the way it is, expect Zimmerman to still receive a monster contract from somebody. However in projecting ahead to 2016, we do have some concerns. The first is the velocity issue and how it made Zimmerman more hittable than ever. Remember that Zimmerman already has a Tommy John surgery in his past and over the last four seasons he has logged right at or slightly more than 200 innings (not counting postseason). Another factor in the velocity drop is that Zimmerman gave up his highest home run total ever in 2015 with 24 as opposing pitchers were able to catch up with is stuff like never before. Turning only 30 in May, Zimmerman is still young enough that he can come back toward his old stellar rates this season but the concerns are legitimate. Ultimately the price is never out of whack when it comes to selecting Zimmerman in the draft but you still want to be a bit more cautious this time around.

2016 PROJECTION: 15-8 3.24 ERA 1.10 WHIP 159 K

28. Danny Salazar: I guess we were simply too early on this one. Prior to the 2014 season, we drooled all over the powerful arm of Cleveland Indians top pitching prospect Danny Salazar. Our extreme excitement over the gas-throwing youngster was echoed all across the fantasy baseball landscape, especially after Salazar opened more than a few eyes the year prior when he debuted with a 3.12 ERA and struck out 65 batters in just 52 innings. With a fastball that has reached 100-mph and with movement that defies the laws of physics, Salazar seemed like a guaranteed breakout candidate for 2014. However we once again were reminded that no young player is ever a sure thing (or even veteran for that matter) as Salazar absolutely fell on his face. While the fastball remained electric, Salazar's control was downright hideous. Things got so bad that Salazar was soon demoted back to the minor leagues in late May, the Indians unable to stomach his 5.53 ERA and 1.62 WHIP any longer. No doubt we had a bunch of egg on our faces for that one but again we were hardly alone there. After a month back on the farm, Salazar returned to the team where he began to lay the framework for his 2015 breakout. Finishing the season with a 3.50 second half ERA and 1.24 WHIP, Salazar began harnessing his pitches which in turn allowed his crackling fastball to dominate hitters. Still as the 2015 season came around, Salazar seemed a bit like old news, so great were the scars endured from those who owned him the previous year. In the latest case of a post-hype sleeper made good, Salazar began the season with a 3.32 April ERA and proceeded to reel off a ridiculous summer performance (2.65 and 2.53 ERA's in July and August) to completely restore his standing as one of the best young power pitchers in the game. Showing much better control compared to 2014, Salazar's fastball went to work in collecting 195 strikeouts in 185 innings. In addition, Salazar had one of the best hit rates in the majors, surrendering just 156 on the season. Still a pup at the age of 26, Salazar has another year or two of ceiling left to launch himself even further up the starting pitcher ladder. 200 strikeouts is a given for 2016 and a lowered composite 3.45 ERA from last season seems certain as well. This is a stock clearly on the rise and going at a rapid pace. Get on board.

2016 PROJECTION: 15-7 3.26 ERA 1.12 WHIP 205 K

29. Francisco Liriano: 2015 made it three seasons out of the last three where previously enigmatic lefty Francisco Liriano pitched like a top-of-the-rotation starter. After washing out with the Minnesota Twins and Chicago White Sox, Liriano found new life in Pittsburgh which has recently become the place where struggling pitchers go to save their careers. Having some of the worst control in all of baseball prior to his arrival there, Liriano instantly turned back the clock to his very early Minnesota days when it looked like he was headed for stardom. Over the last three seasons with the Pirates, Liriano has logged ERA's of 3.02, 3.38, and 3.38 as he was downright impossible to hit at times. With one of the very best hit rates in baseball and major strikeout stuff, all Liriano had to do was curb some of the sky-high walks rates he habitually had. While it was still not perfect, Liriano subtracted just enough there to make his other numbers jump out. Now 32-years-old, Liriano has actually entered into a phase of his career where he can be trusted for the first time as a top SP 2. With his K rate almost touching 10.00 the last two seasons and his first 200-strikeout campaign achieved, Liriano's stuff is as potent as ever. We are sold.

2016 PROJECTION: 14-11 3.31 ERA 1.23 WHIP 197 K

30. Michael Wacha: Heading into the 2015 season, the reality was that the once brightly shining prospect star of St. Louis Cardinals pitcher Michael Wacha had dimmed more than a little. After being labeled as a future staff ace in short order when he debuted in 2013, Wacha only added to the hype by registering a 2.78 ERA, 1.10 WHIP, and 9.05 K Rate that year. 2014 began promisingly as well for Wacha, as he posted sub-3.00 ERA's both in April and May. Unfortunately the good times would cease from that point on as Wacha came down with soreness in his pitching shoulder in a June start that eventually landed him on the DL for a month. Upon returning in September, Wacha got hit very hard as he continued to feel soreness in the shoulder. There was talk that surgery may have been needed but Wacha instead chose to rehab the joint. Rehabbing a shoulder is never a sure thing though and that more than anything is what made Wacha a risky investment for 2015. Wacha would ultimately get the last laugh however as he once again posted sub-3.00 ERA's both in April and May, showing the old shine on his stuff that was there prior to the shoulder problem. The good times kept rolling this time around though, with Wacha staying strong through the summer (outside of a bit of a struggle in August) as September arrived. It was at this point where fatigue became an issue for Wacha, who was in uncharted innings territory after missing such a large chunk of 2014. We are willing to give Wacha a pass on his 7.88 September ERA as he Cards shut him down early and chalk that up to predictable fatigue from someone so young going that deep into the season for the first time in their career. In looking at the big picture, there was a great deal of positives, highlighted by the composite 3.38 ERA and 17-7 record. When you dig a bit deeper, there were some issues that you should be aware of though. For one, Wacha's .272 BABIP was on the lucky side, with his 3.87 FIP ERA being more indicative of where he should have been in that category. On top of this, Wacha's 7.59 K/9 IP was the lowest of his three-year career. We could say that Wacha was pitching more to contact as he matured or we could say his past shoulder issues sapped some strength. We would lean a bit on the latter as Wacha also struggled a bit with control as evidenced by his 2.88 BB/9 IP. Control problems can be blamed on shoulder trouble so Wacha might have lost some feel there. So in essence there are still some concerns about investing in Wacha for 2016 and the safe thing to do is evaluate him on his current state instead of how he was before the shoulder began to bark. We still like the overall pitcher that Wacha remains but only as the third member of your team's rotation. Value him there and you won't get hurt.

2016: 16-8 3.26 ERA 1.20 WHIP 167 K

31. Marcus Stroman: 2015 was all set up to be a year where promising Toronto Blue Jays top pitching prospect Marcus Stroman turned into an upper-level starter. The former 2012 first round pick of the Jays supplied a lot of juice to the hype meter when he pitched to a 3.65 ERA and 1.17 WHIP as a 2014 rookie. Showing off a 95-mph fastball and a vast array of secondary pitches that made MLB personnel departments drool, Stroman went right to the top of the 2015 pitching sleeper list. One spring training base running drill later and Stroman had a torn ACL in his knee that finished his season before it had gotten a chance to start. While everyone else threw in the towel on him, Stroman refused to stop working as he spoke of making a late season comeback. Amazingly Stroman did just that, making his first start on September 12th when he got the win over the Boston Red Sox. While the Jays handled Stroman with kid gloves in his four starts prior to his usage in the postseason, he dazzled again with a 1.67 ERA and 0.96 WHIP in 27 innings. It is all systems a go for this Roy Oswalt clone (both in size and stuff) and we once again are pushing Stroman very hard as a top sleeper candidate. Yes the AL East and calling Rogers Center home are big red flags but Stroman has shown no difficulty thus far navigating those minefields. Be aggressive with the kid.

2016 PROJECTION: 14-9 3.34 ERA 1.12 WHIP 167 K

32. Jake Odorizzi: When it comes to developing young power pitchers, the Tampa Bay Rays are almost without peer. From David Price to Chris Archer to now Jake Odorizzi, the Rays have it covered when it comes to developing strikeouts artists. As far as Odorizzi is concerned, he took another firm step forward in 2015, lowering his ERA to 3.35 and logging a very good 1.15 WHIP in his 169.1 innings. While Odorizzi dealt with some nagging injuries at times, his K rate remained good at 7.97, while his control improved noticeably. Getting back to the K rate, Odorizzi seemed to make the concession in giving up some strikeouts for better control and a lower hit rate, a clear indication of maturity. He could still be on an innings limit for another season but Odorizzi looks primed for yet another step forward in 2016. Getting close to front-of-the-rotation status.

2016 PROJECTION: 10-10 3.30 ERA 1.14 WHIP 167 K

33. Marco Estrada: Some guys just buck all the trends and common reason; with one such case being perennial tease Marco Estrada. A very intriguing sleeper candidate the last few seasons due to some very good strikeout stuff, a low hit rate, and impeccable control, what held Estrada back on a yearly basis was the fact he gave up home runs in bunches. While Estrada pitched decently in 2012 and 2013 for the Milwaukee Brewers, most ran out of patience waiting for him to finally figure things out in an ugly 2014 campaign that helped get him traded to the Blue Jays that winter. Moving from the National League to the American League is always a big negative for any pitcher but that is doubly true when the division is the AL East and the home ballpark is Rogers Center in Toronto. Despite all those negatives, Estrada finally did figure out how to curb his home run habit, moving his HR/9 from 2014's 1.73 to last season's 1.19. That helped Estrada post another useful ERA of 3.13 ERA, which was especially glowing considering his new environment. Alas there was a lot of mirage when it came to Estrada's pitching line. For one thing, Estrada had about as much luck as any starter in all of baseball as shown in his .212 BABIP. That mark is so much in the lucky range that Estrada's FIP was 4.40 and his XFIP an astronomical 4.93. With a K/9 that sank to a career-low 6.51 in 2015, the stage is set for a very ugly 2016 season if the luck normalizes. Once again we will advise you to stay far away from Estrada this season, so loud are the warning sirens emanating around him. Let the guy be someone else's problem.

2016 PROJECTION: 14-10 3.78 ERA 1.08 WHIP 156 K

34. James Shields: By the end of the 2014 season, we were sounding the alarms on veteran workhorse pitcher James Shields. While in the past we were always big fans of Shields due to his high strikeout totals and very solid ratios, we became very alarmed by the numbers by the end of 2014. While his 3.21 ERA and 1.18 WHIP were still impressive, the advanced statistics told a different story. For the third straight season, Shield's K/9 dropped, while his batting average against rose for the fourth straight year. With a string of 8 straight 200-plus inning seasons in the rearview mirror, there was genuine worry that all that wear and tear on Shields' arm were beginning to sap some juice from his pitches. Signing as a free agent with the San Diego Padres prior to last season restored some of the appeal of Shields however, for the obvious benefits of moving from the AL to the NL where he could ward off some of the erosion by facing weaker lineups. Shields predictably bumped up his strikeouts, passing the 200-K mark for the first time since 2012 with 216. Still the red flags remain as Shields saw a tremendous rise in his home run rate despite playing half his games in Petco Park and again pitching in the weaker National League. Compared to his 0.91 HR/9 in 2014, Shields somehow allowed that number to skyrocket to 1.47 as he surrendered 33 bombs. The resulting 3.91 ERA was a big letdown, as was the 1.33 WHIP which is simply unacceptable in the National League. Things got so disturbing that the Padres were already offering up Shields for trade last July despite not even being a full season into his four-year deal. At the age of 34 and with insane mileage on his arm, the fantasy baseball community needs to cash out on the aging veteran.

2016 PROJECTION: 12-14 3.97 ERA 1.27 WHIP 188 K

35. Hisashi Iwakuma: Another veteran starting pitcher who deserves to be included near the top of the All-Underappreciated Team is the ageless Hisashi Iwakuma. Ever since Iwakuma came over from Japan for the 2012 season, he has performed like a front-of-the-rotation arm all four years he has been in the States. Iwakuma's season ERA's during that span have read as the following: 3.16, 2.66, 3.52, and 3.54. That makes Iwakuma's career ERA a stellar 3.16 and his WHIP is just as impressive at 1.08. Needless to say, those look like near-ace numbers to us. While Iwakuma's ERA has jumped a bit the last two years as he reached his mid-30's, the veteran continues to offer tremendous value at the draft table. With the numbers annually pointing Iwakuma toward being an SP 2/3, he has often been drafted at the rate of a 4 which makes the payoff sizable. The 2015 season was not without its challenges though as Iwakuma had a difficult first half that included a DL stint for a strained lat muscle and a first half ERA of 5.22 that led many to believe he was declining badly right before our eyes due to age. Well Iwakuma came back from the DL refreshed in July and proceeded to pitch like a low-end ace the rest of the way with a 3.05 ERA and 1.02 WHIP. Even more impressive is that Iwakuma began to pile up strikeouts during that time frame, recording 91 in his 100.1 second half innings. That performance shows Iwakuma is far from being finished despite the fact he will turn 35 in April. Iwakuma has kept his K/9 in the mid-7.00 range throughout his 4-season MLB stay and outside from an increase in home runs allowed, his other ratios have been right in line with his norms. We will gladly take Iwakuma as our SP 4 any day of the week but keep a watch on him during free agency. If Iwakuma signs on with a National League team, bump him up even more. Moving to an offensive park in the American League though will require a downgrade.

2016 PROJECTION: 14-10 3.50 ERA 1.07 WHIP 150 K

36. Tyson Ross: The development of Tyson Ross as an upper-level starting pitcher continued in 2015 for the San Diego Padres, albeit one that took a step back from his 2014 breakout. After shocking even his most ardent supporters by pitching to a splendid 2.81 ERA and 195 strikeouts in 195.2 innings, Ross seemed on the verge of ace status for the Padres. Unfortunately Ross lost the battle with his control in 2015, walking 84 batters in his 196 innings for a horrible 3.86 BB/9 rate. Be that as it may, Ross still recorded his first 200 K season with 212 strikeouts as his 98-mph fastball tied up more than a few batters. Ross' power arsenal has proven to be very potent the last two years and his 3.26 ERA last season should have even been better due to some poor BABIP (.320) luck. If Ross can knock off about 10-15 walks from his ledger in 2016, he could easily achieve ace-level status with his high K rate and low hit rate. The tools are all there but it is up to Ross to take that next step.

2016 PROJECTION: 12-10 3.17 ERA 1.28 WHIP 210 K

37. Gio Gonzalez: Other than a spike in the WHIP department, it was a typical SP 3 season for Washington Nationals veteran lefty Gio Gonzalez. A better pitcher than he is given credit for, Gonzalez has now logged six straight seasons with a sub-4.00 ERA (with four of them coming with under 3.40). Gonzalez has proven to be a very imposing challenge in terms of yielding hits, as his fastball touches the upper 90's and is complemented by great movement on his off-speed stuff. That movement though gets Gonzalez in trouble with the walks and that has been a career-long problem for him. Putting this into some ugly perspective, Gonzalez has never bad a BB/9 under 3.18 in his career and it has gone as high as 4.13 in a season where he threw for more than 150 innings. Thus while Gonzalez has generated very tidy ERA's as a major leaguer, his WHIP has been another story as his career mark there is an ugly 1.32. 2015 saw one of Gonzalez' worst numbers in that category as he came in with a 1.42 mark, his highest since his rookie season. The 3.79 ERA was also the highest among his six-year streak of having that number under 4.00 but Gonzalez also had some rough luck with the BABIP (.341), one of the highest numbers there in all of baseball. With a FIP of 3.09 and an XFIP of 3.59, Gonzalez was the same pitcher in 2015 that he always has been but with some bad luck thrown in. Finally, Gonzalez has proven to be a very underrated strikeout pitcher, punching out as many as 207 batters in a season. His K/9 has generally always been in the 8.50-9.50 range and that should continue for a bit longer. Other than a recent run where Gonzalez has had trouble pitching in the first two months of the season, his baseline numbers have been pretty steady in his very solid career.

2016 PROJECTION: 14-8 3.49 ERA 1.26 WHIP 177 K

38. Garrett Richards: We were big boosters of Los Angeles Angels hard-throwing righty Garrett Richards entering into the 2015 season, despite the fact he would begin the year on the DL while continuing to recover from the gruesome torn patellar in his left knee suffered last August. With Richards receiving nothing but positive reports during his ahead of schedule recovery, we saw a prime buying opportunity to snag an ace pitcher for a downgraded rate. With the knee injury getting so much of the focus, it was easy to forget the tremendous breakout campaign Richards was engineering prior to that unfortunate incident after a few years of unmet expectations. Finally discovering how to gather a high number of strikeouts with his 98-mph fastball, Richards almost overnight became an ace-quality starter in 2014 as he pitched to a 2.61 ERA and 1.04 WHIP, while also striking out 164 batters in 168.2 innings. Richards would make his 2015 debut on April 19th and proceeded to put together a good but not great season by his 2014 standards. While Richards finished with a solid 3.62 ERA and 1.24 WHIP, both numbers were up more than a little from the year prior. It is not like we can blame fatigue or having a tough time getting a feel for pitches since Richards' injury had nothing to do with his arm. As a result, we might have to look at Richards' 2014 campaign as a bit of an outlier, which makes sense considering how that season was far and away his best ever. A lucky .273 BABIP adds credence to this thought as well. Whereas we were possibly jumping the gun calling Richards an ace pitcher off his 2014, we now should place him more firmly in the low-end SP 2 of solid SP 3 region. The price is never very high here given the lack of a track record and that means Richards is shaping up as a good buy once again.

2016 PROJECTION: 14-10 3.48 ERA 1.19 WHIP 178 K

39. Scott Kazmir: The mid-career renaissance continued for veteran pitcher Scott Kazmir in 2015, as the former Long Island Duck of the Independent League pitched at an ace-level for most of the season. Now 32-years-old, Kazmir has proven that his 2013 comeback from the nether regions of baseball was legit. What got Kazmir forced out of the majors back in 2011 was a fastball that was leaking major mileage, with his K rate sinking all the way to a below-average 5.58 with the Los Angeles Angels. Kazmir went back to work though and perfected a new release that added back the lost mileage which he showed in his eye-opening return to the majors with the Cleveland Indians (9.23 K/9 IP). A 3.35 ERA with the Oakland A's the next season stamped Kazmir as more than a simple flash in the returning pan. With Kazmir re-established to his past Tampa Bay Rays days, the scouting report could be dusted off in terms of his tendencies. For Kazmir, that means a finite amount of excellent pitching before the innings start to pile up and the fatigue sets in. Standing only at a slight 6-0 and 180 pounds, the toll of pitching a major league season usually begins showing up with some rough outings in August and goes into September. That is if Kazmir doesn't come down with injury which has been another constant in his career given his lack of bulk and the stress pitching causes on his body. Both issues were at play in 2015 as Kazmir was once again excellent when on the mound (2.49 ERA/1.12 WHIP the first half of the season) but he also came down with left shoulder tightness that cost him a couple of starts. The slight interruption to his season held off the second half fade somewhat but Kazmir's August (3.94 ERA/1.25 WHIP) and especially September (6.52 ERA/1.79 WHIP) were quite ugly as the trend held true yet again. Yes Kazmir was traded into a more offensive park with the Astros in Houston at the July 31 deadline but no matter the locale, the lefty is a major SELL in July when his value is at its highest. Along the same ways we used to handle Dan Haren and his inevitable second-half slides, Kazmir needs to be owned for just the first four months of the season before you cut him loose to someone else.

2016 PROJECTION: 14-10 3.33 ERA 1.22 WHIP 151 K

40. Jason Hammel: You can go home again. While fellow Chicago Cubs rotation member Jake Arrieta got most of the hype (and deservedly so) going back to the 2014 season, veteran starter Jason Hammel also turned out to be quite a pickup for GM Theo Epstein. After years of injuries and lackluster pitching while making his way through Tampa Bay, Baltimore, and Colorado, Hammel saw the proverbial light switch go on with the Cubs during the first half of 2014 when he pitched like a top-of-the-rotation starter in compiling a 2.98 ERA, 1.02 WHIP, and exploding his K rate by punching out 104 batters in 108.2 innings. Alas the Cubs were not completely sold as they dealt Hammel and fellow starter Jeff Samardzjia to the Oakland A's at the July 31 deadline for top shortstop prospect Addison Russell. From there the stark difference in pitching for the National League and the American League came into focus as Hammel began struggling right away with the A's and never really found a groove as his ERA shot up to 4.26 out West. Upon reaching free agency at the end of the season, Hammel quickly realized his best bet to rediscover what was working so well for him the first half of 2014 was to go back to where it all unfolded with the Cubs. So when the 2015 season got underway, Hammel once again became a first half pitching monster as he put up a

2.85 ERA, 0.95 WHIP, and struck out 105 batters in 103.2 IP. The bottom would fall out for the second season in a row however, as Hammel limped home in the second half with a ghastly 5.10 ERA and 1.49 WHIP. With Hammel pitching so poorly after the All-Star Break two years running, we now have to consider the fact he wears down as the season goes along a la Scott Kazmir or Dan Haren back in his ace heyday. The evidence is pretty telling there and so if you own shares in Hammel next season, prepare yourself to move him sometime in late June. Now as far as the advanced numbers are concerned, a major part of Hammel's success is his incredible control (2.11 BB/9) which when combined with his mid-career strikeout boost (9.07 K.9) make him quite a chore for opposing hitters. No doubt finally operating in the National League and in a non-Coors Field park helped Hammel unleash those strikeouts and at 33 he has another year or two of pitching at this level before he declines. We don't like investing in sharp first half/second half guys like Hammel due to the pressure of trying to move him when others in your league might be aware of the sane trends but there is no doubt Hammel can be a big help for at least three months of the season before the fatigue becomes an issue.

2016 PROJECTION: 14-10 3.61 1.15 WHIP 170 K

41. Steven Matz: The never-ending conveyer belt of New York Met power pitchers being churned out of the team's farm system didn't let up one bit in 2015 as Steve Matz joined the fun with Jacob DeGrom, Matt Harvey, and Noah Syndegaard starring last June 28th. What a debut it was as Matz gave up just two runs in 7.2 innings for the win, while also going 3/3 at the dish with 4 RBI. The power lefty came into his Mets debut with insane numbers at Triple-A Las Vegas, which has the similar offensive and thin air dimensions of Coors Field in Colorado. In his 90.1 innings in Las Vegas, Matz registered a 2.19 ERA while striking out 94 batters. Needless to say Matz was ready to move to the big leagues as the hype machine grew. Unfortunately Met fans were not able to get a decent dose of Matz as he was only able to throw 35.2 innings for the team due to a series of injuries ranging from a torn lat muscle in his side, to stiffness in the same area a month later that threatened his postseason. As great as Matz' stuff is, the injuries are more than a minor annoyance for a guy who already has had Tommy John elbow surgery. Some have pointed out that Matz' delivery needs work and that his lack of an easy throwing motion is what is causing all the injuries. This is something to be keenly aware of when investing in Matz for 2016 as the risk is high for more injuries given what we have seen thus far in his young career. We would advise not getting into any bidding war for Matz on that risk alone, despite the temptation to invest in an ace-level starter that he has the potential to be.

2016 PROJECTION: 12-8 3.15 ERA 1.21 WHIP 159 K

42. Shelby Miller: It was a strange season for new Atlanta Braves SP Shelby Miller right from the start of 2015 and all the way through its completion. He began the season as hot as any pitcher in baseball, logging an ERA of 2.17 and a ridiculous 0.95 WHIP in April/May. In the process, Miller made the St. Louis Cardinals look very bad in dealing him away to the Braves for outfielder Jason Heyward. The Cardinals pretty much gave up on Miller after a down 2014, as struggles with control and home runs the first half of that season overshadowed a strong finish. Be that as it may, the Braves looked like geniuses for buying low on Miller and the hard-throwing righty was back on track as a top young pitcher. As Miller went into the break with a 2.38 ERA, it was easy to understand that a bit of a correction could be coming during the second half as he was pitching a bit over his head and also was benefitting from some generous BABIP luck. Thus it was no shock when Miller's ERA was a more shaky 3.83 in the second half but his overall 3.02 mark was still tremendous. What also changed for the better for Miller was that he was able to cut his BB/9 by a half run and his HR/9 followed a similar path. Somehow though, Miller's record was a horrific 6-17 as he got virtually no run support. The Braves were one of the worst teams in baseball for most of 2015 and that was the main determinant when it came to his lack of wins. Ignore Miller's record as we have gone on many tangents about how the "Wins" statistic is a joke in fantasy baseball due to the high luck factor. Instead push Miller's ERA up to the 3.30-3.50 range this season and go from there when evaluating an investment.

2016 PROJECTION: 11-10 3.34 ERA 1.24 WHIP 155 K

43. Kyle Hendricks: While not on the level of Jon Lester or Jake Arrieta, the Chicago Cubs have gotten a nice back-end boost to their rotation from former Texas Rangers property Kyle Hendricks. The righty made his 80.1 inning debut with the Cubs in 2014 where he opened more than a few eyes by posting a 2.46 ERA and 1.08 WHIP. Despite the nice initial numbers, there was a bit of hesitation by the Cubs to proclaim Hendricks a firm member of the rotation for 2015 due to his ugly 5.27 K/9 and lucky .271 BABIP. However all Hendricks did was go out last season and prove he was legit, raising his K/9 to an above-average 8.35 and fighting though uncharted innings territory to post a solid 3.95 ERA and 1.16 WHIP. While nothing jumps out at you regarding Hendricks, his advanced numbers paint a picture of a guy who doesn't beat himself with walks (2.15 BB/9) or home runs (0.85 HR/9). Investing in guys who are pluses in both those categories is always a good move since it usually is a precursor to tidy ratios like we have seen out of Hendricks thus far. A very good SP 5 right now, there is still some more room for improvement as Hendricks is just 26. Reaching SP 4 status is very possible this season.

2016 PROJECTION: 14-10 3.85 ERA 1.15 WHIP 174 K

44. Justin Verlander: There was not a pitcher we shredded more in these pages a year ago and pretty much nonstop going back to 2013 than Detroit Tigers former Cy Young winner Justin Verlander. With his velocity slipping noticeably starting in 2013 due to some incredible workloads throughout his career, Verlander was arguably the worst pitcher in baseball when you factor in salary in 2014 when he recorded a 4.54 ERA and 1.40 WHIP. With the drop in velocity came a sizable decrease in strikeouts as well, with Verlander going from an 8.95 K/9 in 2013 to just 6.06 in 2014. Yes there was an unlucky .317 BABIP that helped raise the ERA higher than it should have been but we still strongly advised not to get involved with Verlander under any scenario heading into last season. Well Verlander wasted little time making our point as he began the year on the disabled list with a triceps strain and he wouldn't return from the ailment until June. After all that waiting, Verlander's owners were greeted with a 5.09 ERA in June and a 4.73 mark in August. With disaster enveloping Verlander for a second consecutive season, a funny thing happened. After fighting the obvious erosion of his stuff and continuing to rely on a fading fastball, Verlander began to use more on his secondary pitches late in the summer as a concession to his advancing age. The results were immediate as he finished out the year with a 1.50 ERA in August and a 3.27 September to salvage things. Verlander would finish with an impressive 3.38 ERA considering how bad things were early on but all was not as it seemed. For one thing, Verlander's FIP (3.49) and XFIP (4.15) were more indicative of what his numbers should have been in that category if he had not received such a lucky .267 BABIP. Also, Verlander's 7.63 K/9, while an improvement on 2014, was still down more than a bit from his dominant heyday. Throw in increased susceptibility to injury and Verlander looks just as risky as he did prior to 2014. In the National League maybe we would take a shot and hope Verlander could keep up his transition to being more of a pitch-to-contact artist but in the American League we will pass.

2016 PROJECTION: 12-9 3.84 ERA 1.17 WHIP 175 K

45. Michael Pineda: The roller coaster ride that comes with owning enigmatic New York Yankees starting pitcher Michael Pineda continued on in 2015, as the hard-throwing righty mixed a bunch of good with some very ugly bad. The biggest positive of course was the fact Pineda is now two seasons removed from missing two years of action with serious shoulder trouble. Having thrown his second-highest inning total (160.2) a year ago, Pineda's final 4.37 ERA left a lot to be desired. While the ERA turned out to be a bit shaky, Pineda was actually very good early on in the season, highlighted by a 16-K monster gem on May 10th against Baltimore that lowered his ERA to 2.72. Whether Pineda was adversely impacted by such an intense outing, there was no doubt he was much more hittable from that point on. Mixing in another DL stint (this time for the very scary forearm tightness), Pineda was beyond brutal in the second half as he pitched to nearly a 6.00 ERA (5.80). No doubt some of the blame for the latter had to do with Pineda reaching such a personal high in innings, as fatigue caused his pitches to stay up in the zone. Pineda should have a bit more endurance for 2016 but he remains a big an injury risk. However there are also some big-time positives here, namely a K/BB ratio that was phenomenal last season. With one of the best BB/9 rates in the majors at 1.18, Pineda's 8.74 K/9 put him in line to dominate any one start. In addition, Pineda actually pitched better than his 4.37 ERA indicated due to a very unlucky .332 BABIP. That very high number resulted in a FIP of 3.34 and an XFIP of 2.95. Those are excellent ratios and it shows you how good Pineda is underneath all the fatigue and poor luck. Anyone with the kind of power arm and swell control that Pineda possesses is destined for big things, especially in the first half of a season. Still you always have to tread carefully here with the injury risk as Pineda is almost guaranteed to go on the DL at least once. That needs to be factored in any draft price you pay but ultimately you can safely pencil Pineda in as a top SP 4 who has the ability to be a terrific 3 if things break right.

206 PROJECTION: 14-8 3.56 ERA 1.21 WHIP 167 K

46. Yordano Ventura: It was another good but not great season from the powerful arm of the Kansas City Royals' Yordano Ventura. After lighting up spring training in 2014 with his near-100 mph fastball, Ventura claimed a rotation spot right from the get-go. The result was a very impressive rookie campaign highlighted by a 3.20 ERA and 14 wins. While those numbers seemed to suggest Ventura was on his way to possible stardom, his 1.30 WHIP, very poor control (3.39 BB/9) and slight frame that made him at risk for injury muddled the outlook. Also for as hard as Ventura threw (top five in baseball in 2014 when it came to average fastball velocity), the kid only struck out batters at a 7.82 rate as his heater came in somewhat straight. Fast forward to 2015 and while there was still decent interest in Ventura, the hype had calmed down more than a bit. And for the second season in a row, Ventura was a bit of a letdown as his ERA shot up more than a little to 4.08 and the control was lacking quite a bit (3.20 BB9/) that contributed to a second straight ugly 1.30 WHIP. The problem with Ventura seems to be that while he throws very hard, he can't control his pitches. He has yet to make the transition from being a "thrower" to a "pitcher" and until that happens, Ventura will continue to be far from a sure thing. In addition, Ventura has had a few elbow scares going back to 2014, as his small and slight 6-0/180 frame combined with the high velocity makes him the classic Tommy John surgery candidate. Yes there is still a bit of ceiling left with Ventura as he turns only 25 in June but there are quite a few question marks that make him ideally your SP 4 and nothing else until we see improvement.

2016 PROJECTION: 14-8 3.79 ERA 1.29 WHIP 158 K

47. Masahiro Tanaka: There may not have been a more polarizing pitcher in all of baseball during 2015 fantasy baseball drafts than New York Yankees ace Masahiro Tanaka. Choosing to rehab a partially torn UCL in his elbow that ruined the second half of his 2014 debut with the Yankees instead of undergoing Tommy John surgery, Tanaka was right at the top of the list of the biggest injury risks for 2015. After all Tanaka's elbow could possibly blow out with any one pitch and after he got hit hard in his brief return to starting last September, the best advice was to let him be somebody else's problem. Well for those who did cross their fingers and hope for the best in selecting Tanaka, overall they had to be pleased with what they got.   While Tanaka did fight through numerous injury interruptions, he managed to throw 154 innings where he registered a 3.51 ERA, 0.99 WHIP, and struck out 139 batters. Of course those numbers pale in comparison to Tanaka's pre-elbow form with the Yankees in 2014, when his electric fastball and four-pitch arsenal brought forth a sterling 2.51 ERA and 135 K's in 129.1 innings. When you compare the two campaigns, a few things are easy to spot and shows clearly that the UCL tear is having a negative impact on Tanaka's numbers. The biggest issue is the drop in velocity and in turn Tanaka's K rate. Tanaka was down around 2-mph on his fastball from the season prior, also choosing to throw his two-seamer instead of the more stressful four. The drop in K rate from 2014 (9.31) to 2015 (8.12) was even more vivid. And with the diminished velocity came a big increase in home runs given up by Tanaka. In fact the gopher ball became a major issue at times as more than a few of his starts were destroyed by a number of flat pitches that went over the wall. After a 0.99 HR/9 IP as a rookie, Tanaka sailed up to a very ugly 1.46 mark in 2015, which contributed heavily to the jump in ERA. Perhaps the most disturbing number of all was the .242 BABIP Tanaka had last season. That very lucky number means that Tanaka should have ended up being much WORSE when it came to his ERA. Thus while the surface 3.51 ERA was decent, Tanaka was quite shaky when you dissect all of the relevant advanced numbers. So as we look ahead to the 2016 season, we once again will tell you to avoid Tanaka unless you can snag him at least as an SP 3. The threat of injury on any one pitch remains and the DL stint Tanaka had last year due to forearm pain (a usual precursor to Tommy John) is more evidence of how this could go very bad at a moment's notice.

2016 PROJECTION: 12-7 3.61 ERA 1.08 WHIP 165 K

48. Jeff Samardzjia: It was a horror show of a season for former ace starter Jeff Samardzjia in 2015 as he endured a brutal beating to the tune of a 4.96 ERA while a full-time member of the American League with the Chicago White Sox. With Samardzjia having lost some velocity over the last year, his much more hittable pitches began sailing over the outfield wall at a high rate as evidenced by his very high 1.22 HR/9 rate. Another result of the drop in velocity was Samardzjia fighting his stuff more as the walks began to pile up. A free agent as of press time, it is important for Samardzjia to go back to the National League so that he can rediscover some of his lost numbers. While his days of striking out 200 guys could be finished due to the dip in velocity, Samardzjia could still be a very good SP 3 if he ends up in a good pitching ballpark. Major question marks here but still worth looking into under the right circumstance.

2016 PROJECTION: 12-11 3.86 ERA 1.26 WHIP 177 K

49. Julio Teheran: Pretty much nothing went right for the Atlanta Braves in 2015 and that includes the performance from their top pitcher Julio Teheran. After compiling an ace-worthy season in 2014 (2.89 ERA/1.08 WHIP/186 K), Teheran was an unmitigated disaster a year ago. The carnage included a 4.56 ERA first half where Teheran put up a number in that category of at least 4.67 in the first three months of the season that had him making his way to the waiver wire. With a skyrocketing hit rate and unexpected control problems, Teheran was kicked to the curb by more than a few of his owners during that span. Truth be told, Teheran was able to turn things around in the second half, registering a 3.42 ERA from July onward. While his composite 4.04 ERA was decent considering how bad he was early on, the damage was done to Teheran's reputation. Perhaps we overestimated Teheran's 2014, with his very lucky .267 BABIP (adjusted XFIP of 3.72) standing out as a warning that many overlooked. With his BABIP still somewhat lucky but a bit more neutral at .288 last season, it could be that what we saw in 2015 is more of who Teheran is. That is not such a good thing as Teheran had a BB/9 of 3.27 which is a terrible number for any pitcher and his 7.67 K/9 can't make up for that amount of free passes. The Braves are likely going to be bad again in 2016 as they gear up for the opening of their ballpark, which makes owning Teheran very dicey again when you consider what we saw out of him last season.

2016 PROJECTION: 11-10 3.81 ERA 1.16 WHIP 177 K

50. Jose Quintana: When it comes to projecting players each season in fantasy baseball, bonus points always need to be given to those hitters and pitchers who season after season stay in the same numbers ballpark. Bonus points go to those who carry underrated tags as well. One pitcher who fit that criteria in 2015 was Chicago White Sox hurler Jose Quintana who for the third season in a row posted an ERA of 3.51 or lower, a WHIP between 1.27 and 1.22, and a K rate north of

7.30. No matter how you view Quintana, the guy has become an extremely dependable lefty starter who could squeeze out one more season of improvement in 2016 at the age of 27. Despite the very tidy numbers, Quintana has been largely ignored on draft day as he often gets selected in the SP 5 range. That is spectacular value from a guy whose numbers have him in the SP 3 class. With durability also on his side, Quintana is one of the better buys among starting pitchers. Better yet, Quintana's 3.36 ERA was achieved despite some poor BABIP luck (.327). The elevator is still climbing here and outside of the negatives of pitching in the American League and in an offensive park like he does with the White Sox, Quintana is a tremendous investment that could yield nice value once again.

2016 PROJECTION: 11-8 3.30 ERA 1.23 WHIP 179 K

51. Luis Severino: Historically serving as an organization that peddles their top prospects due to chasing veterans to help with their annual playoff push, the New York Yankees made it known around baseball that one prized farmhand who was completely off limits was power righty Luis Severino. With Severino quickly earning plaudits for his dominate pitching at Triple-A (1.91 ERA in 61.1 innings), the Yankees promoted the then 21-year-old at the beginning of August to help them down the stretch of a pennant race. While that would be an immense amount of pressure for such a young pitcher, Severino showed the calm demeanor that was lauded just as much as his 98-mph fastball. Severino helped the Yankees clinch the first AL wild card, logging a 2.89 ERA and 1.20 WHIP in his 62.1 innings with the club. Winning 5 of his 11 starts, Severino showed the overpowering stuff that made him such a highly sought after prospect, punching out 56 batters at an 8.09 K/9. While the Yankees will monitor Severino's innings in 2016 as a full-fledged member of the team's rotation, the upside is immense here. We would be tripping over ourselves trying to get our hands on Severino if he were pitching in the National League but his stuff is just too much of a handful for opposing batters to hit him much more in the American League. Fatigue could be an issue in August which means a sell high could be in order in redraft leagues but otherwise Severino is on the fast track to becoming a major pitching talent.

2016 PROJECTION: 12-7 3.39 ERA 1.22 WHIP 159 K

52. Ian Kennedy: The somewhat volatile career of Ian Kennedy continued on in 2015 with the San Diego Padres, with the lefty running the gamut in terms of numbers. There was some quiet sleeper appeal attached to Kennedy coming into the season, what with him being able to operate in Petco Park for the entire year. Staying true to his form of doing the opposite of what we expected, Kennedy instead came out of the gates by landing on the disabled list with a strained hamstring in his first start of the season (where he got bombed no less). Upon his return in May, Kennedy helped push himself to the waiver wire as he got his head beat in throughout the month (6.40 ERA). From June onward though, Kennedy pitched very well (3.64 ERA/1.26 WHIP/98 K in 84 second half innings) as he further earned the wrath from those who earlier cut bait when they couldn't stomach his early struggles any longer. Despite the solid finish, Kennedy still held a composite ERA of 4.28 which should have been a run lower considering the ballpark. A free agent as of this writing, Kennedy needs to stay in the National League and in a pitcher's park in order to be somewhat interesting again. Historically Kennedy has had some brutal home run rates which got him run out of Arizona and his control betrays him as well on occasion. The strikeout rate has been very impressive since he debuted with the New York Yankees years ago and that aspect is quite underrated when it comes to his statistical numbers. Overall though we don't like the stresses that go with owning Kennedy and prefer someone less of a headache.

2016 PROJECTION: 12-11 4.07 ERA 1.28 WHIP 177 K

53. Chris Heston: When you throw a no-hitter, you get noticed. Engineering his own personal "pay attention to me" moment, San Francisco Giants rookie starter Chris Heston tossed a no-no versus the New York Mets on June 9th. A relative unknown prior to the gem, Heston went on to have a fine debut as he compiled a 3.95 ERA and 1.31 WHIP, while also winning 12 games. Of course Heston was better than the ERA indicated, as his first half ERA of 3.39 showed. Typical of any rookie starter, Heston wilted in the summer when he went into uncharted innings territory and that resulted in a ballooning ERA of 4.91 during the second half. We can give that post-All Star Break performance a mulligan and buy in a bit to the talent. Heston is a ground ball pitcher who doesn't get hurt by the long ball and his 7.14 K/9 was good enough in the NL. While Heston is in no way shape or form in the class of a Tim Lincecum or a Matt Cain in terms of coming through the San

Francisco system as an instant star, he should be better as he gains more experience this season. A move to SP 4 status is likely.

2016 PROJECTION: 14-10 3.79 ERA 1.28 WHIP 156 K

54. Joe Ross: There was quite a bit of pitching talent in the Ross household growing up as little brother Joe joined big brother Tyson as above-average major league starters in 2015. While Tyson has been around for a few years, Joe took his first extended foray into the majors last season when the former first round pick (25th overall in the 2011 draft) was a revelation in pitching to a 3.64 ERA and 1.11 WHIP while filling in for the injury-ravaged Washington Nationals rotation. What is interesting is that Joe Ross shows much better control than his brother, with less of a strikeout knack. Joe is no slack in the whiffs column though, registering a very solid 8.10 K/9 IP last season, with potentially more to come as he further develops. There is a lot to like here and we surely haven't seen the best that Ross has to offer which makes him a very good sleeper investment for 2016. The fact he tossed only 76.2 innings as a rookie has kept the spotlight off of Ross in looking ahead to this season and that makes him one of the better upside plays among starting pitchers.

2016 PROJECTION: 14-9 3.47 ERA 1.08 WHIP 158 K

55. Aaron Nola: The Philadelphia Phillies wasted little time keeping their 2014 first round pick (7th overall) Aaron Nola down on the farm long. With the Phillies clearly among the worst teams in all of baseball from the early stages of the season, the team summoned Nola to make his debut June 21st against the Tampa Bay Rays. Nola wound give up only 1 run in 6 innings with 6 strikeouts in that maiden start and he was thus off and running on what the team thinks will be a career as a possible future ace. In his 77.2 innings with the Phillies, Nola showed tremendous poise and a vast repertoire of pitches that allowed him to register an impressive 3.59 ERA and 1.20 WHIP as he struck out 68 batters. While Nola doesn't light up the radar gun, he rocked a 9.09 K rate at Triple-A last season prior to his promotion and it was a still very solid 7.88 with the Phillies. Also possessing very good control, Nola only has to reign in the home run ball (1.10 HR/9 IP with the Phillies) for him to achieve his optimal impact. While we don't exactly see an ace starter in the future, we will sign off on a potential SP 2 real soon. Trending upward.

2016 PROJECTION: 11-12 3.44 ERA 1.19 WHIP 149 K

56. Andrew Heaney: After not getting much of a chance in the Miami Marlins organization, top lefty pitching prospect Andrew Heaney found a prime opportunity with the Los Angeles Angels in 2015. Long lauded for his top-notch control and underrated strikeout ability, Heaney labored at Triple-A with a 4.71 ERA prior to his promotion by the team. We said at the time that Heaney's high ERA at Triple-A was a classic case of boredom in still pitching in the minors and he proved us right by logging a 3.49 ERA and 1.20 WHIP in his 105.2 innings. Everything checked out from an advanced statistical point of view for Heaney with the Angels, from his 2.38 BB/9 and miniscule 0.77 HR/9. The 6.64 K/9 was a bit on the low side but we fully expect Heaney to make gains there as he continues to gain experience this season. A guy who doesn't walk batters, keeps the ball down, and has a few seasons left of ceiling is very interesting to say the least.

2016 PROJECTION: 14-9 3.40 ERA 1.19 WHIP 138 K

57. Drew Smyly: Few pitchers wanted to turn the page on the 2015 season quicker than Tampa Bay Rays pitcher Drew Smyly, who was only able to log 66.2 innings due to non-stop injury problems. A decent sleeper heading into the season due to a quietly very good run with the Rays (1.70 ERA/0.76 WHIP/44 K in 47.2 IP) after he came over in a 2014 trade deadline deal from the Detroit Tigers, Smyly immediately developed a sore shoulder at the start of spring training that had him placed on the DL to start the year. He would make it back to debut on April 24th but Smyly started only three games before a torn labrum put him on the shelf until mid-August. Once again though Smyly showed good stuff in a limited sample size, putting up a 3.11 ERA and striking out 77 batters in those 66.2 innings. Clearly Smyly has good power behind his fastball and he has shown the ability to miss bats. The control wobbles from time to time but Smyly deserves another look in 2016 given the positives he keeps putting forth when he is on the mound. The cost won't be high in terms of an investment due to all the missed time which makes Smyly an even better late round grab.

2016 PROJECTION: 10-9 3.32 ERA 1.1.6 WHIP 149 K

58. John Lackey: While longtime St. Louis Cardinals legendary pitching coach Dave Duncan may be in retirement, his principles seem to still be fully utilized by the team. There is simply no other way to explain how John Lackey was able to achieve a 2.77 ERA and 1.21 WHIP for the team at the age of 36 after struggling through a rough 2014 that included some severe injuries. The numbers were beyond impressive as Lackey was a rock of dependability for the Cardinals in tossing 218 innings, his most since 2010. After some truly ugly seasons with the Boston Red Sox, clearly getting out of the AL East and the land of the DH as a whole was the key. Lackey has also been able to hold a K/9 over 7.00 and his control was as good as ever at 0.87 BB/9 last season. Now Lackey did get some help in terms of having positive luck with the batted ball and also with his strand rate which needs to be factored into his draft grade. In addition, we always preach about not investing in aging pitchers who suddenly post a season far above their recent performance.

2016 PROJECTION: 14-10 3.57 ERA 1.23 WHIP 165 K

59. Andrew Cashner: Always a prime curiosity in terms of possessing a power arm capable of big-time strikeout totals, San Diego Padres veteran Andrew Cashner fell off the wagon in 2015 when his ERA spiked to 4.34 and the WHIP to an even more troubling 1.44. This came on the heels of Cashner pitching great in both the 2013 and 2014 seasons, yielding one of the lowest hit rates in the game during that span. As promising as Cashner appeared to be, injuries always interrupted the proceedings. Most significantly, Cashner has had some big elbow scares that brought forth Tommy John suggestions in the recent past. Luckily it never came to that but Cashner seemed like a shell of his former self in 2015. With a slight dip in velocity, Cashner all of a sudden struggled in giving up 200 hits in his career-high 184.2 innings last season. In addition, Cashner had zero control as his 3.22 BB/9 would attest. Sure the .330 BABIP was quite unlucky but Cashner seems like a guy whose stuff is a tick or two below where it once was. We love the home ballpark but the Padres tried to deal him throughout last season and into the winter which you have to think is a telling red flag. Always tiring in dealing with his injuries, Cashner now doesn't even offer the upside he once did.

2016 PROJECTION: 10-12 3.84 ERA 1.15 WHIP 165 K

60. Colin McHugh: The follow-up to Colin McHugh's 2014 breakout with the Houston Astros (2.73 ERA/1.02 WHIP/157 K in 154.2 innings) was a bit of a letdown for those who bought in fully on the guy last season. A sliding K rate and some ugly early control sent McHugh spiraling to a 4.50 first half ERA and erased a lot of the positive memories from just a year earlier. McHugh was able to turn things around however, registering a 3.11 ERA from the All-Star Break onward as the Astros locked up a postseason berth. While his composite 3.89 ERA was decent enough, it was more than a run higher than his 2014 number and his K rate sank by almost two strikeouts per nine as well. As a result you could argue that McHugh's 2014 campaign can go in the outlier bin and what he did last season is more in line with his future numbers. While McHugh does a nice job keeping the ball in the park (0.89 HR/9), he is more an SP 4 than anything else.

2016 PROJECTION: 15-10 3.79 ERA 1.24 WHIP 176 K

61. Raisel Iglesias: Sometimes a small sample size of hitting or pitching numbers leave the fantasy baseball community wanting to see so much more. That was the case with hard-throwing Cincinnati Reds starter Raisel Iglesias who announced in a thunderous way in August that he deserves a rotation spot to begin 2016. Capable of unleashing his fastball near triple-digits to go along with a buckling curve, Iglesias put up three straight starts in August where he punched out double-digit batters. Overall in his 95.1 innings, Iglesias struck out 104 for a very impressive 9.82 K/9 IP. That is a number that will get anyone's attention and Iglesias should be a popular sleeper on that part of his game alone. While he needs some improvement with his home run tendencies (1.04 HR/9 IP), Iglesias has the type of electric arm that could make him a significant breakout pitcher for this season. Bid aggressively.

2016 PROJECTION: 10-10 3.84 ERA 1.19 WHIP 167 K

62. Mike Fiers: For the second time in three years, Mike Fiers went into the fantasy baseball season with quite a bit of sleeper appeal attached to his name. Having first made a name for himself with a spectacular second half performance in 2012, Fiers became a hot commodity for the 2013 season. Unfortunately Fiers was miserable from start to finish as his ERA was as bad as you could get at 7.25. On the Milwaukee Brewers at the time, the team sent Fiers back to the minor leagues as a sign of them not being able to stomach anymore of his terrible pitching. Fiers wound up spending the first half of 2014 rehabilitating his stuff but he received a mid-season promotion when injuries struck the rotation. Taking a book out of 2012, Fiers was the epitome of dominant as he registered a 2.09 ERA,

0.84 WHIP, and struck out 71 in 64 second half innings that season. As a result, Fiers became a March draft sleeper as the 2015 season rolled around. Just like in 2013 though, Fiers was hit very hard out of the gates last season in posting an insane 5.79 ERA and 1.59 WHIP in April that quickly got him sent to the waiver wire. Maybe Fiers wants to join the Jon Lester/Cole Hamels April struggles club because from May onward, the guy was pretty darn good in posting four straight months with a sub-4.00 ERA which helped him get dealt to the Houston Astros at the July 31 deadline. While he did struggle in September, Fiers was almost unhittable in August with the Astros (including an actual no-no) and he wound up finishing the season with a very good 3.69 ERA considering where he started in April. As we gaze toward 2016, Fiers as a full-season pitcher in the American League is not overly attractive and his awful Aprils are another big negative to take into account. Still despite having a fastball that only sits in the upper 80's, Fiers misses a lot of bats as he has averaged a K/IP in his career. Over the last two years, Fiers has rocked K/9 rates of 9.54 and 8.98 as he gets a ton of movement on his pitches and has a deceptive release. While his control was lacking at times (3.19 BB/9), Fiers keeps the ball in park (1.20 HR/9) which grows in importance now that he will be full-time member of the AL. We have Fiers as a solid SP 4 for 2016 but just keep a close eye on him next April.

2016 PROJECTION: 14-10 3.77 ERA 1.26 WHIP 179 K

63. Taijuan Walker: Persistent shoulder trouble delayed the much-anticipated debut of Seattle Mariners top pitching prospect Taijuan Walker leading into the 2015 season. After only tossing 38 innings a year earlier due to more shoulder trouble when Walker was a big-time fantasy baseball sleeper, the hype dimmed a bit as last season got underway. Despite all the glowing minor league numbers, you can argue that Walker was among the worst starters in all of baseball the first two month of the season as he registered an April ERA of 6.86 and a May mark of 5.74. In fact Walker was lucky he was not demoted back to Triple-A, so horrific were his results. From that point on Walker alternated a good month followed by a bad until he was shut down in September due to inning concerns. Overall Walker finished with a 4.56 ERA and 1.20 WHIP while punching out 157 batters in his 169.2 innings. In dissecting the numbers, the biggest failure by Walker was not keeping the baseball in the park as he gave up an insane 25 home runs. Walker's 1.33 HR/9 was among the highest in baseball and that was doubly inexcusable with half his starts coming at Safeco Field. On the plus side, Walker's 8.33 K/9 IP showed that his ability to collect strikeouts in the minor leagues could make the jump to the majors. Still only 23, Walker remains an intriguing talent who should improve across the board with more experience in 2016. If Walker can just knock off 5-7 home runs from his total, that alone could push his ERA under 4.00 with a good WHIP. Give him another chance but not until late in the draft.

2016 PROJECTION: 11-11 3.98 ERA 1.19 WHIP 176 K

64. Hector Santiago: Talk about a tale of two halves. There may not have been a more stark first half hero/second half zero performance than what we saw out of the Los Angeles Angels' Hector Santiago last season. Having served as mostly a reliever for most of his career, Santiago's powerful fastball had the Angels curious to see what he could do as a starter. Well at least until late June, the answer was that Santiago could pitch at a front-of-the-rotation level. Overall Santiago was phenomenal during the first half as he posted a 2.33 ERA, 1.10 WHIP, and striking out 98 batters in his 108.1 innings. Getting the fastball up to the high-90's and with knee-buckling off-speed stuff, Santiago's always ugly control was not much of an issue. At the height of Santiago's value in late June however, we warned all of his owners to sell high as he began approaching unchartered innings territory. Having never pitched a full Major League season before, it was a guarantee Santiago would start getting hit hard as the last few months arrived. Boy was that an understatement as Santiago was obliterated from July onward as his ERA climbed to 5.47 and his WHIP to 1.49. The Angels couldn't hardly even stomach having Santiago in the rotation anymore by September which one can understand. As we look to 2016, Santiago once again will have to be handled as a first half asset and a major sell in late June. There are some things to like here such as a very solid 8.07 K/9 but Santiago still makes too much trouble for himself with the walks (3.54 BB/9) and that struggle seems like it will never improve. Ultimately we always advise staying away from the stress that pitchers with this kind of first half/second half split, as you want someone you can depend on all season. Santiago is not that guy.

2016 PROJECTION: 12-8 3.50 ERA 1.25 WHIP 167 K

65. Alex Wood: You can't get them all right. Or might we add, "we can't get them all right." It was in these pages and on our website prior to 2015 where we championed the cause of Alex Wood as the next big breakout pitcher. We had good reason to do so, having seen some very promising signs and indications the year prior that Wood had the stuff to be a front-of-the-rotation asset. It was during the 2014 season where Wood compiled a 2.78 ERA, 1.14 WHIP, and struck out 170 batters in 170.1 innings (8.91 K/9) that made us very excited about his prospects for 2015 with the Atlanta Braves. Alas Wood wasted little time in showing he was not up to those lofty expectations, beginning the season in horrible fashion in putting up a 4.03 ERA and brutal 1.48 WHIP as he lost all semblance of control. In addition to the hits and walks piling up, Wood suddenly couldn't strike guys out as his K rate plummeted. Even with a very good 2.48 May ERA, Wood took much of the shine off of that number with a 1.52 WHIP. Wood was a complete mess on the mound and he showed nothing of the promising hard-thrower he appeared to be just a season ago. Eventually even the Braves got tired of Wood's act, jettisoning him to the Los Angeles Dodgers during the summer trading frenzy. As poorly as Wood threw in April and May, he was somehow WORSE over the summer in putting up a July, August, and September where his ERA was above 4.00 in all three months (and above 4.90 in two of them). No matter how you looked at Wood in 2015, he was a colossal bust. In looking ahead to 2016, Wood remains in a prime pitcher's park with the Dodgers and has a good chance to win games on a perennial contender. However Wood needs to push back up his sagging 2015 K rate (6.60) and lower his suddenly high walk rate (2.80) to even hold SP 4 value. We got burned badly by Wood last season which makes us quite leery of recommending him again.

2016 PROJECTION: 12-9 3.70 ERA 1.24 WHIP 165 K

66. Mike Leake: Another top member of the solid ERA/soft-tossing club is veteran Mike Leake, who reaffirmed that status with another very useful season in 2015 highlighted by a 3.70 ERA split between his stints with the Cincinnati Reds and San Francisco Giants. The sub-4.00 ERA brought to three seasons in a row and four out of the last five where Leake achieved such a mark. What was really surprising is that Leake's ERA was higher while a member of the Giants and their pitching haven park (4.07) than his 2015 tenure with the Reds and their launching pad home base (3.56). As is typical of a Leake season, the K Rate will be in the mediocre 6.00-6.50 range but on the plus side Leake has good control and a solid enough hit rate. A full season with the Giants and the benefits of their park will keep Leake in a tidy ERA bracket but in innings-capped formats he loses a bunch of appeal.

2016 PROJECTION: 12-11 3.36 ERA 1.22 WHIP 138 K

67. Jimmy Nelson: While he was never included in anyone's top pitching prospect list, hard-throwing Milwaukee Brewers righty Jimmy Nelson still put himself on the map with a dominant stretch of pitching in 2014 at Triple-A. Posting a K rate of 9.24, Nelson was virtually unhittable as he posted a 1.46 ERA in 111 innings. That earned Nelson a late-season promotion that carried some fantasy baseball intrigue considering the minor league numbers and Nelson's pedigree as a former second round pick of the team. Alas Nelson was not ready for the jump as he was hit hard to the tune of a 4.93 ERA but the Brewers reserved a rotation spot for him to start 2015 anyway in realizing he had nothing left to prove at the minor league level. While there were some rocky moments along the way like with any young pitcher during his first full MLB season, Nelson acquitted himself quite well in pitching to a 4.11 ERA and 1.29 WHIP while winning 11 games on an awful team. Digging into the numbers, Nelson's minor league K Rate did not make the jump to the majors as he was at 7.40 K/9 IP in 2014 and 7.51 last season. Nelson also was home run-prone as he gave up 18 long balls that helped raise up the ERA. On the positive side, Nelson was stingy with the hits, yielding only 163 in 177.1 innings. This is the key stat as Nelson's stuff is obviously tough for major league hitters to get good wood on and if he can knock down the BB/9 IP (3.30 in 2015) by a full run, the ERA would drop quite a bit. Typically it takes hard-throwing young starters like Nelson a season or two to get the walks and home run ball more under control and if that happens in 2016, we could be looking at a terrific low-cost draft pick. The elevator is pointing upwards here.

2016 PROJECTION: 12-12 3.71 ERA 1.27 WHIP 165 K

68. Nathan Karns: Joining the conveyer belt of power arms coming out of the Tampa Bay Rays system, Nathan Karns became the latest starting pitcher who has the look of a very bright future. While Karns was not a high draft pick (12th round in 2009), his knack for striking out batters in the minor leagues put him on the fast track to the Rays rotation. After cup of coffee stints in 2013 and 2014, Karns began the 2015 season with the Rays and immediately began showing the potential to be a front-of-the-rotation arm. While Karns dealt with some forearm issues the second half of the season, he opened eyes with a final ERA of 3.67 and 1.28 WHIP, while striking out 145 batters in 147 innings. While Karns is a bit older then you may think at 28, the low hit rate and 8.88 K/9 are a nice combination of skills that likely will lead to a bit more improvement this season. In a real shocker though, the Rays dealt Karns to the Seattle Mariners right after the World Series concluded which at least keeps him in a top pitcher's park. This was still a puzzling move considering Karns' recent development.

2016 PROJECTION: 12-12 3.56 ERA 1.26 WHIP 174 K

69. Jaime Garcia: Do yourself a favor and check out the career numbers for St. Louis Cardinals starter Jaime Garcia. We guarantee you will be pleasantly surprised how good a pitcher the veteran has been throughout his 7 year career. With those 7 seasons in the books, Garcia's career ERA is a very impressive 3.31 and 2015 brought his best mark ever in that category at 2.43. While Garcia will never impress you with high strikeout totals, his control is impeccable and the home run rates here are annually under 1.00. Garcia's biggest problem has been his lack of health, having dealt with numerous arm/shoulder/back trouble that has not allowed him to throw more than 170 innings outside of one season and makes owning him volatile. There may not be a better and more affordable SP 5 than Garcia given the numbers and that makes him a terrific late round investment however.

2016 PROJECTION: 12-7 3.59 ERA 1.21 WHIP 110 K

70. Henry Owens: The Boston Red Sox finally unleashed top lefty pitching prospect Henry Owens on the major leagues late in the 2015 season, a clear signal that they are ready to rebuild again after a very disappointing performance by the club. While Owens only got 11 starts, he showed more than enough to think he will be a front-of-the-rotation arm soon enough. The report on Owens is that he has sneaky good strikeout stuff and a vast four-pitch arsenal to keep hitters constantly off balance. What was interesting about Owens is that prior to his promotion, he was not very good at Triple-A Pawtucket as he struggled with his control (4.12 BB/9) and his K rate dropped almost three full runs per 9.0 from the season prior. Truth be told, Owens continued that trend with the Red Sox, walking 24 batters in his 63 innings and posting just a 7.14 K/9. As we have stated numerous times, we are very leery of pitchers who have trouble with walks in the American League, especially the AL East. Being a prospect in the high-profile Boston organization usually leads to some overhype as well, which means investing in Owners for 2016 is anything but a safe pick. Try to avoid the division as Owens is by no means a can't miss guy.

2016 PROJECTION: 12-10 4.04 ERA 1.27 WHIP 137 K

71. Yovani Gallardo: The aging of Yovani Gallardo continued unabated in 2015, as he posted his highest ever WHIP at 1.42 in his first season with the Texas Rangers. Heading into 2015, Gallardo carried the double negative in moving from the National League to the American League (and in Texas of all places) and having diminished stuff. A four-time 200-plus K power ace during his early days with the Milwaukee Brewers, Gallardo only managed 121 strikeouts in his 184.1 innings last season. Gallardo began losing velocity as early as the 2012 season and it has not let up since. While Gallardo is still relatively young at 30, his career-long issue with walks and poor pitch efficiency is more pronounced without the K's. While Gallardo kept the ball in the park last season, his K/9 dropped all the way to a career-low 5.91 which is Kyle Lohse territory. With his 3.32 BB/9 still showing how Gallardo makes trouble for himself, it is imperative he sign on with a National League team in free agency.

2016 PROJECTION: 11-8 3.67 ERA 1.35 WHIP 144 K

72. Clay Buchholz: At least for the first half of the season, it appeared as though Boston Red Sox enigmatic veteran right-hander Clay Buchholz had rediscovered some of his old top-end stuff. After performing like one of the worst pitchers in baseball in 2014 in registering a 5.34 ERA and 1.39 WHIP, Buchholz came out of the gates strong in April and by the All-Star Break was sitting with a tidy 3.26 ERA. Part of the reason for the renaissance was Buchholz posting his best K rate since 2008 at 8.50. Buchholz also dramatically curbed some past issues with the home run ball with a 0.48 HR/9 rate but the good times ended in July as he was diagnosed with a right flexor strain in his elbow. The positive news is that Buchholz was throwing in September which means he will be fine for spring training. What we now have to determine is whether Buchholz can repeat his

2015 first-half. We are hesitant to predict such a thing considering how bad Buchholz had been prior to last season. In addition, he still resides in the worst pitching division in baseball in the AL East and in a launching pad ballpark in Fenway.

2016 PROJECTION: 11-7 3.99 ERA 1.2.4 WHIP 137 K

73. Patrick Corbin: With Tommy John surgery having wiped out his entire 2014 season, Arizona Diamondbacks lefty Patrick Corbin was pretty much a forgotten man entering 2015. Making his debut on June 4th, Corbin went through the usual post-Tommy John ups and downs. Still Corbin did enough nice things in pitching to a solid 3.60 ERA in his 85 innings to remind us all of the interesting path he was on before the surgery. Back in 2013 Corbin seemed like a young pitcher on the rise by registering a 3.41 ERA, 1.17 WHIP, and striking out 177 batters. Unfortunately Corbin couldn't build off that very good campaign when his elbow went bad the following spring. Now almost two full seasons removed from the procedure, Corbin should be at his optimum strength which means he looks like a decent sleeper candidate. Having struck out 78 batters in his 85 innings last season (8.26 K/9), Corbin has stuff that misses bats. Corbin also has very good control which makes him that much more intriguing. The volume has been turned way down here after the surgery but that just makes Corbin an even better sleeper investment.

2016 PROJECTION: 12-9 3.39 ERA 1.119 WHIP 160 K

74. C.J. Wilson: One running joke that has made its way around the Fantasy Sports Boss office is how durable innings-eating veteran lefty C.J. Wilson is either really good or downright hideous in any one start with nothing in-between. Now a full five seasons since his conversion from the bullpen to the starting rotation, Wilson has quietly been very good during that span in registering ERA's of 3.35, 2.94, 3.83, and 3.39 leading into 2015. Unfortunately Wilson took a big dip last season as his ERA climbed to 4.51 amid elbow trouble. It appeared as though four straight seasons of 200-plus innings is starting to manifest itself with poor health for Wilson and at 35 he is not a good bet to turn back to his old SP 3 self. As far as Wilson the pitcher is concerned, he has been quite stingy with the hits given up in his career which account for the low ERA's. However the flip side is that Wilson has had some very spotty control, with his BB/9 IP hovering over 3.00 for four straight seasons (going as high as 4.35). We are always leery of guys with arm trouble in their mid-to-late-30's and Wilson is right near the top of that list going into 2016. Another guy who you want to cash your chips in on as it seems things will only go downhill from here.

2016 PROJECTION: 12-8 3.85 ERA 1.31 WHIP 165 K

75. Wei-Yin Chen: For the second consecutive season, the Baltimore Orioles got a very nice season out of veteran Taiwanese pitcher Wei-Yin Chen. After a mini-breakout 2014 when he posted a 3.54 ERA and 1.23 WHIP, Chen improved on that with 3.34/1.22 ratios last season. Turning 31 in July, Chen won't be doing much of any improving from here on out but his 2015 numbers seem somewhat repeatable. Chen's .290 BABIP was only slightly lucky and his 7.20 K/9 allows him to miss enough bats to get out of trouble. A classic SP 5 candidate who can round out your rotation.

2016 PROJECTION: 10-9 3.75 ERA 1.23 WHIP 149 K

76. Jake Peavy: Despite his advanced age, we did have a smidge of attraction to Jake Peavy as we looked ahead to the 2015 season. After having nothing but struggled as a member of the Chicago White Sox after leaving the San Diego Padres, Peavy was dealt back into the NL West with the Giants late in 2014. While Peavy's stuff was a notch or two below his Padre days, we figured a full season in the spacious San Francisco ballpark could result in a sneaky good SP 4 campaign. While the home run ball has always been a big problem for Peavy (which would figure to be neutralized a bit with the Giants and being back in the NL), the other problem he annually faces with regards to poor health was something that could not be avoided. Peavy would only be able to throw 110 innings in 2015 due to a litany of aches and pains but his 3.58 ERA was still solid enough for him to realize some of the SP 4 outlook we had for him. Now an aging player as he turns 35 in May, Peavy has another year on his deal with the Giants which could result in another tidy ERA. Even being back in the NL did nothing to stop the leaking K rates Peavy has put up recently though, as his number there dropped to a career-low 6.34 last season. Ultimately there is not much shine left on the Peavy stock and SP 5 is about the best we can say about his value for 2016.

2016 PROJECTION: 12-8 3.78 ERA 1.23 WHIP 149 K

77. Edinson Volquez: We were not overly excited about the free agent decision of Edinson Volquez to depart the National League (where he rediscovered his one-time immense potential) to the rougher American League by signing with the Kansas City Royals last winter. After a career filled with unmet expectations and sky-high walk rates that ruined his ratios, Volquez became the latest reclamation project made good with the Pittsburgh Pirates by having a career season in 2014 (13-7, 3.04 ERA, 1.23 WHIP, 140 K/192.2 IP). It clearly looked like the key for Volquez' big year was the fact he finally stopped trying to strike everyone out and instead pitched more to contact. Taking some pop out of his fastball, Volquez also finally reigned in the walks which were a perpetual problem. Still going to the Royals and into the American League was looking like trouble and so we steered away from Volquez for 2015. While there were some rough spots early on, Volquez managed to have a decent season for the second year in a row in posting a 3.58 ERA and 1.31 WHIP while punching out 152 batters. The rise in ERA was not unexpected given the move to the DH-league but it was still a solid number nonetheless. What is interesting is that Volquez IMPROVED his control even more in 2015, lowering his BB/9 to a career-low 3.18. Volquez also kept the ball in the park, posting his second straight sub-0.80 HR/9 IP mark. When you break it all down, Volquez was pretty much the same pitcher he was a year ago and that the ERA rise was simply due to the tougher league and nothing else. While Volquez lacks the flash he had earlier in his career due to the drop in his K rate the last two seasons, he works very well as a top SP 5 option.

2016 PROJECTION: 14-9 3.61 ERA 1.29 WHIP 155 K

78. Cliff Lee: The final stage of the up-and-down career of Cliff Lee doesn't look like it will be very pretty to say the least. The late blooming, Cy Young-winning lefty did not throw a single pitch that counted in 2015 due to tearing the flexor tendon in his elbow during spring training. Now 37-years-old, the Phillies bought out the final year of Lee's contract which puts him on the market with great uncertainty regarding future employment. Even before his 2015 washout, Lee was only able to register 81.1 frames the season prior as he was plagued by more elbow problems to go along with a bum shoulder. Clearly Lee's body is betraying him under the weight of all those 220-plus inning seasons. Even before the series of injuries, Lee's velocity was dipping noticeably, with his walk rate shooting up in the other direction. While Lee was still striking out guys at a decent clip in 2014

(7.97), it is always a terrible idea to invest in aging/injury-prone pitchers whose name value greatly outpaces their current level of performance. Salute the career and move on.

79. Nathan Eovaldi: For at least the first five months of the 2015 season, the New York Yankees made out nicely in their winter trade for the hard-throwing but very inconsistent Nathan Eovaldi. With a career 15-35 record in five previous seasons despite having a fastball average among the very best in the game, Eovaldi was a puzzle that both the Miami Marlins and Los Angeles Dodgers couldn't solve. The big problem with Eovaldi was that despite how hard he threw, the baseball came in straight more often than not which led to a hit rate that was one of the worst in baseball. Moving from a spacious park in Miami to a home run haven in Yankee Stadium didn't engender much optimism that Eovaldi could finally live up to his potential either. In actuality though, Eovaldi was very good the second half of the season after struggling to adapt to the American League during the first half. After an ugly 4.50 ERA first half, the introduction of a splitter to Eovaldi's repertoire led to what was looking like a terrific second half as he threw to a 3.67 ERA and went 5-1. Unfortunately the hot stretch ended at the start of September as Eovaldi was shut down for the rest of the season with a sore elbow. When looking at the numbers as a whole, Eovaldi was still quite underwhelming with his composite 4.20 ERA and the 1.45 WHIP was downright hideous as the hits keep piling up. The worst aspect regarding Eovaldi though remains the lack of K's as he punched out only 121 batters in 154.1 inning, with his 98-100-mph fastball continuing to come in way too straight. Despite the solid second half, Eovaldi is nothing but an SP 5 who will be one of the more frustrating players to own. Guys like this are simply not worth the headache.

2016 PROJECTION: 14-10 4.17 ERA 1.37 WHIP 149 K

80. Jerad Eickhoff: As ugly as the 2015 season was for the Philadelphia Phillies, their rotation has some very promising arms moving forward. Joining Aaron Nola at the front of that line is 2015 acquisition Jerad Eickhoff who the Phils picked up from the Texas Rangers in the Cole Hamels trade. The Phillies threw Eickhoff right into the fire in August and had to be very impressed with what the kid was able to accomplish. Showing off a nice blend of fastball, curve, and slider, Eickhoff more than held his own by pitching to a tiny 2.65 ERA in 51 innings. The 8.65 K/9 stands out, as does a 0.88 HR/9. The fact Eickhoff can keep the baseball in the park is no small thing when you call Citizens Bank your home. Now Eickhoff did get assistance from a lucky .257 BABIP (3.60 XFIP) but the stuff is clear to see. While we don't forecast Eickhoff as an ace for the future, he has the type of arsenal and velocity to be a solid SP 3 as soon as this season. Sleeper alert.

2016 PROJECTION: 11-11 3.59 ERA 1.21 WHIP 149 K

81. Daniel Norris: One of the top pitching prospects coming into the 2015 season, the power arm of Daniel Norris was quite attractive on the surface. However his home ballpark with the Toronto Blue Jays in the offensive haven that is Rogers Center quieted some of the hype surrounding him. A former 2011 second round pick of the team, the Blue Jays bestowed a rotation spot on Norris to begin the 2015 season in a signal that they were sold on his abilities. Unfortunately Norris was not ready as his control completely betrayed him to the tune of 12 walks in only 23.1 innings with the Jays before the sent him back to Triple-A to work through the issue. Despite his ugly 1.50 WHIP, Norris put up a solid 3.86 ERA so it wasn't completely bad. Eventually the Detroit Tigers came calling though as they acquired Norris in the deal for David Price. Given a fresh start in a pitcher's park this time around with the Tigers, Norris again had his debut season interrupted when he landed on the DL with a strained oblique. However Norris successfully lowered his walk rate with the Tigers and his 1.11 WHIP showed this improvement. Ultimately though Norris' 2015 was too chopped up to get a good read on him as a major league pitcher and that makes grading him for 2016 quite difficult. Posting K rates as high as 15.09 in the minors, Norris's 6.87 K/9 IP in the majors last season has room for growth. If Norris can continue to curb the free passes, he should be able to post a decent enough ERA and WHIP next season as he continues to make incremental but not giant gains. We would like Norris so much more if he were in the NL but overall he is worth a late round pick to round out your rotation this season. Finally, kudos to Norris for kicking cancer's butt during the fall.

2016 PROJECTION: 11-8 3.97 ERA 1.17 WHIP 155 K

82. Tyler Lyons: During his first three years in the major leagues, the St. Louis Cardinals seem to be unsure of how to use lefty pitcher Tyler Lyons. Alternating him between the bullpen and rotation based on need, it was more of the same in

2015 as he logged a very nice 3.47 ERA and 1.25 WHIP. A former 2009 9th round pick of the team, Lyons has shown that he can miss bats and possesses good control, which makes him quite intriguing if he were to become a full-fledged member of the rotation. One big problem is that Lyons gives up home runs in bunches which could give the team pause in terms of adding Lyons to the rotation but the kid has done enough good things in his young career for him to be a part of your late round sleeper pool.

83. Doug Fister: The impossible was accomplished by Doug Fister last season during his first full-year as a member of the Washington Nationals rotation. After a string of very good years with the Detroit Tigers in the American League (three straight seasons with an ERA under 4.00), there was quite a bit of hype with Fister facing a complete 2015 in the much easier National League and in such a massive ballpark. Well Fister defied all positive prognostications when it came to his outlook, battling injuries most of the year and pitching poorly when he was on the mound. The resulting 4.19 ERA and 1.40 WHIP were brutal considering the pitching environment and the Nats couldn't wait to move on from him at the conclusion of the season. With Fister being nothing but a mediocre strikeout guy, he is pretty much useless without decent ratios. Looking ahead to 2016, Fister is now just another guy who has a bunch of performance and health question marks attached to his name. Whereas once we were admirers of Fister's, today we look past him with a shrug.

2016 PROJECTION: 12-12 4.05 ERA 1.28 WHIP 146 K

84. Phil Hughes: One of the bigger disappointments of the 2015 season was the performance of the Minnesota Twins' Phil Hughes. Unfortunately this has been the theme in Hughes' career going back to his New York Yankee days. With a home run rate that annually is among the worst in baseball, Hughes is a big inning waiting to happen at any given moment. That makes owning Hughes quite stressful as any one start could turn into a disaster due to a handful of bad pitches. What really was a letdown was the fact Hughes seemed to finally unveil the potential he carried as a former first round pick of the Yankees, using the vast dimension of Target Field to keep the home runs somewhat at bay during the 2014 season. A career-best in ERA (3.52), WHIP (1.13), and strikeouts (186) was the result and that made buying into Hughes for 2015 seemingly less risky than ever before. The home runs returned in full force throughout last season though, with Hughes' 1.68 HR/9 resulting in a hideous 29 long balls. Hence the shaky 4.40 ERA and resumption of Hughes as nothing but a back-end guy for a fantasy baseball rotation. Ideally we would love to see Hughes in the National League at some point but for now he should serve as nothing but a late round grab who offers zero upside.

2016 PROJECTION: 12-10 4.16 ERA 1.26 WHIP 165 K

85. Matt Shoemaker: One popular 2015 sleeper who went completely bust was Los Angeles Angels starting pitcher Matt Shoemaker. While Shoemaker has a live arm that is capable of picking up strikeouts at an above-average rate, he fell squarely into that incredibly frustrating class of pitcher who is prone to the home run. In his 135.1 innings last season, Shoemaker gave up a hideous 24 home runs which made any one start a potential time bomb. While Shoemaker survived a 4.85 ERA first half that made him a pariah in the fantasy baseball community, the Angels finally were forced to demote him back to Triple-A in August (5.66 ERA for the month) in order to try and get his stuff back in order. Unfortunately things didn't really turn around as Shoemaker struggled again when called back up in September and then he came up lame with a sore elbow that finished his season early. While Shoemaker's season was a big disappointment as a whole with his composite 4.66 ERA, beneath the surface there at least were some encouraging signs. His 1.26 WHIP was solid and his 7.71 K rate as well. Still we always strongly advise you against drafting any pitcher who gives up home runs at the rate that Shoemaker does as you can't ever feel comfortable in any one start. Too high maintenance to deal with.

2016 PROJECTION: 11-11 4.17 ERA 1.25 WHIP 137 K

86. Jesse Hahn: If we were to tell you that a young starting pitcher engineered ERA's of 3.07 and 3.35 during his first two major league seasons, you would be more than a bit intrigued. Those ERA's belong to Oakland A's righty Jesse Hahn who has impressed in his short stay as a major league starter. Hahn really first opened eyes as a rookie in 2014 with the San Diego Padres in pitching to that 3.07 ERA and posting a very impressive 8.59 K/9 IP. During that offseason Hahn was dealt to the A's as part of the deal where the Padres acquired catcher Derek Norris. The A's clearly got the better end of the deal, at least during the first half of 2015 before Hahn came down with pain in his forearm that set off a slew of alarms. Ultimately Hahn avoided surgery and by the middle of September was starting to throw again as he prepared for 2016. At only 26, Hahn still has another year or two of ceiling left to his game and his instant success as a major leaguer makes him a very smart pick as a back-of-the-rotation guy. With a miniscule 0.47 HR/9 and good enough 2.33 BB/9, Hahn doesn't beat himself which is why he has been able to post such useful ERA's. While his .273 BABIP was in the lucky range resulting in a higher 3.52 FIP ERA, Hahn looks to be worth your time as a low-cost upside play for the 2016 season.

2016 PROJECTION: 8-12 3.57 ERA 1.19 WHIP 149 K

87. Jesse Chavez: With two seasons in the rearview mirror as a member of the Oakland A's rotation, clear trends are starting to emerge with right-handed pitcher Jesse Chavez. The most obvious is Chavez' sharp contrast as a first half asset and a second half flop in terms of his numbers. Consider that in 2015, Chavez pitched to a very solid 3.40 ERA and 1.22 WHIP prior to the All-Star Break, only to see those numbers crash to the tune of a horrid 5.59 ERA and 1.58 WHIP during the second half. This was the exact trend that manifested itself in 2014 as well which means Chavez is a guy you want to unload sometime in June if you pick him in your draft. Overall Chavez is a solid SP 5 starter who has good control and a slightly above-average K rate (7.80 in 2015, 8.38 in 2014) who again can hold his own during the first three months of the season. After that however you are pushing your luck and that is especially true after he makes as bad a home ballpark exchange after the A's sent him from the comforts of spacious O.Co Coliseum to home run haven Rogers Center in Toronto in an early winter trade.

2015 PROJECTION: 9-12 4.14 ERA 1.32 WHIP 145 K

88. Jon Gray: The number one pitching prospect in the Colorado Rockies system heading into the 2015 season was 2013 first round pick (number 3 overall) right-hander Jon Gray. After a good but not great Double-A campaign in 2014 (3.91 ERA/8.18 K/9), Gray floundered a bit at Triple-A in 2015 in his 114.1 innings there (4.33 ERA/8.66 K/9). With the Rockies performing like one of the worst teams in the major leagues last season, Gray was promoted at the start of August as a means to pacify a very restless fan base. The Rockies were very careful managing Gray's 40.2 frames with the team, only allowing him to pitch into the sixth inning twice in 9 starts though. Taking into effect it was his first foray in the majors, Gray was not very impressive in posting a terrible 5.53 ERA and 1.62 WHIP, while surrendering 52 hits in those 40.2 innings. While Gray kept the ball in the park which is quite important when you call Coors Field home, the kid continues to walk guys at a very high clip (3.23 BB/9 at Triple-A, 3.10 with the Rockies) which is a major issue. Gray has some good strikeout ability though, with his K rate above 8.00 at every professional level he has performed at. Ultimately we would be much more bullish on Gray if he were pitching anywhere else and fair or unfair, he has to be considered a risk due to his home ballpark. While the draft pedigree suggests Gray should have top-of-the-rotation ability, his numbers and location are suggesting more of a future SP 4.

2016 PROJECTION: 8-11 4.26 ERA 1.32 WHIP 146 K

89. Tanner Roark: After the Washington Nationals signed Max Scherzer as a free agent and traded for Doug Fister, there was no room left in the team's rotation for 2014 revelation Tanner Roark. Roark helped save the Nats' season during that season when injuries took out a few members of the rotation, pitching to an impressive 2.85 ERA and 1.05 WHIP in 31 starts. Having won 15 games despite coming into the season with only 53.2 major league innings to his name, Roark seemed to have locked up a spot in the rotation for 2015. The Scherzer signing changed all that as the Nats decided to put Roark in the bullpen instead, a move that neutered any fantasy baseball value he might have had left. Being a good soldier, Roark did what he was told but there is no doubt the demotion to the pen had an adverse effect on his numbers. While Roark did go back into the rotation in late May after a decent turn as a reliever, he got hit very hard which necessitated another move back to the pen. The ultimate result was a lackluster 4.38 ERA and 1.31 WHIP. The Nats are planning to have Roark in the rotation for 2015 after cutting ties with Fister and that alone should get him back onto the fantasy baseball radar when looking for an upside arm for your SP 5 spot. While Roark was very good in his 2014 run, there are some negatives such as a poor K/9 that has not gotten above 6.71 in the major leagues. Roark also gives up some home runs which is not such a big issue in Washington but makes him more of a dicey bet on the road. Those in innings-capped leagues should be less interested than non-capped formats but overall Roark seems ready for a bounce back campaign in 2015.

2016 PROJECTION: 14-9 3.48 ERA 1.16 WHIP 146 K

90. Kevin Gausman: The jury is still out in terms of whether or not Baltimore Orioles hard-throwing righty Kevin Gausman is a Quad-A guy or a major league pitcher. A bullpen arm or a starter. Such is the disappointing mystery when it comes to perennial tease Gausman. We say disappointing due to the fact so much more was expected out of Gausman after he was the 4th pick of the 2012 draft. Having posted some big strikeout rates in the minor leagues (over 9.00 on four different occasions at separate levels), Gausman got hit very hard during his short 2013 debut with the O's (5.66 ERA in five starts). Things began to look up however in 2014 when Gausman was very solid in pitching to a 3.57 ERA in 20 starts. However he battled some injuries and was not a lock for a rotation spot to begin 2015. Thus just like the year prior, Gausman barely threw more than 100 innings for the Orioles but was good again with a 4.25 ERA and career-best 1.23 WHIP. The gains have been there but not sizable enough to think Gausman will ever realize his high draft status. All of the strikeouts he put up in the minor leagues have not completely shown up in the majors (solid but not spectacular 8.25 last season) but Gausman could still push that number up as he gains more experience. The Orioles likely have seen enough out of Gausman to hold a rotation spot for him this season but he seems like nothing more than an SP 5 with some small upside remaining to his name.

2016 PROJECTION: 12-8 3.91 ERA 1.24 WHIP 149 K

91. R.A. Dickey: Now 41-years-old, the knuckleball continues to flutter and tumble for the Toronto Blue Jays' R.A. Dickey. After winning the NL Cy Young in 2012 with the New York Mets in a spectacular season (20-6, 2.73 ERA, 230 K's), most wrote off Dickey when he was dealt to the Blue Jays and their unforgiving ballpark during that winter. Truth be told however, Dickey has done just fine in Toronto and in the American League, finishing the last two seasons with 3.71 and 3.91 ERA's respectively. While Dickey has not come close to touching the 8.86 K/9 that he had with the Mets in 2012, he is still keeping the hit rate down and posting solid WHIP's despite the tougher competition. In fact the 230 K's Dickey had with the Mets when he won the Cy Young was a major outlier number not to be repeated. Dickey really fell off last season with the K rate, going from 2014's solid 7.22 to 2015's ugly 5.29 mark, which speaks to how much erosion is taking place there. While throwing the knuckler is not overly stressful on the arm, Dickey's age has to be a factor in the strikeout drop. Despite the decrease in K's, Dickey still posted a good 1.05 home run rate which is not terrible by any means with Rogers Center as your home ballpark. At his age and the always prevalent feeling of dread when you put Dickey out there in any one start, owning him can be stressful. In the National League we could take one more shot but the drop in K rate makes investing in Dickey as an American League starter very risky.

2016 PROJECTION: 14-11 4.07 ERA 1.24 WHIP 128 K

92. Cody Anderson: A new smoke and mirrors starting pitcher made his way to the major leagues in 2015 in the form of Cleveland Indians 2011 14th round pick Cody Anderson. The soft-tossing righty showed very good poise and control in posting a very impressive 3.05 ERA and 1.11 WHIP in his 91.1 innings considering the stuff Anderson has. When it comes to Anderson's repertoire, he is your classic pitch-to-contact guy who needs a strong defense behind him to succeed which the Indians do have. While Anderson does a nice job not beating himself with walks (2.36 BB/9) and keeping the baseball in the park (0.89 HR/9), his margin for error is razor-thin due to a shockingly low 4.34 K/9. Even the 3.05 ERA has to be taken with a major grain of salt as Anderson's .237 BABIP was extremely lucky. When you consider that Anderson's adjusted FIP was 4.28 and XFIP was 4.58, you can see that the kid was really not as good as his surface numbers indicate. In looking to 2016, Anderson is your classic sparkling ERA debut arm who will burn his new owners royally this season in terms of those who don't see the entire picture. Ignore the ERA and leave him be.

2016 PROJECTION: 10-10 4.19 ERA 1.16 WHIP 119 K

93. Anibal Sanchez: When Anibal Sanchez first made his debut in 2006 with the Florida Marlins, he instantly showed himself to be one of the very best power pitching prospects in the game as evidenced by an early no-hitter. However 2006 was also the start of a very ugly string of elbow/shoulder injuries that included Tommy John surgery. Just when Sanchez appeared to be on the verge of exiting Major League Baseball due to the injuries, the 2010 season arrived. It was during that campaign where Sanchez finally stayed healthy and re-affirmed himself as a very solid mid-rotation pitcher. Eventually getting traded to the Detroit Tigers, Sanchez kept up the good work by posting his first 200-K season in 2013 (202).

Unfortunately the injuries reared their ugly head again in 2014 as Sanchez tossed only 126 innings due to a bum shoulder and things didn't get much better in 2015 as he was only able to throw 157 frames. Things got so concerning that Sanchez was forced to go see Dr. James Andrew last September to find out why the shoulder was still a problem. Luckily Andrews recommended just a PRP injection but Sanchez was finished early for the second season in a row. Now a veteran at 32, Sanchez is entering into a new phase of his career. For one, Sanchez' K rate has fallen to near mediocre levels the last two seasons (7.29 in 2014, 7.91 in 2015) and his walks spiked to 2.81 in 2015 as he fought his control a bit. Less a power pitcher than ever before, Sanchez will have to get by in the tough American League with diminished stuff and a lack of health. Not a good recipe for investment.

2016 PROJECTION: 11-6 3.95 ERA 1.29 WHIP 167 K

94. Brett Anderson: The productive but completely injury-marred career of veteran lefty starter Brett Anderson continued on unabated in 2015, this time with the Los Angeles Dodgers. Expectations were through the roof when Anderson first came up with the Oakland A's as the former second round pick in the 2006 draft combined a vast pitching arsenal with very solid strikeout stuff. Alas after a 175.1 inning rookie year with Oakland (4.06 ERA/1.28 WHIP) that was at times very impressive, Anderson began a never-ending cycle of serious injuries that included Tommy John surgery and major shoulder trouble over the next six years. During that span, Anderson missed an entire year (2011) and never pitched more than 112.1 innings as he became a pariah in the fantasy baseball community. Just when it appeared as though Anderson was on the fast track out of baseball, the Los Angeles Dodgers brought him aboard for 2015 to challenge for a back-end rotation spot. Anderson wound up claiming that spot and began engineering what was a terrific comeback season considering where he was prior. The biggest key of course was that Anderson was able to stay healthy and throw a career-high 180.1 innings, resulting in a 3.69 ERA and 1.33 WHIP. Clearly Anderson still has the stuff to get hitters out and his 2.30 BB/9 showed control that was as good as ever in his career. On the negative side, Anderson's K rate was poor at 5.79, likely a victim of all those shoulder/elbow injuries. He is still crafty enough to hold down a spot as your SP 5 after accepting the Dodgers' qualifying offer but given how injury prone he has been, we don't blame you if you want nothing to do with Anderson this season.

2016 PROJECTION: 8-6 3.57 ERA 1.29 WHIP 111 K

95. Matt Cain: It has been an ugly and very sharp fall from grace for the San Francisco Giants' Matt Cain over the last few seasons to say the least. From the moment Cain arrived on the major league scene as a 21-year-old back in 2005, he moved right to the front of the Giants' rotation on the strength of his powerful four-pitch repertoire and very good control. In fact from 2005 through the 2012 season, you can safely argue that Cain was one of the best starting pitchers in all of baseball as he recorded an ERA under 4.00 in all eight of those years, including four times under 3.00. Possessing a fastball that racked up a high numbers of K's, Cain had all the bases covered when came to serving as an annual fantasy baseball ace. Starting in 2013 however, Cain began a quick and sudden spiral into the statistical abyss, logging increasingly worse ERA's the last three seasons to the tune of 4.00, 4.18, and 5.79 respectively. With velocity that was leaking sharply and his body giving out under a slew of injuries, Cain looks like he is finished at the age of 31. No doubt a major part of the blame goes to the incredibly heavy usage Cain endured from the very beginning of his career. With the Giants making annual postseason appearances that included a few World Series runs, Cain racked up an insane amount of innings on a still developing arm. Basically Cain was an example of what not to do when it comes to young pitching today and he is paying the price now. With Cain unable to stay healthy and his stuff fading quick, there is really no reason to even bother with the guy anymore. Crazy to say at such a young age but Cain looks ready to ride off into the sunset already.

2016 PROJECTION: 10-7 4.27 ERA 1.23 WHIP 150 K

96. Bartolo Colon: The term "ageless pitcher" should have a giant picture of Bartolo Colon under the heading, as the veteran once again defied Father Time by winning 14 games with as decent 4.16 ERA for the NL East-winning New York Mets in 2015. A former Cy Young Award winner, Colon has seen and done it all in his never-ending career. As he gets set to turn 43 this May, Colon is ready to pitch again in 2016, with his standard fare of numbers likely being produced. The aged version of Colon has been in play since his mid-30's now and that is of a rubber-armed righty whose impeccable control help overcome a fastball that struggles to reach even the high 80's. Always susceptible to the home run ball given the velocity challenges, Colon will unfortunately give you those 2-IP/5-ER bombs every now and again. Also you can forget about much in the way of strikeouts as well since Colon's K/9 IP has been under 7.00 since 2011. It would be smart of Colon to stay in the easier National League and in a prime pitcher's park like he was with the Mets in 2015 and his location will almost solely determine if you can sneak one of more decent enough season out of the guy. Check back to see where Colon signs and react accordingly. If he goes to the AL? Leave him be. Stays in the NL and not in a homer-haven? He can work as your SP 5 one more season.

2016 PROJECTION: 12-10 4.39 ERA 1.25 WHIP 128 K

97. Trevor Bauer: Perhaps the most enigmatic pitcher in all of baseball is perennial Cleveland Indians disappointment Trevor Bauer. While few can unleash a fastball with more power, few also have such pronounced control problems as Bauer has had throughout his major league career. A Quad-A pitcher to this point who has dominated at the minor league level but often turns to mush in the majors, it was more of the same for Bauer in 2015 as he registered a 4.44 ERA and 1.31 WHIP, while punching out 170 batters in 176 innings. The former third overall pick in the 2011 draft still has some very good strikeout ability but his BB/9 was hideous at 4.04 last season. We have said for years that Bauer is a waste of time and energy given how undependable he is and that remains the same as we move toward 2016.

2016 PROJECTION: 11-12 4.35 ERA 1.30 WHIP 175 K

98. Jered Weaver: The disintegration of Jered Weaver continued in 2015 as the longtime Los Angeles Angels starter hit new lows with his numbers. Once a 233-K monster ace, Weaver has leaked massive velocity since that magical 2010 campaign. It has gotten to the point now where Weaver is nothing but a liability in the strikeout column, coming in at a career-low 5.09 mark in 2015 which is laughable. With no speed on his fastball to keep hitters honest, Weaver was hit very hard to the tune of a 4.64 ERA, another career-worst. We were telling you to run away from Weaver as far back as 2012 so no need to go any further on this. Put Weaver in the washed up bin.

2016 PROJECTION: 12-11 4.34 ERA 1.24 WHIP 116 K

99. Henderson Alvarez: It was a complete bust of a season for Miami Marlins right-hander Henderson Alvarez in 2015. From the very start of spring training, Alvarez complained of pain and weakness in his throwing shoulder that limited him to just 22.1 major league innings. Some of the blame resides in the 187 innings Alvarez was allowed to throw in 2014, a jump of 47 from the previous year. The extra frames seemed to rob Alvarez of velocity and a 6.45 ERA in those 22.1 innings were proof of this. The 2.65 ERA Alvarez posted in his 2014 rookie season is what stands out here but even that number was quite fluky given the lucky strand rate Alvarez put up. In addition, there is no chance Alvarez will go near that number again when his K rate is below average in the mid-5.00 range. We always like pitchers who throw in spacious Miami but Alvarez hurts you badly in strikeouts and his health now is a clear concern.

2016 PROJECTION: 7-9 3.97 ERA 1.28 WHIP 137 K

100. Taylor Jungmann: Sometimes a pitcher comes out of nowhere and defies all sorts of explanations in terms of performance. This heading no doubt belongs over the noggin of Milwaukee Brewers youngster Taylor Jungmann who came up in the middle of the 2015 season and proceeded to fire shutout innings like they were going out of style. This despite the fact that prior to his promotion, Jungmann was toting a 6.37 ERA at Triple-A and whose prospect star had diminished to almost darkness. Still Jungmann was looking like the real deal (he was a former 12th overall pick in the 2011 draft), registering ERA's of 2.79 in June, 1.77 in July, and 3.12 in August. Despite all this, you got the feeling something very fishy was going on here as the numbers seemed too good to be true. As it almost always happens, the cream eventually rose to the top and trouble began arriving in very bad fashion for Jungmann. He got hit hard in September and his one October start was brutal as well. Fatigue could have been a factor as Jungmann entered into some uncharted inning territory there but we think it more had to do with opposing hitters getting some video on the kid. As we look toward 2016, the Brewers are holding a spot for Jungmann in their rotation, which makes sense considering his low salary and decent overall performance last season. Ultimately we think this has fluke written all over it and that Jungmann will be a major bust. We are not going near the kid.

2016 PROJECTION: 9-12 4.22 ERA 1.23 WHIP 155 K

101. Mark Buehrle: The ageless and tireless rubber arm of Mark Buehrle continued in 2015 as he posted another quality season with a 3.82 ERA and 1.22 WHIP despite pitching in the very rough American League East with the Toronto Blue Jays. Now 37-years-old, Buehrle shows no signs of slowing down despite a fastball that struggles to reach 90. We all know by now that Buehrle doesn't walk batters, keeps the baseball in the park, and generates enough rough swings to stay relevant. You still want to just salute the terrific career and ignore in fantasy baseball.

2016 PROJECTION: 14-10 3.97 ERA 1.29 WHIP 109 K

102. Zack Wheeler: Zack Wheeler became yet another in a recent long line of Tommy John surgery victim's just days into 2015 spring training, finishing his season before it even began. Prior to that, Wheeler was quickly proving himself just as worthy as the other hard-throwing young starters on the New York Mets, registering a 3.54 ERA to go with a very good 9.08 K/9 IP in his first full season in 2014. Now Wheeler is not expected back until sometime in the June/July range as a result of the surgery. A power pitcher all the way, Wheeler has already proven he can rack up the strikeouts with his 98-mph fastball, a skill that is his greatest strength in fantasy baseball. However even before the surgery there were questions about how good Wheeler could become due to poor control (3.84 BB/9 in 2014) and a fastball that comes in straight way too often. A pitcher with shoddy control is always a big concern coming off Tommy John as historically that is the biggest effect of the procedure the first season back. Overall Wheeler looks like more trouble than he may be worth, at least for 2016 despite the vastly lowered draft price.

2016 PROJECTION: 7-2 3.62 ERA 1.28 WHIP 127 K

103. Alex Cobb: No matter how talented a pitcher may be, without good health he simply can't help you. Sounds simple but many in the fantasy baseball community tend to chase potential and possible numbers, while overlooking the injury risks that may go along with that pitcher. Such is the case with the Tampa Bay Rays' Alex Cobb who has a world of talent but who just can't ever stay healthy. He took that theme to a higher level in 2015 as Cobb failed to throw one pitch in the regular season due to needing Tommy John elbow surgery. Cobb is no likely to be ready to pitch until June of 2016 at the earliest but he will again be somewhat alluring when you consider he put up ERA's of 2.76 and 2.87 in 2013 and 2014 while once again fighting injuries in between. As far as Cobb the pitcher is concerned, he has a vast four-pitch arsenal that results in a solid rate of strikeouts (over 8.40 K/9 IP in 2013 and 2014), while also possessing solid control with a career 2.76 BB/9 IP. The draft price will come way down this season which makes Cobb a very interesting late middle round grab but you can't invest here unless he is your SP 5 at best given the injury problems we see every season.

2016 PROJECTION: 9-3 3.37 ERA 1.12 WHIP 149 K

104. Ubaldo Jimenez: There may not be a starting pitcher in all of fantasy baseball who engenders more anxiety and nausea when it comes to past ownership than the Baltimore Orioles' Ubaldo Jimenez. While Jimenez had a very good but brief run as a top-of-the-line pitcher during his early years with the Colorado Rockies, his control has annually been right there among the worst in baseball. With Jimenez having lost velocity over the years, his horrible control is now being joined by a sharp increase in the veteran's hit rate. As a result what you had here for Jimenez was an ERA over 4.50 in two of his previous three seasons going into 2015, leaving him as waiver fodder in almost all formats. That changed early on last season however as Jimenez came out strong with a tremendous 2.81 ERA with 98 K's in 99.1 innings during the first half of the season. While we remained leery, we did say to ride out the hot run until the wheels inevitably fell off. That is exactly what happened during the second half as Jimenez suddenly lost his stuff as he gave up 88 hits in 84.2 innings with 36 walks for an ugly 5.63 ERA. Overall it was still a solid season for Jimenez as his K/9 was helpful at 8.22 and he actually was a bit unlucky with the BABIP at .289 which resulted in a 3.83 XFIP. Now 32 and with his control as ugly as ever, Jimenez has almost no value going into the season.

2016 PROJECTION: 12-11 4.48 ERA 1.37 WHIP 178 K

105. Jon Niese: While he has dealt with his fair share of shoulder injuries over the years, lefty Jon Niese has supplied some very useful seasons for the New York Mets during his career. Now entering his ninth season with the team, Niese has registered ERA's under 4.00 during three of them, with a still solid career mark in that category of 3.91. There are clear limitations here however, starting with the lack of strikeouts. Whereas Niese kept up a 7.00-plus K/9 IP for awhile, the last two seasons have seen that number slip to a below mediocre level. The hit rate is also starting to rise sharply as Niese got absolutely pounded in some outings in 2015. His 4.14 ERA was still decent but the 1.40 WHIP tells the story of a guy who was quite hittable. In NL-only formats you have use for Niese as a member of a very good team. Overall though he leaves you wanting more and he may not even start for the Mets this season due to a suddenly crowded rotation.

2016: 12-10 4.16 ERA 1.41 WHIP 125 K

106. Mat Latos: Amazing that at the still young age of 28, Mat Latos is barely holding on as a major league hurler. It appears that a string of elbow/shoulder injuries over the last two years have sapped the pop from Latos' stuff, as he was hit hard pretty much for all the 2015 season. This after Latos pitched to a terrific 3.25 ERA in 2014 with the Cincinnati Reds, another in a batch of SP 2-worthy campaigns that went all the way back to 2010 with the San Diego Padres. The Reds dealt Latos to the Miami Marlins during the 2014 offseason however which raised some eyebrows around the league. Before the ink was dry on the deal, Latos wound up having to undergo a procedure on his pitching elbow to remove bone chips. While he able to begin the season on time, Latos was instantly a shell of his former solid self as he was hit very hard in a season split between the Marlins and eventually the Los Angeles Dodgers who acquired him during the summer. Just when we thought we had seen the worst from Latos prior to the deal, he went out and put a ghastly 6.66 ERA and 1.52 WHIP that first got him sent to the bullpen and then ultimately designated for assignment. The big red flags even outside of health is the fact that Latos got hammered despite calling two of the best pitching parks in the majors home in 2015. With his velocity down more than a little and injuries continuing to take him away from the mound, Latos is barely just a number 5 starter in real-life baseball. Realize firmly that Latos' current level of pitching is not even in the same hemisphere as to where he was just two seasons ago.

2016 PROJECTION: 7-10 4.48 ERA 1.34 WHIP 144 K

THE REST

107. Scott Feldman: There are some pitchers who take up space every season on the waiver wire who actually have some ability that can help in certain formats. One such guy is veteran Scott Feldman who has posted ERA's under 4.00 in three of the last four seasons. While Feldman doesn't do any one thing that moves the interest needle, the guy can give you 180 or so innings with a decent ERA and WHIP. Depending on where he ends up next season, that means Feldman can work as a back-end starter in AL or NL-only setups.

108. A.J. Burnett: If 2015 really was the final major league season for A.J. Burnett, the veteran certainly went out with terrific numbers as he recorded a 3.18 ERA in his 164 innings. While his K/9 dropped under 8.00 last season (7.85), Burnett was still able to overpower enough hitters to stay a top member of the Pittsburgh Pirates staff. Burnett turns 39 in January so he certainly has a ton of mileage on his arm and that bolsters the retirement talk. While the ERA was impressive, Burnett also showed his age with a 1.36 WHIP. When you see the strikeouts ebbing and know that Burnett has historically struggled with his control, you have to be very cautious if you invest here if he does return. Grade Burnett as an SP 5 if he decides to gives it one more shot.

109. Chris Tillman: While we have spent more than enough time talking about pitchers who get stronger as the season goes on, such as the Chicago Cubs' Jon Lester and Texas' Cole Hamels, a lesser-known member of that club historically has been Baltimore Orioles lefty Chris Tillman. While Lester and Hamels struggle badly in April before turning it on, Tillman goes a step further by also pitching poorly in May and June. This results in Tillman almost universally being sent to the wire early on, where those in the know would then smartly pick him up as they enjoy the inevitable resurgence. For his career, Tillman has a 1.44 first half WHIP compared to a 1.22 mark in second half. While the ERA's are closer (4.42/4.00), Tillman usually earns some solid reviews from July onward. 2015 went right along with that script but not completely. Tillman was so bad the first half (5.40 ERA) that his 4.55 second half mark was still a decent improvement. Alas a 4.55 ERA is still quite high and Tillman overall had a poor season overall. We will chalk some of Tillman's struggles up to simply being a bad season, as he has had an ERA under 4.00 from 2012 through 2014. Also turning just 28 in April, there is no erosion to worry about in terms of age. Those in AL-only formats should be much more interested in Tillman's second half, while those in mixers can ignore him until July arrives.

110. Derek Holland: It was another season filled with health problems for Texas Rangers lefty Derek Holland in 2015, with shoulder and finger woes cropping up this time around. Over the last two seasons Holland has only been able to throw a combined total of 95.2 innings for the Rangers which surely have stunted what was looking like nice some very good initial growth. It was not that long ago in 2013 where Holland seemed to finally be living up to the sizable hype attached to his name when he first started making his way up the minor league ladder (3.42 ERA/1.29 WHIP/189 K) but the last two seasons have been a complete wreck. No longer a prospect at 29, Holland is just a late round speculative grab in mixed leagues. While Holland has put up some big-time strikeout rates in the minor leagues, that ability has not followed him to the majors with his 6.29 K/9 last season serving as a reminder. We hate the ballpark as always and the constant injuries make Holland just another name.

111. Anthony DeScalfani: The Cincinnati Reds uncovered a decent innings eater during the 2015 season in the form of righty starting pitcher Anthony DeScalfani. A virtual unknown even to the most hard-core fantasy baseball addict, DeScalfani became a popular name off the waiver wire in April when he came out of the gates with a 1.01 ERA and a 0.77 WHIP. One month was all opposing hitters needed though to get a firmer read on DeScalfani's stuff and they battered him hard the rest of the way. In fact DeScalfani did not finish any one month from May to the end of the season where his ERA was under 4.00. That tells you DeScalfani was solved a bit by major league hitters and that makes him nothing but a low-end starting pitching option in NL-only formats.

112. James Paxton: Sometimes you just get tired of waiting for a promising young pitcher to get things going and that would be an understandable feeling concerning Seattle Mariners lefty James Paxton. The hard-throwing Paxton first put himself on the map with a big spring training that won him a rotation spot to begin 2014. Paxton wound up acquitting himself quite well in registering a terrific 3.04 ERA and 1.20 WHIP but he only was able to toss 74 innings due to a series of injuries that kept him a mainstay on the DL. Fast forward to 2015 and pretty much the same thing took place, with Paxton putting up a sub-4.00 ERA (3.90) and striking out guys at a decent 7.54 clip. However Paxton spent three months on the DL with arm trouble and then came back to make two starts before sitting the rest of the year with a torn fingernail on his pitching hand. Pretty much anything that could go wrong health-wise for Paxton has happened and it is getting tough to stomach any more of this from the angle of fantasy baseball.

113. Josh Collmenter: The Arizona Diamondbacks' Josh Collmenter is another one of those guys who season after season posts solid ERA's and WHIP's but who no one ever seems to want. 2015 was no different as Collmenter recorded a 3.79 ERA and 1.26 WHIP in 121 innings, with little to no fanfare attached. That made it a perfect 5/5 for Collmenter in terms of finishing a season with an ERA under 4.00 which is saying something when you consider the offensive tendencies of Chase Field. There are warts though, such as a very poor K rate (4.69 in 2015, 5.77 in 2014) and an increase in Collmenter's home runs per nine (1.34) is a scary development in his offensive home park.

114. Travis Wood: Back from the abyss, Chicago Cubs veteran Travis Wood continues to entice us with decent ratios and a K rate that is more than impressive considering his lack of flash. After a 5.03 ERA washout in 2014, Wood didn't look like he had a role with the Cubs as the 2015 season got underway. Wood wound up playing an important role for the Cubs though, splitting his season between the bullpen and the rotation. Collecting four saves and a bunch of strikeouts as reliever, Wood also won 5 games as a starter in serving as a do-everything arm for the team. Overall Wood recorded a terrific 118 strikeouts in his 100 innings with an ERA of 3.84 on a playoff team. In looking ahead to 2016, Wood will likely be in the bullpen again, while also being an insurance arm when injuries open up a spot in the rotation. In NL-only leagues Wood has some interesting appeal due to his K rate but in mixers he should only be looked at if he gets a chance to start.

115. Tom Koehler: The Miami Marlins look determined to see out the development of hard-throwing but flawed pitcher Tom Koehler over the last two seasons, continuing to trot him out every five days despite some very mediocre results. While Kohler has been good enough with ERA's of 3.81 and 4.07 the last two years, his WHIP has been over 1.30 during that span and point to a guy who has a very limited ceiling. There were rumblings that Koehler might have been tried as the team's closer last season when Steve Cishek washed out but it never came to pass. Ultimately I think that is where Koehler belongs as his 98-mph fastball can be that much more effective in the pen and in short doses. Until that happens, Koehler has almost zero value.

116. Kyle Lohse: The longtime king of the "Soft-Tosser/Good Ratio" club, the bottom finally fell out for aging veteran Kyle Lohse in 2015. After posting four straight seasons with an ERA under 4.00 going back to 2010, nothing went right for Lohse last year as that number shot way up to 5.85. Lohse showed diminished velocity and that was especially deadly for a guy who couldn't strike batters out even before the dip. As a result Lohse was hit very hard, with the worst number being his sky-high 1.71 HR/9. In addition to his major troubles there, Lohse fought his stuff like never before in compiling a 2.54 BB/9 which added to the misery. With his K rate as mediocre as ever at 6.38, Lohse seems like he is toast at the age of 37.

117. Matt Garza: Despite all of the rampant injuries and very high home run rates throughout his career, veteran starting pitcher Matt Garza always seemed to come up with a solid ERA in the mid-3.00 range to make himself useful in fantasy baseball. Unfortunately, this did not happen in 2015 as Garza's ERA spiked to 5.63 as his stuff seemed to finally abandon him. Garza has been leaking velocity for years and it really bit him last season as his K/9 dropped to a very low 6.30. That is quite a drop from the 7.88 Garza achieved in 2013 and you have to think all those years of arm troubles have started sapping the juice out of his stuff. While home runs remain a problem, Garza fought his control like never before in 2015, posting a horrific 3.45 BB/9. While he is still young at 32, Garza is looking finished as even an SP 5.

118. Dan Haren: It is up in the air whether or not Dan Haren will come back to pitch one more season, as he has been hinting at retirement going back to the start of 2014. Still Haren has proven to be effective enough to hold down SP 5 value even through last season when he logged a 3.67 ERA in a year split between the Miami Marlins and Chicago Cubs. Long one of our favorites in these pages due to his ace numbers and extreme durability, Haren has been the rare power pitcher who reinvented himself into a still effective starter despite the leaking velocity. Here is a salute to a tremendous career.

119. Danny Duffy: It was a letdown season for anyone who owned Kansas City Royals lefty Danny Duffy in 2015. A renowned strikeout monster in the minor leagues who struggled with terrible control problems when he made his way to the majors, Duffy had settled in during the 2014 season when he logged an excellent 2.53 ERA in 149.1 innings while splitting his work between the bullpen and rotation. The Royals gave Duffy a chance to be a regular rotation member for 2015 but early struggles eventually had him bouncing back and forth from the bullpen once again. The ERA also jumped sharply to an elevated 4.08 and walks rate spiked to a very high 3.49 BB/9. Perhaps most disappointing is that all the strikeouts Duffy had in the minors have not made the trip to the majors as his K/9 has generally stayed in the high-6.00 range the last two seasons. Without those strikeouts, Duffy is nothing but a mediocre pitcher whose best value could lie in the bullpen where his fastball would become more of a weapon.

120. Chris Young: While most probably thought the pitching version of Chris Young was retired, the veteran starter was in fact still hanging on in Major League Baseball as the 2015 season got underway. A minor league deal with the Kansas City Royals gave Young one last chance to stay a big-league starter after years of injury derailments and ugly pitching results. Like everything that has happened with the Royals lately, Young came up smelling like roses for the team in posting a shockingly good 3.06 ERA in his 123.1 innings. A giant of a man at 6-10, Young has always been a chore for major league hitters due to his long stride and arching release which makes the baseball feel like it is jumping right out at them. While his fastball has historically struggled to reach 90, Young has had a slew of good to very good K rates going back to his early San Diego Padre days. Now aging as he turns 37 in May, Young gets by more on keeping the ball in the park (1.17 HR/9) and with a decent hit rate. However the fact of the matter is that Young was a major fluke last season in terms of his sparkling ERA, mainly due a ridiculously lucky .209 BABIP that was as low a number for a pitcher over 100 innings as we have seen in quite awhile. As a result, Young's FIP and XFIP were both over 5.00 which speaks to how fortunate he was with the batted ball. That number will regress heavily in 2016 if Young finds another starting spot with the Royals or elsewhere and that makes him a terrible investment on that issue alone.

121. Brandon Finnegan: The Cincinnati Reds are hoping they have a new future ace to replace longtime number 1 Johnny Cueto after the latter was dealt away to the Kansas City Royals at the July 31 deadline. The main return for Cueto was former 2014 first round (17th overall) power righty Brandon Finnegan. Having a fastball that can reach the upper 90s, Finnegan did well in his cup of coffee run with the Reds in posting a 4.18 ERA and striking out 24 batters in 23.2 innings. Capable of picking up a good amount of K's with his hard stuff, Finnegan just needs to work on his control (3.94 BB/9) to start realizing his potential. Worth a very late round pick based on the upside.

122. Kris Medlen: Now with two Tommy John elbow surgeries in the bank, veteran starting pitcher Kris Medlen was just another name when 2015 fantasy baseball began. Making his way back after missing all of 2014 from the second such procedure, Medlen returned in late July to make 15 appearances for the Kansas City Royals split between the bullpen and rotation. Still young enough at the age of 30, Medlen was decent with a 4.01 ERA and 1.27 WHIP in his 58.1 innings. We will always hold Medlen's second half of 2012 in extremely high regard given how dominant he was (0.94 ERA/0.82 WHIP with 95 K in 95.1 innings) but that inflated expectations to unrealistic levels the next season. A 6.17 K/9 last season is indicative of how much Medlen's stuff has eroded due to the two surgeries and counting on him to hold up for even half a season has been foolish. On stuff alone Medlen can be a solid SP 5 but you ideally want to invest in more stable arms.

123. Miguel Gonzalez: The Baltimore Orioles have been a surprising source of some very good pitching values during the Buck Showalter era. While we always suggest avoiding AL East pitchers unless they have ace or number 2 ability, the Orioles have fielded rotations over the last few years that have had some classic SP 4 or 5 starters. One such case was righty Miguel Gonzalez who in his first three major league seasons registered ERA's of 3.25, 3.78, and 3.23 which work in any fantasy baseball format. Pitching to high contact, Gonzalez was a bit limited when you went past the ERA, as his 1.28 career WHIP was getting to shaky territory, and his K rate has always resided in the mediocre mid-6.00 range. Unfortunately Gonzalez couldn't make it four seasons in a row with a sub-4.00 ERA in 2015, as he was hit hard throughout with that number ballooning to 4.91. Gonzalez lost his control completely, posting a horrific 3.17 BB/9 IP and he also yielded 24 home runs in 144.2 innings. While Gonzalez is still young at the age of 32 in May, we wouldn't go anywhere near the guy unless you take part in an AL-only format.

With no upside to speak of and possessing a very shaky K rate, there really is nothing to talk about here if the ERA is not under 4.00.

124. J.A. Happ: Annually one of the worst starting pitchers in the game each season, somehow J.A. Happ managed to post a 3.61 ERA in a 2015 split between the Pittsburgh Pirates and Seattle Mariners. It was the move to the Pirates where Happ had the stretch that pushed his ERA down to his best mark since 2009, recording a 1.85 mark with the team in his 63.1 innings. Be that as it may, we all know Happ is a rough pitcher to own when it comes to his numbers, with his career WHIP an unsightly 1.37. While we commend the run Happ had last season, his career trends are pretty well-defined with regards to him being nothing more than waiver fodder.

125. Rick Porcello: Anyone who has a clue about fantasy baseball knew that Rick Porcello signing with the Boston Red Sox was a disaster waiting to happen. A soft-tossing/K-averse pitcher operating in the AL East is about as bad a matchup as a hurler can get in terms of environment and the results with predictably horrendous. When the carnage finally ended, Porcello sat there with a pathetic 4.92 ERA and a horrific WHIP of 1.36. While Porcello still possesses very good control and a decent enough HR/9, he is a batting practice pitcher more often than not in the AL East. Things will be just as ugly as long as he continues to don the Boston uniform.

126. Vidal Nuno: Already somewhat of a journeyman with three major league stops in three seasons, the Seattle Mariners' Vidal Nuno is barely holding onto a rotation spot. Obviously this means you should be looking past him when perusing some possible SP 5's.

127. Matt Moore: Even before the Tampa Bay Rays' Matt Moore underwent Tommy John elbow surgery early in the 2014 season, he was a guy we always tried to avoid for a number of reasons. While there was no denying the potent fastball that induced a high number of strikeouts, Moore had some big red flags. The biggest was a complete and utter lack of control that led to high walk rates and early departures from starts due to poor pitch efficiency. Costing him wins in the process, Moore was a WHIP-killer whose K upside was simply not worth checking out under those setups. His 57 inning return in 2015 was an abomination as well, as he clocked in with a 5.84 ERA. While Moore continued to walk guys at a high rate (3.00 BB/9), his K rate tumbled to a pedestrian 6.63 K/9. Without the strikeouts as part of the package, Moore really has nothing left to offer you anymore.

128. Robbie Ray: The Arizona Diamondbacks will likely take another long look at Robbie Ray for 2016 and they should given the fact he was quite solid in pitching to a 3.50 ERA and striking out 111 batters in 123.1 innings. Having already made his way through the Washington Nationals and Detroit Tigers organizations, Ray made the most of his chance last season. A real key in Ray's success was that his home run rate was very low at 0.66, doubly important in a launching pad like Chase Field. A 3.50 BB/9 needs a lot of work but Ray helps offset that with his 8.10 K/9. While we are not blown away by any means regarding Ray, he at least should be watched early on to see if he can build off his 2015 season.

129. Jeremy Hellickson: Not all pitchers who come through the Tampa Bay Rays system become stars and that certainly has been the case with Jeremy Hellickson. While Hellickson did come up with some hype when promoted by the Rays, he eventually fell out of favor due to rampant injuries and underwhelming pitching results. After moving through the Arizona Diamondbacks organization and now the Philadelphia Phillies after coming over via trade, life has not gotten much easier in the National League as he finished 2015 with a very ugly 4.62 ERA and 1.33 WHIP. That brought to three the amount of consecutive seasons Hellickson has had an ERA over 4.50. At 29-years-old there is no ceiling left to be had here which makes Hellickson just another average pitcher not worth your time or attention.

130. Robbie Erlin: You always have to pay attention to any San Diego Padres starting pitcher due to the benefits of throwing in Petco Park, a trend that has yielded some good values in the past. There are some limits to this however as Robbie Erlin doesn't belong among this group. After three seasons of cup of coffee runs with the team, Erlin has yet to keep his ERA under 4.00 despite the ballpark boost. Next.

131. Roenis Elias: Through two seasons as a member of the Seattle Mariners rotation, Roenis Elisa has done enough to be worthy of SP 5 status. After a 3.85 debut in 2014, Elias was only slightly worse in 2015 with a 4.14 mark. While Elias walks too many batters, his mid-7.00 K/9 offsets that a bit and he keeps the baseball in the park. A durable and solid late round selection.

132. Tommy Milone: Veteran righty Tommy Milone is quite easy to project and at the same time very straightforward when it comes to his usage. With a career ERA of 4.35 on the road and 3.56 at home, Milone is a strict play only in his own ballpark and a complete bench guy on the road. With a middling K rate and no statistic that jumps out, Milone is better left for those in AL-only setups.

133. Matt Bolsinger: The Los Angeles Dodgers got an unexpected boost to the back end of their rotation when they promoted unheralded pitching prospect Mike Bolsinger in late April. There may have been some unfamiliarity factor in terms of opposing hitters having no book on Bolsinger but he was phenomenal with a 1.05 ERA in 25.2 May innings. Eventually though hitters began to adjust and Bolsinger had two very rough months out of the last three (not counting August when he was sent back to the minor leagues before returning in September). The Dodgers eventually put Bolsinger in the bullpen where he pitched in long relief and that seems to be where he is destined for in terms of 2016. Bolsinger was not an impressive prospect outside of some good K rates and the Dodgers don't even seem sold on him as a member of their pitching staff.

134. Wily Peralta: After a nice 2014 season that put him on the fantasy baseball map, Milwaukee Brewers right-hander Wily Peralta had a disastrous 2015 campaign that made him a waiver wire mainstay. A 4.72 ERA and 1.54 WHIP is useless even in NL-only formats as Peralta struggled in almost every aspect of the pitching game. From giving up 14 home runs and walking 37 batters in only 108.2 innings, Peralta was also not fooling anyone in giving up 130 hits. He also could not help himself with one of the worst K rates among all starters in 2015, posting a ridiculously poor 4.97 K/9. A late season oblique injury mercifully ended the carnage early. Not to be touched.

135. Zach Davies: A late round name to keep in mind in your draft this season is 23-year-old Milwaukee Brewers farmhand pitcher Zach Davies. With the Brewers in full rebuild mode in 2015, Davies got a late season look without a bunch of expectations attached to the former 2011 26th round pick. Davies wound up opening some eyes however in his six starts, logging a 3.71 ERA and picking up 3 wins. A heavy ground ball pitcher, Davies keeps the ball in the park which helps him avoid big innings and overcome shaky control (3.97 BB/9 IP). Despite the solid run of outings, Davies' season was a very small sample size that should not be overblown. Worth a late round pick in very deep mixed leagues only.

136. Tim Lincecum: It was another ugly season for Tim Lincecum in 2015, as he combined more bad pitching with poor health that ended with hip surgery in August. Prior to the surgery, Lincecum posted his fourth straight season with an ERA over 4.00 (4.13), while his 1.48 WHIP was one of the worst marks among all starting pitchers. Over the last four seasons now Lincecum's ERA has come in at 5.18, 4.37. 4.74, and 4.13; while the WHIP's registered 1.47, 1.32, 1.39, and 1.48 during that span. In other words Lincecum is truly one of the worst starting pitchers in all of fantasy baseball and really the only thing he has left is name brand coming from his two Cy Young Awards that seem like a lifetime ago. By now it is obvious all those years of not icing his arm after starts and the Giants allowing him to throw such high amount of innings at a young age have completely ruined his career.

137. Hyun-Jin Ryu: Talented but injury-prone Los Angeles Dodgers Korean hurler Hyun-Jin Ryu didn't even throw one pitch in the major leagues in 2015, as he complained of pain in his throwing shoulder at the start of spring training and eventually needed season-ending surgery. Ryu is expected to be ready for the start of 2016 but there is serious doubt as to whether he still has the impressive stuff he showed in his 2013 and 2014 campaigns. Remember that Ryu posted K rates over 7.00 in both of those seasons, with ERA's coming in at 3.00 and 3.38 respectively. Unfortunately Ryu's shoulder has been a persistent problem from the very beginning and it seems like it will forever be an issue with varying severities. Worth a very late round speculative grab but even that is stretching it.

138. Jarred Cosart: Tough to justify owning a guy who sports a 4.52 ERA and 1.38 WHIP, while calling the spacious ballpark in Miami home as Jarred Cosart did in his 69.2 innings last season. Sporting some of the worst BB/9 IP marks in the majors during his brief career to this point, Cosart can't help himself either with strikeouts due to his shaky 6.07 BB/9 IP mark from 2015.

139. Mike Pelfrey: If you were to ask this peanut stand who the worst starting pitcher in the major leagues has been over the last seven years prior to 2015, Minnesota Twins veteran Mike Pelfrey would have been on the short list. After all

Pelfrey has been a human batting practice machine through big chunks of his career, having posted FIVE seasons with an ERA over 5.00. Making things even more horrific, Pelfrey doesn't even do anything in the strikeout department, habitually posting season marks under 5.00 in the K/9 IP column which is almost hard to believe. As a result of all this, we completely ignored the somewhat respectable 4.00 ERA Pelfrey posted in the first half of 2015 and were not shocked when his number there rose to 4.66 in the second. His place as one of the worst starters in baseball remains secure.

140. Chad Bettis: Owning any Colorado pitcher is a always a dicey proposition and the same held true with former 2012 second round pick Chad Bettis. Having been absolutely annihilated when given a chance to pitch at the major league level briefly in 2013 and 2014, Bettis got a decent look last season when he threw 115 innings with the team. Still Bettis was pretty unimpressive with his 4.32 ERA and 1.41 WHIP. Control has been a career-long problem for Bettis going back to the minors and that alone makes him radioactive given the home park.

141. Chase Anderson: After finally making his debut with the Arizona Diamondbacks in 2014, Chase Anderson has done enough to hold down the number 5 spot in the team's rotation with his average numbers (4.18 ERA/1.33 WHIP in 267 career innings). There is nothing that stands out here regarding Anderson as he is quite mediocre across the board. He will give you innings but not much in the way of K's (6.54 in 2015) and his ratios are not stellar either. Really holds usage in NL-only formats and nothing else.

142. Brandon Maurer: Petco Park has been directly responsible for supplying some useful back-end-of-the-rotation arms over the years, even from guys who are middling to bad starters when pitching on the road. Yet another addition to this growing group was Brandon Maurer who put up a 3.00 ERA in his 51 innings with the Padres last season. A below-average prospect while working his way through the Seattle Mariners farm system, Maurer keeps the ball in the park and strikes out enough guys to make less work for himself. Alas a bout with shoulder inflammation stalled the second half of his season but at the very least Maurer put himself in contention for a 2016 roster spot. Could work as a home stream in NL-only formats.

143. Charlie Morton: There is an annual "soft tosser" class of fantasy baseball pitchers each and every season who often carve out useful roles as SP 5's. Often these pitchers post decent enough ERA's and higher WHIP's, to go with mediocre to poor K rates. While in innings capped formats these pitchers should be avoided, in non-capped leagues you can own one or two to round out your rotation. One such pitcher is Pittsburgh Pirates veteran Charlie Morton who posted a 3.26 ERA in 2013 and a 3.72 mark in 2014 to put himself on the fantasy baseball map. In reality though, Morton is a very limited pitcher whose career-high in strikeouts is a poor 126. With such a razor-thin margin for error, Morton needs decent BABIP luck and excellent control to get by. He did not get either in 2015 as he posted a bad 2.86 BB/9 and his .309 BABIP was slightly unlucky. The result was a 4.81 ERA that is a non-starter in any format. Now 32, Morton can safely be ignored this season.

144. Kyle Gibson: One of our favorite whipping boys among pitchers in fantasy baseball is perennially overmatched Minnesota Twins starter Kyle Gibson. Having some prospect buzz while coming up the Minnesota system, Gibson quickly proved himself to be a below-average pitcher who was truly pathetic at times in registering 6.53 and 4.47 ERA's his first two Major League seasons. The problem with Gibson is that he can't miss any bats, having posted K/9 rates at very ugly levels as a professional pitcher. In fact the 6.70 K/9 IP Gibson posted in 2015 was his career-high which is not saying much since he was under 6.00 his first two years in the league. On top of the lack of K's, Gibson has horrible control, with BB/9 rates of over 3.00 in two of his first three seasons. While Gibson did manage to put up a solid 3.84 ERA in 2015 with the Twins, that can be taken with a bit of a grain of salt due to a lucky .287 BABIP. Gibson clearly has to get out of the American League to have any semblance of value but he is a shaky bet even in a streaming situation. Ignore completely.

145. Brandon Morrow: What was once looking like a very promising career as a power pitcher has devolved into a complete injury mess for Brandon Morrow. Numerous shoulder/elbow problems, along with a diagnosis of diabetes have prevented him from throwing more than 55 innings in each of the last three seasons. The latest roadblock was Morrow undergoing shoulder surgery over the summer that will keep him out for 3-4 months. He could claim a minor-league deal by the spring but Morrow is nothing but old news.

146. A.J. Griffin: Griffin joins Jarrod Parkers as early 2015 Tommy John surgery victims who didn't pitch at all last season. Making matters more difficult, Griffin then dealt with shoulder issues while beginning his rehab in late summer. Nothing to see here.

147. Steven Wright: R.A. Dickey now has some new company in the knuckleball fraternity as the Boston Red Sox gave an extended look to pitch tumbler Steven Wright in 2015. Like almost all knuckleball pitchers, Wright was often either completely shelled or excellent with no in-between. A minor league lifer who is already 31, Wright registered a decent 4.09 ERA and 1.29 WHIP last season. Alas Wright doesn't have the hard knuckler that Dickey has which means he was a liability in the strikeout column as shown by his 6.44 rate. You can never feel comfortable using a knuckleball pitcher in any one start and that is especially true for one in the American League. Pass him by.

148. Tyler Skaggs: The hard-throwing Skaggs has had a tough time getting going as a major leaguer after being a first round pick of the Los Angeles Angels back in 2009. After rocking some big strikeout rates while coming up the minor league ladder in the Arizona Diamondbacks organization, Skaggs was hit incredibly hard during his cup of coffee appearances with the team in both 2012 and 2013. Eventually getting dealt back to the Angels for the 2014 season, Skaggs again struggled when given a chance to pitch with the team at the major league level. Disaster would then strike in terms of Skaggs needing season-ending Tommy John surgery which wiped out his entire 2015 campaign. Skaggs is expected to be ready to go for the start of spring training but his prospect shine has almost completely dimmed. While those 11.00-plus K rates at the minor league level remain impressive, Skaggs has to first prove he can stay healthy, stop walking so many batters, and cease with the gopher ball issue. Those are a lot of conditions for possible ownership. In other words, don't bother.

149. Joe Kelly: It was nothing short of a disaster for Joe Kelly in his first full go-round with the Boston Red Sox last season. After coming over as a midseason trade acquisition the year prior, Kelly was given a firm spot in the Boston rotation to begin 2015. From start to finish, Kelly was hit hard, posting a hideous ERA of 5.20 or higher in three of the first four months of the year. Eventually the Red Sox were forced to send Kelly back to the minors as a last gasp attempt to right the ship. The one bright spot was Kelly coming back up and pitching to a 2.68 ERA in August and a 3.86 mark in September ERA but the lefty still finished with a hideous 4.82 mark overall. Kelly also dealt with pitching shoulder weakness that ended his season early. In short Kelly was simply one of the worst starters in baseball. Avoid completely.

150. Jorge De La Rosa: Long a pariah in the fantasy baseball community due to his brutal control, sky-high ERA's, and home ballpark in Coors Field with the Colorado Rockies, you really have to be desperate to ever get involved with the erratic power pitcher. Now entering into his 13th MLB season, De La Rosa still has not changed much over the years which of course is a very bad thing. His 2015 included a 3.93 BB/9 IP rate which was his worst mark since 2009, his 1.36 WHIP was a joke, and he continued having trouble staying healthy in registering just 149 innings. Now aging at 35, De La Rosa should stay on the waiver wire for all of 2016 unless you want to intentionally lose this season.

151. Manny Banuelos: After seemingly being stuck in neutral in the New York Yankees' minor league system as rampant injuries continued to dim Manny Banuelos' once impressive prospect hype, a 2015 offseason trade to the Atlanta Braves supplied a prime opportunity for the erratic lefty to put down roots on a rebuilding team. After beginning the season in the Braves farm system, Banuelos got called up to make his Atlanta debut in July. It appeared initially that the Braves stole Banuelos away from the Yankees as he quickly posted a 2.49 ERA in 4 July starts, striking out 16 in 21.2 innings. Unfortunately it all went downhill from there as Banuelos' body betrayed him yet again as he made only two more ugly starts (17.36 ERA) the rest of the season. Banuelos wound up needing surgery to remove a bone spur from his left pitching elbow but he is expected to be fine for the start of camp. As far as the small sample size of numbers Banuelos put up in his 26.1 innings in 2015, a very ugly 6.49 K/9 IP and an even more hideous 4.10 BB/9 IP show you just how diminished Banuelos' stuff is after all of the injuries. Might be of some use in NL-only setups but even that is stretching it.

152. Mike Foltynewicz: The guy with the impossible to spell or pronounce last name had a very rough ending to his debut major league campaign with the Atlanta Braves in 2015. Foltynewicz unbelievably had to have a part of one of his right ribs removed to stop rampant blood clots from infiltrating his right pitching arm late in the year. While he was slated to be fine for spring training, the rib issue was pretty much the only thing worth talking about when it came to Foltynewicz' performance last season. An ugly 5.71 ERA told the whole story about how hittable the 24-year-old was and that bloated number took the shine off of what were some very interesting 2015 Triple-A numbers (3.49 ERA/10.01 K/9 IP). While Foltynewicz has every right to improve, we can't recommend going near him until he shows any sort of sign of figuring things out.

153. Adam Morgan: The Philadelphia Phillies ushered in the future during the 2015 season, calling up a bunch of their top hitting and pitching prospects to replenish what had become one of the more decrepit rosters in the majors. Included in that bunch was mid-level starter Adam Morgan whose 2014 shoulder surgery dimmed his light prospect status a bit. The former 2011 third-round pick was hit around during his 84.1 innings with the Phillies, posting an ugly 4.48 ERA and a terrible 5.23 K/9 IP rate. In actuality, Moran was not much better at Triple-A prior to his promotion, posting an even worse 4.74 ERA with Lehigh Valley. Flat out, Morgan is nothing more than a soft-tosser who will barely qualify as an SP 5 with the Phillies and even less than that in fantasy baseball. In fact if Morgan was a right-hander, no one would even be talking about the kid.

154. Drew Hutchison: We always talk about pitchers who have exemplary ERA's and WHIP's but who fail to get wins due to a lack of run support. Rarely do we mention the flip side where a guy gets hit hard throughout a season but also receives a fluky amount of wins due to the offensive potency of his team. We present to you the 2015 version of Drew Hutchison, whose Toronto Blue Jays teammates put up a ton of runs whenever he took the hill as evidenced by his 13-5 record. For Hutchison to win 13 games despite carrying around a bloated 5.47 ERA tells you all you need to know about what happened here. While Hutchison has had moments when you wanted to add him in the past, 2015 was a complete abomination. Even outside of the offensive dimensions of Rogers Center, Hutchison didn't help himself with a very high 1.28 HR/9 and he lost more than a K/9 from 2014, going from 8.97 to 7.78. Move right along.

155. C.C. Sabathia: There is no need to go over what has transpired here again when it comes to the vast disintegration of New York Yankees veteran lefty C.C. Sabathia. Once a perennial fantasy baseball ace, Sabathia now can't be owned in any format given how horrific his numbers have been across the board since 2013. Sabathia is the poster child for how massive inning totals eventually sap the arm strength and turn a pitcher into a human batting practice machine. Over the last three seasons Sabathia has logged ERA's of 4.78, 5.28, and 4.73 and his body is breaking down everywhere. Enough said.

156. Rich Hill: While few were still paying attention by that late juncture in the season, an amazing story took place in the Boston Red Sox rotation last September. With the Red Sox putting the finishing touches on a brutal 2015, they promoted off-the-street lefty starter Rich Hill from the minor leagues in order to eat up some innings in a meaningless September. Well it was not a meaningless finish for Hill however and the veteran took full advantage of his first chance to pitch in the major leagues since a 5.1 inning stint with the New York Yankees in the bullpen a year earlier. Having been pitching for the Long Island Ducks in the Independent League prior to being signed by Boston, what Hill accomplished in his four starts was impossible to believe. First came a one-hitter with 10 strikeouts in a win over the Tampa Bay Rays, followed by another 10-K outing in a win over the Blue Jays when he gave up three runs in 7 innings. A meeting with the Baltimore Orioles brought forth more insanity as Hill struck out 10 batters for the third start in a row while pitching a two-hit shutout that netted his third straight win. Hill would finish out with 2 runs given up in 6 innings as he took a tough luck loss. The grand total came out to a 1.55 ERA and 36 strikeouts in 29 innings for a 13.29 rate. Now 36 and having made his way through too many organizations to count, Hill's latest stop comes with the Oakland A's who signed him to a one-year deal. The bottom line here is that some unfamiliarity allowed Hill to pitch as well as he did and that he really is not worth anything more than a last round speculative pick.

157. Josh Tomlin: Now a veteran at the age of 31, the Cleveland Indians' Josh Tomlin can hang his hat on his best ever season in 2015 when he put up a 3.02 ERA and 1.15 WHIP in an abbreviated campaign. Still Tomlin's career ERA remains ugly at 4.65 and he really carries value just in AL-only formats.

158. Martin Perez: While he showed some flashes of ability (including a no-hitter) early in his career, Texas Rangers righty Martin Perez is now nothing but waiver fodder after undergoing Tommy John surgery in 2014. While Perez did make his way back in the middle of last season, his 4.46 ERA and 1.42 WHIP shows that he is not someone you want to get involved with.

159. Alfredo Simon: While no one can take away the tremendous All-Star first half of 2014 that Alfredo Simon shockingly accomplished (12-3/2.70 ERA/1.05 WHIP), there has been nothing but disaster since that time. Not only did Simon get destroyed during the second half of that 2014 campaign (4.52 ERA/1.44 WHIP), he carried his struggles into the next season with the Detroit Tigers. Moving from the National League to the American League was already a big red flag going into the season for a guy who doesn't strike people out but Simon outdid himself with a 5.05 ERA and 1.44 WHIP. A free agent as of press time, Simon has to go back to the National League to even possibly get a look as an SP 5. He just doesn't even deserve that kind of valuation.

160. Ervin Santana: It was not the start to the 2015 season that veteran hurler Ervin Santana envisioned after he signed late with the Minnesota Twins in spring training. Busted for a failed drug test, Santana was suspended the first 50 games of the year. Already just barely an SP 5 in fantasy baseball circles, Santana was sent packing to the waiver wire en masse as a result of the violation. No one wound up missing Santana either as he came back to pitch in his customary underwhelming manner. With a 4.00 ERA and 1.30 WHIP, Santana oozed mediocrity. The guy has made a career with some wild swings in production, almost alternating good and bad seasons for years. Now aging at 33 and with a K rate that has sunk under 7.00/9, there is no longer any reason to be involved with this anymore.

161. Rubby De La Rosa: When you give up 32 home runs in 188.2 innings, you have no business being on a fantasy baseball team in any setup. Such is the life of Rubby De La Rosa who over the last three years has had ERA's of 5.56, 4.43, and 4.67. The numbers say it all and that is to put De La Rosa at the very bottom of any deep pitching sheet you create.

162. Aaron Brooks: The main return on the Ben Zobrist trade to the Kansas City Royals, pitching prospect Aaron Brooks received a baptism by fire when brought up by the team late in 2015. Brooks was a complete mess as evidenced by his 6.67 ERA and tiny 6.18 K/9. You know what to do.

163. Kyle Kendrick: With one of the highest career ERA's among all starting pitchers entering 2016, the only reason you should own Kyle Kendrick if is you league gives out prizes for finishing in last place.

164. Aaron Harang: Another year, another team, and another disaster for veteran starter Aaron Harang in 2015. Now turning 38 in May, Harang could be out of the league by the time you read this.

165. Justin Nicolino: The Miami Marlins trotted out prospect Justin Nicolino for 12 starts in a rebuilding 2015 season but the results were underwhelming. A 4.01 ERA and 1.24 WHIP were not terrible but Nicolino only managed to strike out 23 batters in 74 innings which is pathetic. Guys with such pronounced soft-tossing tendencies should be avoided completely.

166. Ivan Nova: The return from Tommy John elbow surgery was not pretty for Ivan Nova in 2015. Already quite hittable before the procedure, Nova was a complete mess as he was pulled from the rotation after a series of beatings. Nova doesn't miss bats which is a big problem in the AL East and that will continue to be his downfall going forward. Ignore the youth and let Nova stay on the wire.

167. Colby Lewis: Having now fully made his way back from 2012 Tommy John surgery, veteran Texas Rangers starter Colby Lewis has struggled quite a bit over the last two years after sitting out for all of the 2013 season. While Lewis has given Texas innings, his ERA's during that span have come in at ugly 5.18 and 4.66 marks. Now in Lewis' defense, he was noticeably better in 2015 as he moved further away from the surgery. His 1.24 WHIP showed some positive signs but Lewis has a ton of mileage already on his 36-year-old arm. A former Japanese League veteran, Lewis's K rate has been dropping sharply and the home runs are always a problem. The age and numbers say clearly you should avoid Lewis completely this season.

168. Adam Conley: A big start to the Triple-A season earned Miami Marlins pitching prospect Adam Conley a promotion at the end of June, as the team once again began looking toward their prospects after another year of non-contention. While he made just one appearance each in June and July, Conley was brought back up to stay in August where he showed some intriguing ability by registering a composite 3.84 ERA and striking out 57 batters in 61 innings. The pedigree is certainly there as Conley was is a former 2011 second round pick of the Marlins and his 8.41 K/9 is an attractive number as well. The ballpark is also obviously a draw and Conley will be given every chance to stake his claim to a rotation spot from the start of the season. Has the look of a worthwhile late round pick.

169. Matt Wisler: The truly horrific season the Atlanta Braves had in 2015 got to the point that they were giving starts to guys who didn't belong in the major leagues. That was clearly the case with righty Matt Wisler who put up a 5.11 ERA in 100.1 innings and who likely pitched himself out of any chance to be in the rotation for 2016. He didn't belong there anyway.

170. Tyler Duffey: The Minnesota Twins got a nice boost to their rotation down the stretch last season, promoting the former 2012 fifth round pick at the start of August. While there were some rocky moments, Duffey acquitted himself nicely by putting up a 3.10 ERA and striking out 53 batters in just 58 innings. Duffey was dominant all season at the minor league level prior to his promotion (2.56 ERA at Double-A, 2.53 at Triple-A) which makes what he did in his cup of coffee run with the Twins not a complete mirage. Duffey is capable of getting a good amount of swings and misses as his 8.22 K/9 showed and his tiny 0.62 HR/9 was stellar. Walks are a problem like most young starters but Duffey should be on your radar, especially in AL-only setups.

171. John Danks: We won't waste much time here. Basically if you own veteran starter John Danks in even AL-only formats, you are looking to finish at the bottom of your league. Whereas Danks at one time briefly held some value early in his career, things turned quite sour when he began to leak velocity. The numbers have been ugly for awhile now for Danks, with 2015 bringing a 4.71 ERA if you needed to be convinced. As bad a pitching investment as one can make this season.

172. Justin Masterson: When your ERA is over 5.50 for each of the last two seasons, there really is nothing to say when it comes to Justin Masterson and 2016 fantasy baseball. Even before Masterson fell on his face, we spoke at length about how overrated he was. While Masterson has had some decent moments through the years, he was always very hittable and he couldn't get lefties out. Having undergone arthroscopic shoulder surgery this past September, Masterson is now barely hanging on as a major league pitcher. Nothing but waiver waste.

173. Mike Minor: It is almost like the 2013 season never even existed for the Atlanta Braves' Mike Minor. It was during that season Minor seemed to take a giant step towards being a front-of-the-rotation starter in registering a 3.21 ERA and 7.96 K rate in 204.2 innings. It appears as though Minor's first 200-plus inning campaign sapped the strength in his pitching shoulder as he was a 4.77 ERA train wreck in 2014. Always prone to the home run ball, Minor's 1.30 HR/9 IP was insane. Things only got worse as Minor missed the entire 2015 season with a torn labrum in his shoulder, an injury that didn't allow him to start throwing again until late September. While Minor should be ready to go for spring training, any type of shoulder injury is always a major red flag you want to avoid. We have seen in cases such as Mat Latos, and prior to that Josh Johnson and Tommy Hanson how once-promising careers have quickly bottomed out once the shoulder goes bad. That could be the future for Minor as well given what we have seen. Avoid.

174. Williams Perez: It was a very unimpressive rookie debut for Atlanta Braves righty Williams Perez in 2015, as the native of Venezuela was rocked to the tune of a 4.78 ERA and 1.55 WHIP. The Braves were stripped down to nothing when it came to their rotation as they went fully into their rebuild mode and that is more or less the reason Perez got a long look. With a hideout 5.63 K/9 IP and even worse 3.93 BB/9, Perez should only be on a roster if your goal is to finish in last place.

175. Jarrod Parker: Parker is just the latest in a recent long line of young pitchers whose careers look over before they even really got started due to a string of major surgeries. Now with two Tommy John procedures under his belt before the age of 27, Parker can be safely avoided in all formats this season.

176. Bronson Arroyo: Arroyo was the very rare case of an aging veteran pitcher who needed to undergo Tommy John surgery. Prior to the surgery, Arroyo was quite possibly the biggest workhorse pitcher in the game who racked up tremendous inning totals with decent enough ERA's. Now 39-years-old, Arroyo is more likely to retire than throw a pitch for you this season.

177. Brandon McCarthy: A big second half run with the New York Yankees in 2014 (2.89 ERA/1.15 WHIP/82 K in 90.1 IP) landed McCarthy a massive/overinflated contract from the free-spending Los Angeles Dodgers that offseason. After historically being a middle K rate guy during his stints with the

Oakland A's and Arizona Diamondbacks, McCarthy changed his repertoire on the fly with the Yankees, using his four-seam fastball and sinker more which he cited as the reason for the sharp uptick in his K rate. Unfortunately McCarthy has proven to be one of the more snake bit pitchers in the game. First it was the scary skull fracture he suffered from a comebacker which was then followed a few seasons later by Tommy John elbow surgery only 23 innings into his 2015 Dodgers tenure. McCarthy won't return until near midway through the 2016 season and thus he has very little appeal to speak of until then.

178. Jason Vargas: Vargas is expected to miss most or all of 2016 after undergoing Tommy John surgery. Take him off your cheat sheets.

179. Lance Lynn: Yet another Tommy John victim bites the dust.

RELIEF PITCHERS

Draft Strategy: Perhaps no other position in fantasy baseball is drafted more incorrectly each and every season than the classified closers who collect saves for the 30 respective major league teams. By now we are getting tired of hearing ourselves remind you how incredibly volatile the closer fraternity is each and every season, with more than half of the Opening Day ninth inning arms losing their role at some point during the year due to injuries, poor performance, or trades. Some continue to argue that the high turnover rate among closers makes it imperative to grab a proven one early in the draft but again this is not the way to go since saves have been proven to show up all season long for your to stay very competitive in the category if you work the wire. And once again in most standard ROTO mixed leagues, closers only really impact one category (saves) as they don't pitch enough innings to greatly move the needle much in the ERA and WHIP columns. That means you are using an early round pick on a player who will help in just one statistical column, while the rest of your league shores up on three-to-four category weapons. Needless to say, a major waste of a pick for sure. So once again we suggest you start looking for solid middle-tier closers in the middle rounds and use the late rounds to pick up some sleepers or the leftovers options. There will be double-digit closers who show up all season around baseball which means as long as you stay active on the wire, you will be just fine in terms of having a good total of saves by the end of the year.

New York Yankees (Andrew Miller): In a bit of a shocker, New York Yankees manager Joe Girardi went with free agent signee Andrew Miller as the closer to start the 2015 season over the presumed favorite Delin Betances, with those who invested in the latter more than a little perturbed. The fireballing lefty was more than up to the task though as he dominated from start to finish in compiling a 1.90 ERA, 36 saves, and recording an insane 14.59 K/9. The latest in a very impressive line of failed starters turned into All-Star closers, Miller has been virtually unhittable over the last two years which coincided with his full immersion into the bullpen. With top control and a tiny 0.73 HR/9, Miller is as good as it gets among the closer fraternity.

Baltimore Orioles (Zach Britton): Baltimore Orioles stopper Zach Britton has more than shown you don't have to possess a 98-mph heater to make it as a top closer in today's game. Using a sinkerball that is as good as there is in baseball, Britton has pitched to dominant 1.65 and 1.92 ERA's the last two seasons. Still Britton shot way up in the K/9 category in 2015, pushing past the 10.00 mark for the first time in his career at 10.83. When you consider Britton's number there a year earlier was a modest 7.31, you can see just how well he has adapted to the closer role. While no ninth inning pitcher is ever completely safe, Britton can be trusted more than most.

Tampa Bay Rays (Brad Boxberger): It will be interesting to see what the Tampa Bay Rays do with their closing situation for the 2016 season, as favorite Brad Boxberger was anything but consistent last year. While Boxberger is no doubt a strikeout machine (14.47 and 10.57 K/9's the last two years), his penchant for giving up home runs is a big problem in the ninth inning. There is also the double whammy of Boxberger having terrible control as he put up a nasty 4.57 BB/9 last season which added to the drama when he tried to close out games. Despite the up and down nature of his season, Boxberger held onto the gig throughout as he finished with 41 saves. A 3.71 ERA from a closer is quite high though and Boxberger could easily be replaced.

Boston Red Sox (Craig Kimbrel) In the "Early Offseason" version of our 2016 draft guide, we spoke about how risky the fading Koji Uehara was in terms of counting on him as a prime closer for this season in fantasy baseball. Well apparently the Red Sox realized the issues Uehara presented as they swung a deal with the San Diego Padres to being in Craig Kimbrel to take over the ninth inning. After three straight seasons where he pitched to an ERA under 2.00 and recorded insane K/9 rates between 13.16 and 16.66, Kimbrel was without peer. However like everything else that went wrong with the Padres last season, Kimbrel was a bit less than anticipated as he was more hittable than ever before and saw his ERA rise to a quite high for him 2.58. Kimbrel was still missing a ton of bats as the K rate stayed stellar (13.20) but he started giving up home runs, which is doubly disappointing considering he called Petco Park home. Also over the last two years there have been a few injury scares with Kimbrel and that is something to absolutely be aware of heading into the new season. Relatively young as he turns only 28 in May, Kimbrel has at least had a bit of aura taken away.

Toronto Blue Jays (Roberto Osuna): The award for the most chaotic ninth inning (at least in the first half of the year) went to the Toronto Blue Jays who pulled lefty Brett Cecil from the role one game into the season and then proceeded to go through a few other failed options before hard-throwing rookie Roberto Osuna got a chance. At only 20-years-old, Osuna was terrific as he nailed down 20 saves with a 2.58 ERA and 9.69 K/9. The ratios all check out here as Osuna has good control (2.07 BB/9) and keeps the ball in the park (0.90 HR.9), which is especially crucial in Rogers Center. There was some talk emanating about Osuna possibly being converted into a starter for 2016 but until that happens he is the guy to own when it comes to collecting saves on the AL East champs. If a conversion is in fact made however, Aaron Sanchez becomes the leading fallback option.

Detroit Tigers (Francisco Rodriguez): The late-career renaissance of Francisco Rodriguez continued on unabated last season as the veteran was nearly flawless in converting 38 saves, while his 2.21 ERA was the lowest mark in that category since 2010. It was just a few years earlier where Rodriguez looked finished as his velocity dropped badly and his ERA spiked to 4.38. A change in delivery brought back some life to the fastball however and Rodriguez has been terrific ever since. Now a clear veteran as he turns 34 in January, Rodriguez looks primed for another very good season in 2016. For one thing, his 9.79 K/9 was better than his 9.66 mark the year prior. In addition, Rodriguez improved both his BB/9 and HR/9 last season which further validates how he remains a good investment. The best part about Rodriguez perhaps is the fact that since many in the fantasy baseball community will think he is going to fade again, his draft price should be decent. Based on the metrics, that fade is not ready to happen. Perhaps the only slight negative is that Rodriguez is moving back into the tougher American League after the Detroit Tigers swung a deal for him but that is just quibbling.

Chicago White Sox (David Robertson): The Chicago White Sox opened up the vault for free agent closer David Robertson during the 2014 offseason in an attempt to correct what had become a tremendous problem for them. The All-Star lefty was anything but smooth though as he registered an elevated 3.41 ERA and struggled to keep the baseball in the park. Robertson did collect his usual stellar amount of strikeouts though(12.22 K/9), so his stuff was still quite potent but the guy performed a tick or two below his Yankee levels. Be that as it may, Robertson is still one of the better closers out there and his leash is as long as anyone in the game given his track record and contract.

Cleveland Indians (Cody Allen): A popular closer upside play for 2015 was Cleveland Indians youthful stopper Cody Allen. Already coming off a big 2014 when he posted a 2.07 ERA and logged 24 saves, Allen was a brutal right at the start of last season. By the end of April, Allen was a sitting with an unfathomable 11.57 ERA and his job was in trouble. Allen was ultimately able to turn things around though, pitching two months with an ERA under 1.00, with the other two being in the mid-3.00 range. The overall season turned out all right as Allen's composite ERA still came in under 3.00 at 2.99 and his K/9 was the highest of his career at 12.85. Yes there was a bunch of volatility thrown in but Allen should once again be the guy to close for Cleveland in 2016.

Kansas City Royals (Wade Davis): Finally the Wade Davis Closing Era is upon us. While no one would ever question how good Greg Holland has been as a closer for the Royals, he simply was not right at any point during the 2015 season. Eventually a torn UCL was discovered which led to Tommy John surgery and a complete absence from the 2016 season. That meant Davis would move into the ninth inning as the no-questions asked closer; a role he was destined for all along after some truly incredible numbers in setup. Over the last two years, Davis' season ERA's have come in at 1.00 and 0.94. No that is not a misprint. Simply put, there was not a better bullpen arm in all of baseball during that span. What makes Davis such a chore for major league hitters is his very high K rate (13.63 in 2014, 10.43 last season), not to mention his hard to believe home run numbers. In 72 innings pitched in 2014, Davis did not give up a single long ball. Last season? Try a 0.40 HR/9 rate. Already we can say that Davis is a top tier closer for 2016 fantasy baseball and it would not be a surprise if he ended up as the top guy altogether.

Minnesota Twins (Glen Perkins): It was another very solid season in 2015 for veteran Minnesota Twins lefty Glen Perkins, as he nailed down 32 saves for the surprising contenders. A deeper look at the numbers though reveal some issues that need to be discussed, many of them not good. Over the last two years Perkins has seen his ERA rise to the mid-3.00 range after being under that mark from 2011 through the 2013 seasons. In addition, Perkins' K rate is taking the wrong path as it fell all the way to 8.53 in 2015 which was his lowest ever as a closer. Finally, Perkins has been dealing with increasing health woes over the last two years as he starts to get up there in age (33 in March). Clearly Perkins' arm and stuff are eroding right before our eyes and again you want to always get off the ride a year early instead of a year too late. Trouble is brewing here.

Seattle Mariners (Joaquin Benoit): After enduring the horror show that was Fernando Rodney in the closer role the first half of last season, the Seattle Mariners took a later look both at Carson Smith and old friend Tom Wilhelmsen. While we have seen the Wilhelmsen show before and were not very impressed, Smith on the other hand pitched well with a 2.31 ERA and 1.01 WHIP. However the Mariners traded for San Diego Padres setup man Joaquin Benoit who now looks like the favorite for saves in 2016. Now 38, Benoit is aging like a fine wine and over the last three seasons his ERA has come in at the following dominant numbers: 2.01, 1.49, and 2.34. The K rates during that span? 9.81, 10.60, and 8.68. Clearly Benoit has the goods to get the job done in the ninth inning and he only has to beat out the up-and-down Wilhelmsen and the much more potent Smith. Smith is actually a good threat to the closer role as he was very good himself in setup for the Mariners in 2015 but the experience of Benoit should win out there. Benoit has always been on the verge of long runs as a closer before but never has gotten a decent chance due to trades, injuries, and other factors. This time around he looks like the very good value play he was prior to last season before Kimbrel arrived to changed the outlook. Put Benoit in a prime spot in your closer rankings for 2016.

Oakland A's (Sean Doolittle): Pretty much nothing went right for lefty closer Sean Doolittle in 2015, as persistent shoulder trouble shelved him for all but 13.2 innings. It was nice however to see Doolittle get his closer job back as he finished off four saves, which should place him as the ninth inning favorite for 2016. Keep in mind that it was just a year prior where Doolittle posted his monster breakout campaign (2.73 ERA/12.78 K/9/22 saves) and his strikeout/control ability doesn't get much better that what we saw during that overpowering season. Of course shoulder problems like Doolittle had in 2015 are a potential landmine that can crop up at a moment's notice, so his future is anything but secure. Bad shoulders also tend to sap strength and one can get at least mildly concerned when witnessing Doolittle's K rate drop three full strikeouts from 2014 to 2015. Be that as it may, his draft price will fall quite a bit this season and that makes Doolittle a decent comeback investment.

Texas Rangers (Shawn Tolleson): The Texas Rangers were kidding themselves when they went into the 2015 season with the washed-up Neftaliz Feliz as their ninth inning man. It didn't take long for Feliz to predictably throw away the opportunity which opened the door to the nice story engineered by setup man Shawn Tolleson. The steady veteran proved to be a quick learner as the team's closer, locking down 35 saves and posting an ERA of 2.99. As we look toward 2016, there is a bit of trepidation regarding Tolleson though in terms of him being able to duplicate that kind of performance. The 9.46 K/9 checks out nicely for a closer but the 1.12 HR/9 not so much. Tolleson could be the latest in a long line of guys to fade right into the background again after a surprising season as an effective closer but on numbers alone, he is squarely in the third tier at best among this group.

Houston Astros (Luke Gregerson): After years of terrific work as a top setup man with the San Diego Padres and Oakland A's, Luke Gregerson finally got a much deserved chance to close games after signing on with the Houston Astros as a free agent prior to the 2015 season. Gregerson proved to be money well spent as he locked down 31 saves for the playoff-bound Astros, while pitching to a solid 3.10 ERA. The season was not without some rocky moments for Gregerson though, as he had some extended slumps that pushed the ERA over 3.00. A mediocre 8.70 K/9 lessens the margin of error for Gregerson but he gets a ton of chances on an Astros team that usually winds up playing close games. We won't make it a point to draft Gregerson but we also would not mind having him once the top 10-12 closers are off the board.

New York Mets (Jeurys Familia): Stupidity + opportunity combined together to give Jeurys Familia a prime opportunity to serve as the New York Mets' close right from the start of the 2015 season. Of course we are referring to the mindless PED suspension of incumbent stopper Jenrry Mejia that placed Familia in the ninth inning in the first place (and a second PED bust that cemented his status) and the results were beyond spectacular. Familia dominated from the start, posting a 1.85 ERA, 9.92 K/9, and locking down 43 saves for a division winner. Other than a tiny blip right after the All-Star break, Familia was as safe a closing option as there was in the game. With Mejia likely on his way out of the organization, there is zero threat to Familia's job with the Mets. With a very good 2.19 BB/9 and 0.69 HR/9, Familia is set to be a top tier closer this season.

Washington Nationals (Jonathan Papelbon): Papelbon finally got his wish with regards to being shipped out from the rebuilding Philadelphia Phillies, heading to the Washington Nationals where he displaced the postseason skittish Drew Storen in the ninth inning. Of course the Nats fell flat on his face after Papelbon got into town and his season ended in ugly fashion when he was suspended three games for plunking Manny Machado. In addition, Papelbon fought with Bryce Harper in the dugout, putting his hands around the star outfielder's neck which added to the chaos of his season. As far as what Papelbon did with a baseball in his hand, his 2.13 ERA and 1.03 WHIP were fantastic. Now 34, Papelbon has more than successfully transitioned from a fireballing closer to one who gets by more on guile and off-speed stuff. Just to show you in terms of numbers regarding how the profile of Papelbon has changed, his K rate was down to a career-low 7.96 in 2015. Remember that Papelbon was a 12.17 guy in that category as recently as 2011 but leaking velocity and a rough 2013 forced him to change. The transition has been a smashing success as Papelbon's 2.04 and 2.13 ERA the last two years were his two were the third and fourth lowest totals of his career. While it seemed dicey to invest in Papelbon coming off his 2013 as he looked to be in clear decline, he is now just as good as ever with a different approach.

Miami Marlins (A.J. Ramos): It was a swift and decisive melting down of veteran Miami Marlins closer Steve Cishek early last season, as leaking velocity and terrible control eventually got him sent down to the minor leagues (and eventually shipped out via trade). That opened the door for the Marlins to tab setup man A.J. Ramos to take over the ninth inning and generally speaking, the guy performed very well. Already a veteran at 29, Ramos was able to finish 32 games on a bad team, while posting a tiny 2.30 ERA and striking out batters at a very impressive 11.13 clip. Those numbers pass the eye test in terms of Ramos' ability to continue finishing games at a high level but he does have to work on his control which was very spotty throughout the year (3.33 BB/9). As long as the walks are managed, there is no reason Ramos can't be a terrific closer value for 2016.

Atlanta Braves (Arodys Vizcaino): After trading All-Star closer Craig Kimbrel right before the season got underway, the rebuilding Atlanta Braves began auditions for who could be the future for the team in the ninth inning. The guy who stuck out the most was youngster Arodys Vizcaino who came up from Triple-A and impressed with a 1.60 ERA and 9 saves in just 33.2 innings. While that puts Vizcaino in the driver's seat in terms of closing games, he is anything but a sure thing after he previously washed out of the Chicago Cubs organization. Given how the Cubs have churned out prime prospects like they are going out of style, one has to give pause to anyone who failed to come through there. Also the 33.2 innings were a very tiny sample size and in no way portends to success over the course of a full season. Ultimately Vizcaino should be one of the last closers off the board in your draft and it would be no shock if the Braves had someone better by the season gets underway.

Philadelphia Phillies (Ken Giles): After finally moving Jonathan Papelbon to the Washington Nationals at the trade deadline, the Philadelphia Phillies welcomed in the Ken Giles era as the team's closer. There is no doubt whatsoever regarding Giles' ability to be a high-end closer given the fact his stuff is classic ninth inning material. In his first two major league seasons, Giles has recorded ERA's of 1.18 and 1.80 as he has stuck out batters at better than an 11.00/9 K rate during that span. Even more impressive, Giles doesn't give up home runs as evidenced by the 0.20 and 0.26 HR/9 marks his first two years in the league. The only thing you can knock Giles on is that he fights his control a bit but that figures to iron itself out as he matures as a major league pitcher. There is top five upside here as we think Giles is prime for a huge season.

Chicago Cubs (Hector Rondon): Joe Maddon took his quirky ninth inning maneuverings from the Tampa Bay Rays to the Chicago Cubs last season, first demoting Hector Rondon from the closer role, worked his way through veteran Jason Motte, and then eventually came right back to Rondon again to complete 2015. Truth be told, Maddon was a bit too harsh in pulling Rondon from the closer role in the first place. Yes Rondon is still feeling his way as a young closer but he wound up finishing with a miniscule 1.67 ERA, making it sort of laughable that he was even taken out of the role at any point. Now Rondon is not perfect by any means as his K rate has not reached the 9.0 mark in his three major league seasons. However Rondon generates a bunch of ugly swings and his terrific 0.51

HR/9 mark shows that he doesn't beat himself. With the Cubs set to be big contenders again in 2016, Rondon should be the recipient of a high number of save chances this season. We think he is up to the task.

Pittsburgh Pirates (Mark Melancon): It was a bit of a strange but ultimately dominant season from the National League's top closer in 2015, as Pittsburgh Pirates closer Mark Melancon almost didn't make it out of April when it came to pitching the ninth inning. For some reason Melancon couldn't harness his stuff during the first month of the season, as his 5.23 ERA and .290 BAA against bore out. There were whispers that Melancon was a blown save away from losing his job but fortunately it never came to pass. What happened from that point on though was pure pitching dominance as Melancon registered a 0.71 ERA in May and then proceeded to not give up a single earned run in June AND July. While he sputtered a bit at the end probably due to some fatigue (4.51 September ERA), Melancon has more than established himself as one of the best closers in baseball. Looking at the advanced numbers, there were some issues believe it or not. For one thing, Melancon's K rate sank to a very mediocre 7.28 last season after coming in at an even 9.00 in 2014. In addition, Melancon's 0.47 HR/9, while still terrific, was his highest mark there since 2012. Be that as it may, Melancon was still getting it done with his 2.23 ERA and 51 saves. While we don't consider Melancon a top tier closer, he fits snuggly in the tier 2 range.

St. Louis Cardinals (Trevor Rosenthal): Having completely abandoned the idea of converting Trevor Rosenthal into a starting pitcher, the St. Louis Cardinals have wed themselves to the fireballer as the team's stopper now and into their long-term plans. With a rocket for an arm that can touch 100-mph with his fastball, Rosenthal is a natural fit in the ninth inning to say the least. However he has not been a complete lock down guy just yet, fighting through inconsistency in 2014 that netted a high 3.20 ERA and then in 2015 continued a pattern of poor control with a 3.28 BB/9. Still when it came to collecting saves, few were better as Rosenthal logged 48 last season and he helped himself with a 10.88 K/9. Having lowered his composite season ERA from 2014's 3.20 mark to last year's 2.10, Rosenthal is on the cusp of being a top 5 guy. The biggest concern we have has nothing to do with stuff as Rosenthal has had a few injury scares over the last two years. Since he throws so hard and puts immense torque on his arm, the threat of elbow/shoulder trouble is real. Ultimately though on pure ability, Rosenthal is as good as it gets.

Milwaukee Brewers (Will Smith): With the Milwaukee Brewers expected to on paper be one of the worst teams in baseball in 2016, it made no sense for them to hang onto All-Star closer Francisco Rodriguez. Thus it was no shock when they dealt him away to the Detroit Tigers early in the Hot Stove season, in the process opening up the closer spot for the very promising Will Smith. The very hard-throwing lefty has been one of the better setup men in baseball over the last three years and his high strikeout and low hit rates make him a perfect match for the ninth inning. Last season was indicative of what Smith is capable of as he pitched to a terrific 2.70 ERA and 1.20 WHIP while striking out a crazy 91 batters in 63.1 innings. Smith does battle walks on occasion but he is set up to be the very best closer value of 2016. On talent alone, Smith has the stuff to be a top ten closer this season.

Cincinnati Reds (Aroldis Chapman): Cincinnati Reds nuclear closer Aroldis Chapman proved once again in 2015 that when it comes to the art of striking out batters, nobody is better. Since arriving in the majors from Cuba in 2010, the LOWEST K/9 rate that Chapman has ever recorded was his rookie mark of 12.83 which is still immense. The last two seasons? Try 17.67 and 15.74. Truly ridiculous numbers from Chapman who should be the number 1 closer off the board in all formats. With a 1.63 ERA and 33 saves last season, Chapman is as dominant as ever and he remains in the early stages of his prime since he turns just 28 in February. While the BB/9 is never great (4.48 in 2015), Chapman more than makes up for it with the bets hit and K rates in the game.

Colorado Rockies (OPEN): If the Colorado Rockies could have convinced Dennis Eckersley to come out of retirement to close out games last season, the Hall of Famer would have been the team's best ninth inning arm by a mile. The Rockies went through a slew of mediocre to horrific options at closer last season, with some guys being tried more than once. Better yet, the Rockies need to look to free agency for a solution as their in-house candidates look as shaky as the options they had in 2015. The worst closing situation in the baseball as of this writing.

Los Angeles Dodgers (Kenley Jansen): While he doesn't get mentioned often enough when the subject comes to the best closers in baseball, the Los Angeles Dodgers' Kenley Jansen is more than deserving of being included in that class. Part of the reason Jansen doesn't get the credit his numbers warrant is due to perennial injury/health woes but when on the mound, his high-octane fastball piles up the strikeouts at a very high clip. 2015 was no different as Jansen recorded a 13.76 K/9 and registered a tiny 2.41 ERA while locking down 36 games. In his prime at the age of 28, Jansen will be a top five guy for a number of years and outside of health, there is no reason to not make him one of the top closers off the board.

Arizona Diamondbacks (Brad Ziegler): It is up for debate whether the Arizona Diamondbacks will go into the 2016 season with submarine veteran Brad Ziegler as the team's closer. Still on numbers alone, Ziegler deserves another look as he registered a 1.80 ERA in 2015, his best number there since his 2009 rookie year with the Oakland A's. Ziegler's approach is about as anti-closer as it gets, with his 4.76 K/9 rate the worst among last season's closers. What Ziegler has going for him is his difficult delivery which makes the baseball very tough to pick up for the hitters. In addition, Ziegler helps himself with a miniscule 0.40 HR/9 and solid 2.25 BB/9 rates. Again the Diamondbacks could look for more of a strikeout closer for the ninth inning but Ziegler has to be considered the one to own here at this stage.

San Francisco Giants (Santiago Casilla): It was rocky at times but Santiago Casilla successfully held onto the San Francisco Giants' closer role for the duration of the 2015 season. Long considered one of the very best setup men in the game, Casilla has struggled in the past when given chances to close out games. There were no such issues last season as Casilla logged a 2.79 ERA and nailed down 38 saves for the contending Giants. What really gave Casilla a boost was the fact he raised his K/9 rate northward by a sizable margin, going from 2014's 6.94 mark to last year's 9.62. The latter number is clearly in outlier territory since Casilla has generally been around the former and at the advanced age of 35 we have to doubt that the veteran all of a sudden learned some new tricks. We are quite a bit concerned about investing in Casilla for 2016, given his history of past closer struggles and for the fact that control has been an issue. Throw in his advancing age and there are a lot of issues that could derail Casilla's 2016 campaign.

San Diego Padres (Kevin Quackenbush): With the San Diego Padres having dealt away All-Star closer Craig Kimbrel to the Boston Red Sox early in the winter, the opening at closer for the team could fall to the intriguing Kevin Quackenbush. A towering righty at 6-4, Quackenbush certainly misses enough bats to man the ninth inning as he struck out 114 batters in his 112.2 career innings through two MLB seasons. Quackenbush does have some shoddy control which is always something to fret over when it comes to a closer but he should be given the first crack to man the spot for the Padres in 2016. Decent upside sleeper this season.

Los Angeles Angels (Huston Street): The narrative remains the same for veteran closer Huston Street in terms of health being the only issue that can hold him back from annually being one of the best stoppers in baseball. A frequent visitor to the disabled list throughout his career, Street had his 2015 season ended early due to a Grade 1 groin strain suffered in mid-September. Prior to that, Street was quite shaky at times in posting an elevated (by his career norms) 3.18 ERA and 1.16 WHIP while finishing 40 games in 45 tries. The Angels are always right at the top of baseball in save chances year after year so owning Street is attractive on that front. However Street is now 32 and coming off his highest ERA since 2011. There are some other red flags here as well, with Street's BB/9 last season of 2.89 being his highest since he first was breaking into the majors back in 2008. Want more? How about a lucky .263 BABIP which means Street's ERA should have even been higher (XFIP of 4.16). It is getting tough to make any more excuses regarding Street and his future is looking more uncertain than ever.

THE LAST WORD

So the draft is finished, your roster is set, and you love your team. Unfortunately no fantasy baseball league titles are handed out right after the draft and in actuality your work has really just begun as the six-month marathon to October commences. While we take great pride in our annual draft guide, we also once again recommend you follow us all season long on our website at www.thefantasysportsboss.com. Each week of the fantasy baseball season, we feature articles, analysis, and news breaking items to help you stay on top of all the latest happenings around the game. Some of these weekly features include:

Closing Time (Monday): Join us for our weekly look at all the latest news and notes from the always volatile world of the closer.

Weekly Adds (Thursday): Each week we also share with you our prime weekly pickups to help you to stay on top of your roster in order to maximize its effectiveness.

Status Report (Daily): Throughout the season we continually post updated "Fantasy Baseball Status Reports" where we check in on hitters and pitchers who are in the news based on their recent performances.

Crisis Point (Daily): We also continually post this feature on a daily basis, which goes in-depth on hitters and pitchers who are encountering major trouble with their numbers in an attempt to figure out what statistical direction they will be taking.

Welcome To The Show (Daily): This feature is where we take an initial look and profile prospects who are called up from the minors to make their major league debuts.

News Breakers (Daily): Each day of the season we post up-to-the-minute news breaks regarding lineup changes, injuries, demotions, and anything else that can impact a player's value.

All of this and so much more as "The Fantasy Sports Boss" looks to set the standard for the best and most in-depth news from the game we all love. Be sure to bookmark the site and revisit us daily.